Reading, Writing and Reasoning

A guide for students

Reading, Writing and Reasoning

A guide for students

THIRD EDITION

Gavin J. Fairbairn and Christopher Winch

Open University Press

Open University Press
McGraw-Hill Education
McGraw-Hill House
Shoppenhangers Road
Maidenhead
Berkshire
England
SL6 2QL

email: enquiries@openup.co.uk
world wide web: www.openup.co.uk

and Two Penn Plaza, New York, NY 10121–2289, USA

First editon published 1991, second edition 1996, this edition 2011

A catalogue record of this book is available from the British Library

ISBN: 978-0-33-523887-3
eISBN: 978-0-33-523889-7

Library of Congress Cataloging-in-Publication Data
CIP data applied for

Typesetting and e-book compilations by
RefineCatch Limited, Bungay, Suffolk
Printed in the UK by Bell and Bain Ltd, Glasgow.

MIX
Paper from
responsible sources
FSC® C007785

The **McGraw·Hill** Companies

Contents

Preface

Most students have to produce written assignments at some point. For some, including students of disciplines such as philosophy, history, politics and literature, the essay will be the chief means by which they persuade their teachers, not only that they have learned something, but also that they have thought about what they have learned. Students of other subjects, on the other hand, will often have to undertake a wider range of academic and professional writing, including research and experimental reports. Whether this writing is undertaken over a number of weeks or in the context of a formal exam, students who have taken the trouble to develop skill as writers, who can make good use of what they have read to construct well-reasoned arguments, are more likely to succeed. This book is intended to help with the development of such skills. It is intended, also, as a source of ideas for tutors who want to extend their repertoire of ways of providing such help directly to their students.

We decided to write the first edition of this book, because, as new lecturers in the mid-1980s, we were disturbed by the poor quality of writing produced by many otherwise intelligent students. No matter how articulate they were in class, many of our students always seemed to be unable to convey their ideas successfully in writing. Sometimes this may have been because they did not know how to do so; sometimes it may have been because they did not wish to expend the effort necessary to do so. Thirty years on, things are just as bad. Despite the fact that many universities and colleges in the UK now have support services for students who have difficulties with key skills, including literacy skills, most seem to expect the majority of their students to be able to read, write and think at an appropriate level, without too much input from their teachers. This is curious, given the prevalence of despair among lecturers about poor standards of writing they come across, day in and day out.

Although there are many books on various aspects of study (some of them excellent, some of them less than excellent), none of these books focuses, as our book does, on the '3 Rs' of 'Reading, (w)Riting and Reasoning'. That is why we believe that this book is as relevant today as it was when the first edition was published in 1991. Our idea at that time was that since students are usually assessed via written work in which they are expected to show evidence of both reading and thought, we would write a book to help them to develop skills in reading, writing and reasoning. Such help is probably even more essential now than it was in the past.

Until universities take seriously the need to provide teaching in basic study and literacy skills, it will be up to individual students to develop such skills for themselves. Smart students realize that investing time in learning to read, write and think better will pay off in the long run, both by helping them to get a better qualification and, perhaps even more importantly, by enabling them to be more efficient in undertaking the work necessary to gain a qualification of any kind.

Although we wrote *Reading, Writing and Reasoning* with undergraduate students in mind, we are aware that in both its first and second editions, it found an audience among A level students, students on access courses and postgraduate students, as well as among professional academics. In this third edition, we have included more opportunities to practise the central literary skills of reading, writing and reasoning. This, we are sure, will make it even more useful for all of these groups.

Our aims in this third edition of *Reading, Writing and Reasoning* are thus threefold:

- To facilitate the development of skill in writing clear, careful and persuasive prose, through the use of a clear and effective style and an awareness of the requirements of cogent argument.

- To help readers to develop skill in the reading and evaluation of analytic and descriptive texts, including the sympathetic and critical appraisal of arguments.

- To enable our readers to develop their ability to track and evaluate the arguments by which others try to persuade, and to develop skill in the construction of rational arguments.

How should you use this book?

How you use this book will depend partly on what you hope to get out of it, and partly on your experience and skills as a reader.

If, for example, you have never before given any real thought to the best way of making a book work for you, you might choose to begin at the beginning and to read the text in the order in which we have presented it. On the other hand, if your main concern is to seek help in developing your skill as a writer, it might make sense to read Part 2 first; however, it will be important to follow this by turning to Parts 1 and 3, because skill in academic writing depends both on the ability to read effectively and to make use of what you have read, and on the ability to construct cogent arguments.

If your main reason for reading the book is to find help in understanding and constructing arguments, you might want to begin by reading Part 3. However, it is important to realize that Parts 1 and 2 also contain material that might be helpful, especially Part 2, because your development of skill in the construction of written arguments will usually depend very much on the development of clear and effective literary style.

Finally, you might take a much less strategic approach to the book, dipping in and out at various points, or if you have very specific areas with which you are seeking help, you might try to locate sections that seem relevant to a particular problem, using both the contents list and the index, which we have tried to make as useful as possible, with this possibility in mind.

We hope that for at least some people, reading this book front to back, from cover to cover will be an agreeable, informative and at times challenging experience. However, since in Part 1 we discuss various ways of approaching a text and emphasize our belief that reading a book from cover to cover is not necessarily the best way of using study time, we will be delighted if readers use the book in any of the different ways we have described.

Whatever approach you take to reading, you will notice that throughout the book we invite you to undertake a number of tasks. Some are designed to get you to reflect on issues that we think are important in reading, writing and reasoning; others are intended to give you the opportunity to practise skills. In relation to many of these tasks, we provide responses at the back of the book.

The gender problem: minding our language and avoiding offence

It is now almost universally expected that texts of an academic or professional kind, whether published or not, will avoid the generic use of the masculine pronouns 'he', 'him' and 'his', because of the offence that this can cause to those who have noticed that the world contains women and girls as well as men and boys. Along with this comes the need to avoid the use of words such as 'chairman' or 'fireman', and of the words 'man' and 'mankind' to refer to the human race.

It is relatively easy to avoid the generic use of masculine nouns, for example, by substituting firefighters for firemen, and chairperson or more commonly chair for chairman, and talking of humankind rather than mankind. However, the problems caused by the generic use of masculine pronouns are a little more difficult to address. The most popular approach involves the use of two steps:

- using plural forms, such as 'they', 'them' and 'theirs', rather than the singular forms 'he', 'she', 'him', 'her', 'his' and 'hers'; and

- using 'he/she', 'him/her', 'his/hers' and the un-sayable 's/he' whenever an individual being referred to occupies a role that could conceivably be occupied by either a female or a male (that is, unless the role – for example, being a father or mother – is one that only a man or a woman could occupy).

In our view, while taking these steps certainly addresses the concerns of many people, they each have a tendency to make text cumbersome and inelegant. In spite of this, you may well be required to adopt either one or both of these steps in your essays. However, if you are not given such instructions, there is another strategy that you might find useful.

> Try, as far as is possible, to alternate generic uses of masculine and feminine pronouns.

This is what we have done in this book. No doubt this convention will not satisfy everyone. For example, although we have not taken the trouble to check, we may actually have used more male pronouns than female pronouns, in which case a feminist might accuse us of sexism; if, on the other hand, we have erred in the opposite direction, a chauvinistic man might point out that the convention we have adopted does not accurately portray the way things are in the real world. However, we have done our best.

And finally: an invitation

In the final stages of writing the first edition of this book we began to worry about the possibility that having offered advice to others about how to write, we might ourselves have written, at times, in ways that made us look ignorant of that advice. And so we apologized to our readers for the fact that we are mere mortals, subject to the same weaknesses as everyone else. More than that, since in the event of the book reaching the stage of a second edition we wanted to be in a position to remove some of these mistakes, we invited readers who spotted stylistic infelicities or mistakes to write to us, and offered 50p per mistake, for the privilege of being told where we had gone wrong. In the second edition we raised the stakes a little and increased our 'own goal' rate to 75p. Though no-one has ever clamed the financial rewards we offered, wee doubt that this means weave been entirely successful in avoiding problems, even off a simple kind, such as mistake with speling, grammer; or punctuation? That is why invite you too get in touch if notice mistakes, of any kind, including stylistic gaffs; occasions when words order appear in the wrong, as well as simpler mistake, including missing woods the use of the wrong wards.

Acknowledgements

Thanks were and still are due to a number of people for their help in the production of this book, including Cathy Winch and Bob Solomon who offered helpful comments in relation to the first edition; Martin Stafford who offered detailed advice about the final draft of that edition, and Graham Haydon and Keith Sharp who made suggestions that helped us to improve the second edition. Susan Fairbairn discussed the first edition repeatedly while we were writing it and undertook a detailed reading of the final draft; in addition, she put in a day's unpaid work in correcting proofs of the second edition. She also generously agreed to our borrowing some ideas from this book's first cousin *Reading at University: A Guide for Students* (Fairbairn and Fairbairn, 2001) for this edition. Our work on this edition benefited greatly from detailed suggestions offered by the reviewers appointed by the Open University Press. We are also grateful to colleagues at the Open University Press, who believed in the book enough to invite us to prepare first a second and now a third edition, and to help us on the way to preparing it, including Shona Mullen, Melanie Havelock and Katherine Hartle, whose patience was invaluable. We would like to thank all those people – colleagues, students and reviewers – who in different ways shared with us something of what they thought about the first and second editions; it is always good to know that your work has been noticed and even better to know when it is liked.

The four Haiku that appear on page 00 came from *Haiku for People* (http://www.toyomasu.com/haiku/#murakami), and we are grateful to Kei Grieg Toyomasu for allowing us the freedom to use them.

Gavin J. Fairbairn   Christopher Winch

Introduction: Reading and writing; talking and thinking

We begin, not with reading, writing or reasoning, but with talk, which is a more complicated business than most people realize. Of course, being unaware of the full complexity of talk will not stop you communicating effectively in writing. However, it means that you will not be able to take account of the differences between communicating in speech and doing so in writing. As a result you may be less good at conveying your meanings in writing than you might be otherwise. Indeed, some of the most common problems that students have in writing arise because they have failed to think about these distinctions.

Task 1: How is writing different from talking?

Take a moment or two to write down the differences that you think exist between communicating through speech and communicating in writing.

- What advantages, if any, does talk have over writing?

- Does writing have any advantages over talk? If so, what are they?

[Our response appears on page 246]

Thinking about talk

Consider for a moment what goes into a conversational exchange between two or more people. Naturally, there are the words spoken, but the how, when and where of their being spoken is just as important in communicating meaning as the mere words the speakers use. In other words, there is more to talk than talk. When we speak our tone of voice, facial expression and body language convey attitude and emotion, whether we intend them to do so or not.

Conversations take place in a particular context and a certain amount of background knowledge, common to speaker and listener, can often be taken for granted. For example, recalling an incident in the café in which she and Jill are having lunch, Mary might say, 'You remember the time when ...', leaving the rest of the sentence unsaid, but employing a grimace or a wry smile to evoke an occasion, many years before, when they realized that neither of them had enough money to pay for their coffee. In such situations, a nod and a smile from the listener is enough to show the other person that she understands, because she remembers this aspect of their shared history.

What is left unsaid is often as important as what is said. For example, although the remark 'Jimmy isn't drunk today' could be a simple factual statement about Jimmy, if it was uttered with a knowing look and in a certain tone of voice (perhaps with a stress on the second syllable of 'today') it could be used to imply that he is drunk every other day. Simply changing the way you say something is often enough to alter the meaning conveyed. Consider, for instance, the different meanings that would be conveyed depending on whether the first or the second word in this sentence was stressed:

You were going to do it[1].

You can even communicate the opposite of the meaning that the words you are using would have if taken at face value. For example, someone who says, 'That's very kind of you' in the appropriate circumstances and with a shocked look, a bitter tone of voice and a stress on the first syllable of 'very', may well mean, 'That's very *unkind* of you'. Most native users of English are aware of linguistic subtleties of this kind, because skill in interpreting nuances of meaning in spoken communication is something that we learn as we grow up.

So talk takes place in a certain context. There is a speaker, a listener, and the social and physical situation that they are currently in. One of the most important features of face-to-face talk is that there is the possibility of immediate interaction between speaker and listener. Among other things, this means that if we don't understand what a person is saying, we have the opportunity to clarify what they meant, for example, by asking them to explain something we didn't understand, or to fill in missing information. Another important aspect of face-to-face talk, as we saw in the story about Mary and Jill, is the possibility of conveying meaning through body language, including both facial expression and bodily gestures. Things are different when we can't

---

[1] The 'it' referred to in this sentence could be almost anything: 'collect the cat'; 'pay the telephone bill before we are cut off'; 'make the bid on the house'; 'buy food for tea', or 'book the holiday while the offer is still on'.

see the person with whom we are speaking – especially, for example, when we are talking over the phone.

Task 2: How is talking face-to-face different from talking on the phone?

Take a moment or two to write down the differences that you think exist between talking face-to-face and talking on the phone.

[Our response appears on page 246]

Face-to-face talk and telephonic talk

When we were writing the first edition of this book in the late 1980s, we drew attention to some of the differences between face-to-face and telephonic talk. For example, we pointed out that when we are talking over the phone voices may sound unnatural; people may feel uneasy and pressed for time, and the possibility of referring to objects physically by a gesture or a demonstrative such as 'this cup' or 'that book' is unavailable. In particular, we noted that whereas body language, including facial expression, typically makes a strong contribution to the communication of meaning when we are speaking face-to-face, this was impossible when talking over the telephone. So, for example, we pointed out that although we might think we detect doubt, insincerity or anger in a person's voice when we are talking to her over the phone, we could not read it in her face, as we might were she in the same place as us. As we write this in early 2011, it is still true that other than the words she is using, tone of voice is usually the only thing that will allow us to guess at the mood of a person to whom we are speaking on the phone. This is in spite of the fact that more and more people are now using mobile phones that have the possibility of good quality video connection and that video calling on the Internet is an everyday event for many people.

The absence of visual clues in much telephonic talk has both advantages and disadvantages. On the one hand, the fact that the person to whom you are speaking cannot pick up clues from your body language, facial expression and gestures makes it easier to conceal your true feelings from her during telephone conversations. This is clearly useful at times. Consider, for example, how much easier it is to tell a lie or to turn down an unwanted invitation over the telephone, than to do so face-to-face. Or imagine a situation in which you are trying to convince someone about something that you know to be untrue, using lines like these:

I'm going to be a bit late. It's dreadful; the queue stretches for miles; I think there must have been an accident.

I've been in the library all day working on my essay, but I'll be home as soon as I can.

I'm going to miss my tutorial today, because I've been really unwell all weekend and I still don't feel right.

Can you please tell Professor Winch I'm going to be late with my essay, because: my gran died last week/I've had bubonic plague for a fortnight/I lost all my data when my laptop was hit by lightning.

Many people (perhaps most) will, on occasion, have said things like these over the telephone to others from whom they wanted to conceal the truth (or at least the whole truth) for whatever reason. In such circumstances, the relative poverty of telephonic talk, and in particular the absence of visual clues, is a considerable advantage. However, the tables are turned when we are on the receiving end, when this feature of telephone talk becomes a disadvantage.

Most people will have been duped by another who wished, for whatever reason, to deceive them during a telephone conversation. That is why, if it is possible to do so, it is best always to communicate about important matters in a face-to-face setting, when it is easier to assess whether a person is being truthful or not. This can be really useful at times. For example, if you could see his uneasy facial expression you might have less confidence in the car mechanic who tells you in a breezily confident tone that 'first thing tomorrow I will be able to get the new phalanges I need to get your car back on the road by tomorrow afternoon'.

How are talking and writing different?

Talking face-to-face and writing are different, because like telephone talk, written communication is impoverished by the absence of visual cues. When we are reading we can see neither the face nor the body language of the person who wrote the text; nor can we gain information from his tone of voice. The possibility of immediate clarification, which exists both in telephone talk and in face-to-face talk, is also absent from most forms of written communication. Two exceptions to this would be the 'conversations' that are possible via text messaging and email, though both have built-in delays as the people involved take turns in writing; and of course in each case there is also the possibility of editing. Written communications that are even closer to genuine spoken conversations include the hybrid forms that sit between talk and writing, using Internet services, such as Windows Live Messenger and Facebook Chat.

Our familiarity with speech, the fact that we feel so much at ease with the spoken word and the fact that it 'comes naturally' to us, make it difficult for many people to adjust to the different requirements of writing, and especially to the more formal writing that is found in academic contexts. Because the clues that are supplied by context in spoken communication are not available to her readers, the writer has to make do without them and communicate effectively nonetheless. This involves substituting (if possible) for tone of voice, the physical presence of the listener and the possibility of interaction. For example, since you cannot look or sound firm in a letter, you have to convey firmness by choosing your words carefully, for example, by writing 'I am absolutely determined that …' And since your reader can't see what you can see and has no opportunity to ask for further explanation, clarity is much more important in the written word than it is in speaking. In other words, not only will you often have to give more complete descriptions of places, objects and people in writing than would be necessary if you were communicating the same ideas face-to-face, but striking the right balance between what to leave out and what to put in can be crucially important. All of this means that writing takes a great deal of care, both in ensuring that what and how you write is suitable for your audience, and in ensuring that you give enough information to meet their needs.

The points we have drawn attention to so far may strike you as rather elementary aspects of the difference between making oneself understood in face-to-face speech and in writing, but they are often overlooked, particularly by people who do not write very often, or who are uneasy about writing. Even accomplished writers, who are well aware of the kind of pitfalls we have been discussing, may ignore them when the subject matter about which they are writing is very familiar. In such circumstances, particular problems arise when a writer misguidedly assumes that her readers are at least as knowledgeable as she is about her subject matter. A writer may refer to a book, an argument, an individual or even a topic, wrongly assuming that her readers will know about it. For example, she might refer casually to 'Zukowski's well-known recent monograph on the sexual habits of Outer Mongolian Lepidoptera', when in fact the reader has never heard of Zukowski or Outer Mongolian Lepidoptera, and has no interest whatever in their sexual habits. Unfortunately, there is no immediate way in which the reader can correct this impression. He has to make do with what is on the page in front of him.

Task 3: Communicating directions to your new address

As a way of further exploring the distinctions between communication face-to-face, over the phone and in writing that we have raised in this brief introduction, spend a moment or two thinking about how you would communicate the same information in different ways.

Imagine, for example, that you want to tell a friend how to get to your new address. What difference would there be between doing so face-to-face, on the phone, or in writing?

[Our response appears on page 246]

Part 1

Reading as a student

The ability to read is an art acquired, if we are lucky, when we are young. As a result, by the time they enter higher education, most people should be reasonably competent readers. And so, for example, as well as being able to decode print in a way that allows you to guess how unknown words will sound when spoken, you will be able to guess at the meanings of words with which you are unfamiliar, and to infer meanings that are implied although not stated. It is likely also that you will be able to predict at least some of what is coming as you read. Finally, much of the time you will probably be able to 'catch' the meaning intended by authors without reading every word, although you may revert to doing so when you come across ideas with which you are unfamiliar, especially if technical language and jargon are used.

Although most students will have decent reading skills when they enter university, it does not follow that they will make the best possible use of them, or that they will have developed them as much as they can. Indeed, our experience suggests that most students, at all levels, can benefit from improving their reading skills. That is why, in Part 1, we offer advice about how you can make the best use of the time you have available for reading, along with a number of tasks and exercises, that can help you to think about and develop your reading. Spending a few hours on these will save you time in the long run, because doing so will allow you to become a more effective reader, better able to harvest information from texts to use in the essays and other assignments through which you will be assessed.

Learning to read more effectively will help you to become a better writer.

1.1

Finding meaning in written texts

We read in order to gain meaning. Of course, in a language like ours, there is a sense in which it is possible to 'read' without understanding. This is because the alphabet we use in writing and printing, and the *alphabetic principle* that governs our script and our spelling, allow us to reproduce sounds from print by following rules that enable us to convert print into sound. Consider, for example, the sentence:

A dog sat on a log.

This sentence can be spoken by 'sounding out' each word in turn, that is, by saying the sound associated with each letter in a smooth sequence:

A   d-o-g   s-a-t   o-n   a   l-o-g.

Perhaps you remember 'sounding out words' when you were first beginning to read? Of course, our spelling system is much more complicated and much less regular than this simple example suggests[1]. Nonetheless, the general

---

[1] Think, for example, of how much more difficult another apparently simple sentence is to sound out:

The cat sat on the mat.

It is more difficult simply because it contains a word ('the') that cannot be sounded out letter by letter. Of course, if the cat in question was a brown cat or a sleeping cat, and/or if the mat was turquoise and orange, things would be even more difficult, because as is the case with 'the', words like 'brown', 'sleeping', 'turquoise' and 'orange' cannot be read simply by sounding out individual letters.

alphabetic principle holds. That is what allows us to 'sound out' the above sentence without understanding a word of it.

Being comfortable with the basics of reading is both a good and a bad thing. It is good because it means that we can give most of our energy to the attempt to understand what the author wanted to communicate to us. However, it can be a bad thing, because unless we are careful it can lead us into slovenly reading habits, as we allow the sound and even the meanings of a text, the words and sentences that make it up, to drift past in a haze so that we find after reading for a time that we have little idea of what we were reading about. Have you ever had this experience? It's a little like driving somewhere on 'automatic pilot' and finding when you arrive that you can't remember much about the journey.

Task 4

Think for a moment or two about times when your attention drifts when you are reading, so that, having arrived at a certain point in your journey through a text, you can recall very little about the ideas, arguments and facts that you encountered on the way. What do you think is going on at those times?

Write a few suggestions to yourself, about what you think you can do to avoid this experience, thus improving your performance as a reader[2].

Finally, try to think a little about why, when it is important to understand what an author is trying to say, it is sometimes so difficult to concentrate enough to allow you to do so.

[Our response appears on page 247]

A few years ago one of us was emailed a short passage by his daughter, Faith (Fairbairn, 2005). Unfortunately, she didn't know its provenance – that is, who wrote it, where, when or for what reason, so our thanks are due to the author or authors, whoever they are. It is an interesting passage:

Aoccdrnig to rscheearch at Cmabrigde Uinervtisy, it deosn't mttaer inwaht oredr the ltteers in a wrod are, the olny iprmoetnt tihng is taht the frist and lsat ltteer be at the rghit pclae. The rset can be a total mses and you can sitll raed it wouthit a porbelm. Tihs is bcuseae the huamn mind deos not raed ervey lteter by istlef, but the wrod as a wlohe. Amzanig huh? (Author unknown)

---

[2] You might, for example, find that there is a particular place where reading of a productive kind is easiest for you, or that reading at a particular time of day is most likely to be helpful.

Did you manage to read the passage and understand it? If you did, try to think a little about what was going on when you did so. Do you think that this passage demonstrates the alleged claim of the researchers at Cambridge to which it refers?

Task 5: Read the passage that follows and answer the questions

Toby was neu years old and had a holl of oun ret. His greatest vilt was a tecture called Fred. Toby lev Fred each yak and gave him holls of welt to pock, he even beck him cutch peus when he could get them from his kult. Fred was mump enough to pell in the gelt of Toby's fing and remp his juges.

Answer the following questions in full sentences:

1 How old was Toby?

2 What did Toby have a holl of?

3 What did Toby do to Fred each yak?

4 What did Toby give to Fred?

5 Why was Fred able to pell in the gelt of Toby's fing?

6 What did Fred remp?

Note: This exercise comes from Raban (1982).

[Our response appears on page 247]

Anyone who is able to read this book will be able to read the passage about Toby and his vilt Fred, and to answer the questions about them, even if they don't understand them or the passage itself. In their book *Reading at University: A Guide for Students*, Fairbairn and Fairbairn (2001, p. 21) write that:

> without knowing what 'oun ret' is, you will be able to work out that Toby had a holl of it, and though you have no idea what Toby's 'fing' is or where it is to be found, you will know that Fred was able to pell in its gelt, because he was 'mump enough'.

The reason that like any competent reader, you will be able to read Raban's passage and to answer questions about it, is that perhaps without being aware of having done so, you have developed a sophisticated understanding of the way our language works. Indeed, even if, like many people, you feel ignorant about grammar, you probably know a lot about the ways in which words of different kinds (nouns, verbs, adjectives and so on) function. Whether you know it or not, and whether or not you are familiar with these simple grammatical terms, you know about the ways that these and other kinds of words function to allow the communication of meaning. Fairbairn and Fairbairn (2001) point out that:

> although you can only guess at what they mean, you know that 'lev' and 'pell' are verbs, and that 'vilt', 'kult' and 'tecture' are nouns; you are likely, also, to be able to guess that while a 'yak' is a measure of time, a 'holl' is a measure that is used in relation to materials such as 'oun ret' (or perhaps 'ret') and 'welt', whatever they are. (p. 21)

Task 5 illustrated that it is possible, at times, to answer questions without having any idea what they mean, or even what the words in which they are asked, mean. This spells danger for students who sometimes develop the habit of trying to look more erudite than they really are, by attempting to persuade others that they know and understand things that they do not in fact know and understand.

It works like this (just in case you don't already know)

First, you find some book or article that addresses (or worse still, seems to address) the topic of an essay you are writing. The topic is difficult to understand, and so you don't put too much effort into trying to do so, probably because you've got too much work on right now; perhaps you've left several assignments until the last moment, so now you just have to get something – anything – written before the cut-off date. But, of course, you want a good mark, and you have learned that in general this means persuading your lecturer that you can use big, complex and important sounding words. So you either copy or paraphrase some bits from the text you've found and add them to your assignment, all the while hoping that your lecturer won't read it too carefully.

Literal meaning

Much of the meaning that we gain from what we read is 'literal' in character. Consider, for example, the following sentences:

John went for a walk.

The laptop is on the table.

The poem had five stanzas.

The sandstone was formed in desert conditions.

Our cat Jackson plays the piano better than any other cat alive.

In each of these sentences the meaning is obvious, because words are used in their everyday meanings, in a straightforward way. Reading and understanding them requires no special knowledge, and no interpretation; if we know the literal meanings of the individual words used, and understand how they fit together in our language, we know what these sentences mean.

Literal meaning is important, and in many types of writing it plays a crucial role, particularly where precision is required, because it is important that there should be no misunderstanding on the part of the reader. It is, for example, necessary that court reports, car assembly manuals, insurance claims and scientific hypotheses are not misunderstood through vagueness, the use of difficult metaphors or ambiguity. That is why, in writing of these kinds, literal meaning tends to predominate.

Of course, we do not always fully understand what we read, even if it is written in a way that depends solely on literal meaning. Sometimes this will be due to a fault on the part of the author, who may have been unclear. For example, it may be that his use of a particular word or phrase leads to ambiguity, or that the way in which a passage is structured – the order of words – leads to a lack of clarity. And sometimes, like all of us, you will fail to understand what you are reading, because the writer has used a word or words with which you are unfamiliar. At such times you will find a desktop dictionary (such as the *Concise Oxford Dictionary* or the *Concise Collins Dictionary*) or thesaurus invaluable, and you should ensure that you have access to both, even if you are in the habit of researching the meanings of words using the internet.

Metaphorical meaning

So far we have been considering the importance of literal meaning, where an author communicates by using words in their everyday sense to convey meaning in a straightforward way. Literal meaning is less important in other contexts, for example, when the writer is trying to be witty or entertaining, where part of the effect of the writing may well depend on brevity, ambiguity or the use of metaphor. Consider for example, these two sentences:

Until Rick's band hit the big time, his job in the HMV shop was his bread and butter.

After she injured her toe Jill was a dead duck in the race.

In these sentences the expressions 'bread and butter' and 'dead duck' are being used in a metaphorical rather than a literal way. Most native English speakers from the United Kingdom will thus realize that the first sentence is intended to communicate the fact that Rick used to make his living as a shop assistant, and that the second means that when she injured her toe, Jill had to withdraw from the race, because she was incapable of going on. When we read the sentence about Rick we do not believe for a moment that his job in the shop was literally bread and butter; nor, when we read the sentence about Jill, her toe and the race, do we believe for a moment that she became a dead duck.

Don't mix literal and metaphorical meaning

It is important to avoid confusing literal and metaphorical meaning. For example, you should never write something like:

The university was literally caught with its trousers down.

A university could be caught with its trousers down in a metaphorical sense (that is, it could be caught in a state of embarrassing unpreparedness). But as it stands this sentence is a piece of nonsense, which shows with painful clarity the writer's lack of awareness of the distinction between literal and metaphorical meaning. The word 'literally' should never be used in contexts where a metaphor is intended, as for example it is in the following sentences:

John's tutor literally blew his essay out of the water.

The Dean literally erupted when she heard how many staff had failed to file their expenses claims on time.

In these examples, literal meaning and metaphor are clearly confused, unless in the first, the writer's intention is, for example, to report that John's essay was lying somewhere offshore and that his tutor subjected it to an artillery barrage, and unless in the second, the Dean began not only fuming, but spewing molten rock all over the room. (Both seem unlikely, but if you have evidence to the contrary please let us know.)

1.2

Cultural literacy

As we have shown above, when an author writes metaphorically, his readers need to know more than the simple meaning of the words he uses, if they are to understand him. Another situation where knowing the literal meaning of words is not enough to 'catch' what an author intends to communicate is where its meaning depends upon a certain amount of prior knowledge. In the sentence below, although meaning is conveyed in a literal way and metaphor is not used, many readers will not understand what the author means.

During the highland clearances many crofters were driven off the land.

Although any reasonably competent reader of English prose will know what many of the words in this sentence mean, they will only be able to grasp the author's meaning if they understand the terms 'crofters' and 'highland clearances'. 'Crofters' are tenants who farm small areas of land in the Scottish Highlands and Islands, and the term 'highland clearances' refers to specific historical events that took place in the eighteenth century, when crofters were evicted to make room for sheep. A reader who does not know these facts will have to research this information, merely to understand an otherwise simple sentence. The term 'cultural literacy' is often used to describe acquaintance with a common store of knowledge that any reasonably educated member of our society might be expected to have.

If you possess reasonable general knowledge and a broad understanding of your subject, you are likely to be much more effective as a reader, so it is worth cultivating the habit of reading widely, from the outset of your studies. For example, it would be worthwhile reading a simple history of Europe and the UK, a compendium of science and a simple but comprehensive geography text. Such general reading to bolster your ability to get through reading that throws up lots of new information is especially important if you frequently find yourself confused by references to facts, including people, events, dates and places of which you are unaware, in what you read. Easy reading books like Bill Bryson's (2004) *A Short History of Nearly Everything*, could prove especially worthwhile.

Reading a serious newspaper, whether in paper form or online, along with both a popular science and current affairs weekly or monthly will also be invaluable in helping you to improve your general reading ability, by helping you to build up a store of background knowledge with which to make sense of what you read. Among the daily newspapers in the UK, you might look, for example, at *The Times*, the *Daily Telegraph*, the *Independent* and the *Guardian*, all of which offer reasonably impartial presentations and analysis of current news, although the political leanings and the views expressed are, of course, very different. Among the weeklies, *The Economist, Prospect* and the *London Review of Books* are typical of the kind of reading that might be valuable. In other countries, of course, the choice of newspapers and weeklies will be different. For example, in the US *The New York Times* and the *New York Review of Books* would be two worthwhile choices. Current affairs programmes and programmes about scientific, geographical, historical and aesthetic topics on television and radio and accessing reliable websites, including the BBC website, are also invaluable as ways of building up background cultural knowledge.

Disciplinary literacy: learning the jargon

At times, especially in the early part of your course, you will probably find that you cannot understand some texts because they use specialized vocabulary, including technical terms, with which you are unfamiliar. Imagine, for example, that you were faced with any of the following sentences, which are drawn from a range of academic areas:

> Farrer (1964) argues that fideism and rationalism are both inadequate responses to the possibility of God's existence. (MacSwain, 2006, p. 37)

> Once the gas returns to a hydrostatic configuration, this entropy step manifests itself as a jump in temperature and density of the form seen, while the gas pressure would be continuous across the edge. (Markevitch et al, 2000, p. 549)

> The nested paradigm underscores the need to look consistently at the broader context of systemic issues. (Lederach, 1997, p. 59)

> There is some literature on reflection to guide the novice. Reflexivity, in its various guises, occupies a central place in participatory action research, ethnography, hermeneutic and post-modern approaches to inquiry, taking different forms and raising different questions. (Koch, 1998, p. 1185)

Recent corporate governance reforms have not adequately tackled director liability or accountability because directors in rare cases are paying out of their pockets for their breach of fiduciary duties and shareholder class action lawsuits are often settled before trial. (Rezaee, 2009, p. 410)

Within objectivist linguistics and philosophy, meanings and linguistic expressions are independently existing objects. (Lakoff and Johnson, 1980, p. 206)

Anyone who is unfamiliar with the technical terms used in these sentences – both those for whom the topics in question are totally unfamiliar territory, and students of those topics who have not yet learned these terms – is likely to need help in working out what they mean.

Do you have any idea at all what these terms mean?

'continuous across the edge'; 'corporate governance'; 'ethnography'; 'hydrostatic configuration'; 'fideism'; 'fiduciary duties'; 'hermeneutic'; 'independently existing objects'; 'nested paradigm'; 'objectivist linguistics'; 'participatory action research'; 'post-modern'; 'rationalism'; 'reflexivity'; 'shareholder class action lawsuits'; 'systemic issues'

All academic disciplines have specialized language, often referred to as 'jargon', and although in Part 2 we advise strongly against its use when plain language would communicate your meanings just as well, it will be important for you to become familiar with at least some of the specialized terms that are used in your area of study. What we might call 'disciplinary literacy' – knowing a bit about the language of your discipline – is essential for success, whatever your discipline, even if wherever possible you try to speak and write in ordinary language.

If you find yourself confused by unfamiliar technical terms that you come across, it is important to do whatever it takes to rid yourself of your confusion. It is also important to avoid the feeling that you must be stupid, because everyone else seems to understand. The likelihood is that some of your friends will be just as confused as you are. The only way to find out is to ask them and so you should do so. If they know what the terms in question mean, and can explain their use to you, your problem will be solved. If they don't, you will probably find it helpful to scan some other texts to see whether you can locate places where the words or terms with which you are having difficulty are being used in contexts where it is easier to work out what they mean. Failing this you should ask your teachers for help, without embarrassment. After all, you are a student and their role when they are teaching is to help you to learn. In this, as in anything else connected to your studies, an honest request for help is a sign of intelligence, because it shows that you realize that there is something you don't know, that you need to know. On the other hand, failing to ask for help, because it would be 'too embarrassing' to do so, indicates an amazing degree of stupidity, since it suggests that you would rather be ignorant than risk embarrassment.

1.3

Thinking about what, why, when, where and how you read

Like most students, you are almost bound to have very little time for reading. This is a fact of life and you are going to have to learn to live with it. After all, you have lots of other things to do as well. Apart from all the assignments you will have to get written, as a student you have lots of music to listen to, and lots of eating, drinking and socializing to do. And so, if you are ever going to get through even a fraction of the stuff that you have been told you must read, or decide for your own reasons that you must read, you are going to need help.

To use your time as a reader as well as you can, you will have to think about:

- What you read, and how to make wise decisions about what will repay your effort.

- Why you read – your aims and purposes as a reader.

- When you read and where you read.

- How you read – the strategies and skills and attitudes you adopt as a reader.

Over the next few pages we will raise questions about all of these areas, which overlap substantially with one another. For example, developing a range of skills in reading in different ways and at different levels, including skimming and scanning texts, can help you to decide which books, articles and web pages are most likely to repay your effort.

What should you read as a student?

Whatever reading you have done in the past, and whatever contact you have had with academic books, the reading you will be expected to undertake at university will be rather different. You will probably be directed to some reading by your lecturers – through 'reading lists' for particular courses or modules, and through references in lectures. However, you should expect to take much more responsibility for deciding what you should read than you did, for example, on your A Level or Access course. In the past most of your academic reading will have been undertaken with textbooks and handouts. At university you will have to read a much wider range of material, including books and journal articles in which academics explore original ideas and present new findings. Whenever you write as a student, you will be expected to demonstrate familiarity with a range of such sources.

Try to undertake at least some reading to follow up your lectures and tutorials. We are not talking, here, about reading that is set by your teachers, but reading that is intended to extend or clarify what was discussed in class. This reading need not be especially detailed, and it is unlikely that you will manage to do it every time. However, doing a little is a good habit to establish, and at times it is essential, for example, when you are unclear about something that was said or discussed.

Throughout this book we argue that it is important, when you are writing as a student, to avoid the temptation to try to fool your tutors into believing that you know things that you don't know, or understand things that you don't understand. If you are lucky, you might come across a tutor who doesn't read your work very carefully, but who instead looks for evidence that you are using the right kinds of vocabulary and mentioning the right authors. On the other hand, you are also very likely to meet with tutors who really do read your work in detail, who will notice when you stray into territory in which you feel uncertain. It is much better to write as clearly as you can about aspects of your topic that you understand, than to try to pretend that you understand what you don't. This is especially true if the attempt to do so involves the use of specialist language; referring to well known sources or major ideas, important events or other significant features of your discipline or profession, with which you are not really familiar.

If you find that your lecture or tutorial notes on a topic that you need to mention in an essay are sparse, perhaps because you were asleep or nearly asleep on the day your tutor covered it, make sure that you fill in the gaps in your knowledge and understanding before writing about it. Otherwise you invite disaster, as did the four unfortunate students who star in the examples that follow:

Milly's social psychology tutor was at first mystified by a reference to an idea that she referred to as the 'edifice complex', and which she attributed to Freud, in an essay. Then it dawned on him that she was actually referring to what is known as the 'Oedipus Complex', which, roughly speaking is a difficult period that psychodynamic thinkers believe little boys go through, during which they are particularly close to their mothers and have a kind of rivalry with their fathers. Milly's mistake was especially foolish, because it made it obvious that having taken notes about the Oedipus Complex in a lecture, she had failed to follow it up by reading further.

Andrew, a student in cultural studies, referred in an essay to a book called *The Oranges and Peaches*, which he attributed to Darwin. It is difficult to comprehend what could have been going through Andrew's head as he made this mistake about one of the most famous books in the English language, *The Origin of Species*. Whatever it was, his lecturer was unimpressed.

More worrying, perhaps, than the mistakes made by Andrew and Milly, were mistakes made by two student nurses – Ruth and Gloria – in essays about disability, in the context of which Ruth referred to the *Orwell Strategy* and Gloria talked about 'rest bite' care. Gloria's mistake was fairly simple to fathom, and like silly Milly's and Andrew's mistakes, clearly resulted from simple mis-hearing of the everyday term 'respite care'. However, when he was marking Ruth's work, their lecturer was more confused, because try as he might, he could not work out which strategy Ruth was talking about, until it dawned on him that she must have been trying to refer to the *All Wales Strategy* for the care, treatment and education of people with learning difficulties.

Milly and Andrew both looked ignorant. But in contrast to Gloria and Ruth, at least they weren't studying for a professional qualification where mistakes might have negative effects on people's lives.

The temptation to use knowledge and ideas, and even words that you don't really understand, because you think doing so will make you sound clever, is particularly common among those who are fond of technical language and jargon, and have formed the deluded idea that its use necessarily conveys an aura of sophistication and the impression that one has mastered one's topic. Of course, not everyone who writes in this kind of way does so deliberately to deceive others about what they know (and in an attempt to pull the wool over their eyes, about what they don't know). Some do it because they are unwilling to own up to the fact that they cannot understand some complex and difficult ideas that they read about.

Why do you read as a student

The amount of reading you are expected to undertake will depend on your subject. Some, such as history, philosophy, literature, sociology and psychology, will involve a lot of reading. Others will usually involve considerably less. The subjects you are studying will also affect the kind of reading that you have to undertake. For example, students of literature will have to read many non-academic texts, which in a sense provide the 'raw data' for study; philosophy students will have to read and understand detailed argument, and law students will have to spend time reading reports of legal cases.

Your reasons for reading are likely to be influenced both by the level of study you have reached, and by your subject and the people who are teaching you. Some will be personal to you. However, many will be common across students of all subjects and stages. Some of your reasons for reading will be positive and helpful; some will be less positive and perhaps even detrimental to your academic development.

Task 6: What are your reasons for reading as a student?

Close this book for a few minutes and 'brainstorm' all the reasons you can think of that you might have for reading. As you are doing so, try to think about which seem to you to be good reasons for reading.

Not all reasons for reading are equally valid and not all reading that you do at university will be worthwhile. For example, it will be a waste of time if you understand what you are reading so little, that by the time you get to the end of the text, you haven't learned anything. And it will always be worthwhile if you read for a particular purpose and find at the end that you have achieved that purpose, however small; say, for example, if you have managed to find the answer to a specific question.

Make sure that you always read for good reasons and that you read in ways that will help you to get something out of the effort you put in.

Reading can stimulate your thinking. This is a good thing, as is the fact that it can help you to improve your writing style, both by learning from the good or even great style in which others write, and by allowing you to avoid mistakes made by others. Another very positive reason for reading is the wish to relate what you are thinking to what other people have said or done, argued, discussed or suggested. Academic writing at all levels – from undergraduate essays to the learned books produced by important scholars – is always better if it relates the arguments and points of view that the author presents to what others have written. Unfortunately, this very positive reason for reading is closely related to what we consider to be one of the most negative reasons for reading as a student – the intention to 'trophy hunt' for impressive references and apt quotations with which to decorate essays. The point here is that such reading is rarely about getting to grips with what others have said. It is about giving the impression of scholarship, rather than actually being about scholarship.

Where and when should you read?

If you are going to make the best use possible of the time you can give to reading, it is important that you should think about where and when you find it easiest to read. Places can have an effect on the way we feel and not all locations are equally conducive to reading. So, for example, while you might manage to undertake serious reading during a train journey, you might find that buses are never good places to do so. In a similar way, you might find that whereas you find reading relatively easy in the morning, you find it almost impossible late in the day.

Task 7: Where and when do you read as a student?

Take a few moments to jot down some notes in response to the following questions:

- Where do you find it easiest to read? In the bath? On the bus? In bed? At the kitchen table?

- Can you read in the library?

- Where do you find it hardest to read? Do you ever read there? Why? Could you make changes that made it easier to read there?

- When do you read?

- When do you find it easiest to read for your course? Why?

Try to note when you are reading successfully, and when you are having difficulty concentrating on text, and then try as far as possible to timetable yourself so that you do your reading at the best times of day and in the places that suit you best. Try to arrange that possible distractions – such as friends, impending hunger or thirst, tiredness, feeling either too cold or too hot – do not have the chance to intervene between you and your reading goals.

How should you read?

We turn, finally, to the question of how you should read. But first we offer some advice about skills, disciplines, attitudes and ways of thinking that will help you to become a more efficient and more productive reader, we want to invite you to reflect a little about the kind of reader that you are at the moment.

What kind of academic reader are you?

Radcliffe (2000) thinks that as readers, some people are rather like cloakroom attendants who collect ideas from different sources, sort them out and organize them on various pegs from which they can be retrieved later. This is an evocative metaphor, which relates to a discussion of different kinds of teacher by Postman and Weingartner (1977) in their elderly but still startling book *Teaching as a Subversive Activity*. They talk, for example, about the teacher as a bucket filler (who views his job as being to fill empty minds with knowledge) or as a lamplighter (who views his job as being to illuminate young minds).

Some of Postman and Weingartner's metaphors also lend themselves to a discussion of different kinds of reader, including the reader as a bucket filler, who views reading as a way of filling her mind. Unfortunately, bucket filling readers are often rather undiscriminating and are as likely to fill their minds with rubbish as they are to fill them with worthwhile and well-fashioned ideas; even more unfortunately, when they are students they may, as a result, also fill their essays with rubbish. Students who embrace the bucket model of academic reading usually have a limited relationship with the texts they read. This will probably show in their writing. When they visit books and articles, they are likely to simply harvest ideas, information and nice sounding quotations with which to fill their assignments, rather than allowing the texts they read to bring about lasting changes in the ways they think, or in the things they know.

Fairbairn and Fairbairn (2001, p. 44) discuss a number of new metaphors for different kinds of reader, including 'excavators', 'archaeologists' and 'grand prix drivers'.

Excavators dig into what they read with little finesse. They are primarily interested in collecting large amounts of stuff to dump into their essays and are not particularly concerned to ensure that what they dig up is worthwhile – what matters for them is that they give evidence of reading and the more the better. The reader as archaeologist would be appalled. Rather than mechanically digging out what he can from the books and other texts he reads, the reader as archaeologist digs slowly and carefully, sifting through the rubbish until he finds what he is looking for. Then he will catalogue and label it carefully with other, similar finds, noting down the precise spot where he found it. The reader as archaeologist is interested in gathering evidence to support the theories and arguments he wants to construct, and he will probably compare evidence from several sites in doing so.

The reader as grand prix driver is quite different. He believes in speed. His goal is the end of the chapter, the article, the book or the reading list. He wants to be done with the business of reading as quickly as he can, doesn't have time to collect souvenirs or take snap shots, and in general pays little attention to the intellectual, factual and argumentative scenery he passes through. Some years ago he probably took a speed-reading course and he is very proud of how fast he can travel through text. The grand prix reader notches up books as he passes by, but after a few days can hardly remember their names, never mind what they looked like or the ideas they contained. He will be able to tell you about how much he reads but unless he changes gear quite a lot – when, for example, he comes to difficult sections, he will be able to tell you little about the places he visited; he may not even know that they exist.

Task 8: What kind of academic reader are you?

What kind of reader are you? Are you more than one, depending on the reading task? Sometimes, for example, you might be a bit of a bucket filler, say in the early stages of working for an essay, whereas at other times you might be more discerning, taking the time, like an archaeologist, to sift slowly through the material you unearth.

Take some time to reflect about what kinds of reader you are and about the characteristics that distinguish each. You might, for example, discover that you have something in common with:

- The reader as a juggler (who is good at keeping lots of ideas in the air at once).

- The reader as an explorer (delving deep into unknown and some-times risky intellectual territory).

- The reader as a gardener (who plans carefully, preparing the ground by thinking of questions he wants to ask of the text he is reading; nurturing strong ideas he comes across while weeding out weak specimens).

- The reader as a detective (tracking down arguments and lines of thought, both within and between texts).

- The reader as a lover (who generously and lovingly massages what she finds into use in writing her assignments).

- The reader as map-maker (who is involved in sketching out the features of a source, locating its high points and low points, its interesting features, to allow himself to find his way round during future visits).

Is learning to read fast worth it?

Some students, convinced by speed-reading gurus, believe that reading faster necessarily means reading better. They are mistaken. Although some people can benefit from reading fast some of the time, trying always to read as quickly as possible can lead you to sacrifice understanding for the sake of speed. Woody Allen offers a neat summation of the benefits of speed reading:

> I took a speed reading course, learning to read straight down the middle of the page, and I was able to go through War and Peace in twenty minutes. It's about Russia. (From *Love and Death*; cited by Williams, 1989, p. 26)

For most people, the urge to read faster is at best an unhelpful distraction from the business of trying to make one's reading better, in order to maximize the extent to which it is helpful as a means of learning and developing understanding. Speed has little merit in itself. So although they may get through print in a shorter time, those who focus their reading development on the ability to read faster, may not actually read more, in the sense of gaining more meaning and information from the words that they process. Although they are jetting through the pages, they may be doing so without touching down to pick up any cargo. Indeed, the whole exercise may begin to seem so pointless that they actually begin to read less. In general, it is better to develop skills that allow you to read efficiently at a pace that allows you to engage with and absorb more of the ideas you are meeting, and to understand them better, than to read faster while taking in less.

We hope that you agree with our view that it is never a good use of the time you spend reading to 'cover the ground' without taking some heed of the intellectual scenery through which you are travelling. Barnes (1995, p. 50) quotes a student who is clearly aware that reading is about picking up intellectual cargo, but seems dissatisfied with the result:

> I'm so busy trying to skim the page as fast as I can that I don't remember anything. I keep thinking 'I've got to hurry ... I must remember this, I must remember that ...' so I don't remember anything in the end.

Do you identify with this student's experience? If you do, it is time you thought about the best use of the time you spend reading.

In spite of the fact that we entertain some scepticism about the value of speed reading, we recognize that slowness in reading is no more a virtue than speed. That is why we want now to suggest some steps that should help you to read faster if you find that slowness is causing you problems; the simple suggestions we will make should help you to increase your reading speed without reducing your ability to absorb meaning, perhaps even enhancing it.

1.4

Approaching reading in different ways and at different levels

Rather than dashing more and more quickly through more and more written material, it is better to be selective, to read less and to make sure that you understand, retain and make good use of what you read. We are not insisting that all reading must be slow and painstaking, taking in every nuance, every detailed argument.

> Make sure that you read at a speed and depth that suits your purposes.

Aim to develop skill in discriminating between times when what is required is detailed knowledge and understanding, which calls for deliberate, step-by-step reading of a systematic kind, and times when all you need is a general impression of the author's view, which you will often be able to gain by skipping quickly through the text, reading odd sections that catch your eye because they contain key words relating to your topic.

Reading systematically for understanding demands patience and is time-consuming. However, using reading techniques such as skimming, scanning and sampling, it will often be possible to work out whether a text is worth reading. In addition, it will often be possible to gain an impression of its content, style and likely merit by using organizational features such as, in the case of a book: the contents list, index and the blurb on the back cover or dust jacket, and in the case of an article, the abstract, which introduces the highlights of the content and the reference list, which gives some indication at least of how it relates to other work in its field.

Skimming, scanning and sampling

Most books about study skills include discussions of reading techniques such as 'skimming', 'scanning', 'sampling' and so on, although there is a great deal of variability in the ways in which these terms are used. We do not intend to enter into a detailed discussion of the differences between these approaches, but it is important to say something about their usefulness.

Skimming is described in different ways, which belong to a family of approaches, and you probably skim-read quite a lot of the time, both when you are reading in connection with your course and, for example, when you are reading magazines and newspapers. For example, it might be described as:

- allowing your eyes to pass down the middle of the page taking in important words on either side, which involves gambling that the omission of words from the edges of the page is not too significant and that you will be able to guess at their meaning from what you do take in;

- disciplining yourself to fix your gaze, say, three or four times a line, and perhaps only every third or fourth line, so that inevitably you also take in a certain amount of information from the lines above and below the one you are reading;

- reading only a percentage of the text, perhaps every fifth sentence, or every second paragraph;

- allowing your eyes to roam freely across each page in turn, to pick up its general sense.

Some people might insist that only the first two of these techniques is really skimming, and point out, for example, that the third is really sampling, because it involves reading 'samples' of the text in a methodical way. However, others would want to use the term 'sampling' to refer, more specifically, to the technique of building up a sketchy overall picture of an article or chapter by, for example, reading the first and last paragraphs, followed by the first and last sentences in every paragraph. The fourth technique they might refer to as scanning and it is easy to see why, although we would prefer to use 'scanning' to refer to the attempt to locate particular words or ideas in a passage, which will often be a precursor to skimming text when you turn to an index entry for a word or phrase. Scanning is usually more cursory than skimming, and whereas one may scan a text from back to front, skimming is usually carried out in the direction of the text. Whatever approach you adopt, you should allow yourself the freedom to change gear and read more systematically, when you light upon some word or idea that is of interest to you.

Is skimming worthwhile?

Skimming, in all of the manifestations we have outlined above, is not only worthwhile but absolutely essential, because it is a quick way of gaining sufficient information to make a reasoned decision about whether the text is likely to be useful for your purposes and about how best to extract the information and ideas it contains. It also allows you to avoid the possibility of reading difficult sections out of context, because by skimming you can gradually build up an idea of the text as a whole. When you come across difficult sections you will then have more chance of understanding them, thus reducing the likelihood that through panic you might put aside a useful resource just because you do not feel confident about using it.

> Skimming a text to gain an overview is like sending a scout ahead of an expedition, because it can give you a feel for the territory ahead. It can allow you to make reasoned decisions about both:
>
> - the sections that might be worth investigating in detail, and
> - where your detailed reading should begin.

In general, it is best to begin with whatever material is most relevant to your purposes or interests, or with sections of text that you understand or that seem to be just about understandable (there usually are such places if you look for them carefully). Focusing on sections of a difficult text that relate to what you already know and understand, or in which you have a particular interest, can help you to gain a good enough idea about what it is about; this, in turn, will help you to decide how to go about tackling it in detail.

Task 9: Circuit training for reading

Every so often, take the time to engage in a bit of 'circuit training' aimed at developing your stamina and strength as a reader. Set yourself some small tasks relating to reading. In each case, give yourself a prescribed time to accomplish the task, preferably a bit less time than you estimate it would take to do a thorough job. Here are a few examples of things you might decide to do:

i   Give yourself a short time (perhaps 15–30 minutes) to write some notes about the main points in a chapter or article that you want to read.

ii Give yourself one hour to write brief notes on six journal articles. You could do this using online versions of journals. However, since reading from paper is generally easier, the best place to do this is probably your university library, using paper versions of journals.

iii Write a brief overview of a book that is new to you, but which you really want to get to know; your overview should remind you of the main points and the main locations in which you will find them. Take no more than an hour.

iv Set yourself a topic about which you would like to write an essay, and take one hour to find three books (or three articles) in the library that will help you to find out about it; note down keywords and pages where you can find them.

v Give yourself a short time to re-read an essay that you have written, noting down keywords (the words without which the essay could not say what you want to say), and prepare a three-minute presentation about your views for someone who knows nothing at all about this area (you might even want to try making this presentation to a friend, or your cat or the mirror in your bedroom). Make sure you stick to the key points.

Approaching academic reading

The most important thing in your development as a reader is that you should find ways of reading that suit you. This will include making choices about where and when to read for different purposes; what kinds of material to read, and how much to read; whether you should always read on your own, or whether you should sometimes share your reading with friends. Fairbairn and Fairbairn (2001) point out that choices of this kind depend on a number of factors, which include:

- The stage that your relationship with the text has reached – whether, for example, you are good friends, or have just met in a corner of a library or bookshop.

- The time you have available – whether you savour the time you spend together, or rather (like illicit lovers) you have to snatch odd moments together.

- Your reasons for reading – for example, whether you are assessing the text for relevance, are looking for particular information, or are studying it as a set part of your course.

(Fairbairn and Fairbairn, 2001, p. 69)

> Don't be a passive reader and don't take what you read at face value.

Many students believe, or act as if they believe, that while the academic authors whose books and articles they read have something to say and knowledge to share, their job is merely to access and assimilate such knowledge. If you share this belief we want to encourage you to abandon it, because you are much more likely to succeed academically if you demonstrate that you have engaged with the authors you read, subjecting them to critical appraisal, rather than accepting what they say, blindly.

> To be successful in your university career you will have to develop skill in reading critically, and in making well-founded decisions about the views you read about, and about the evidence and arguments that their authors use in presenting those views.

Rather than viewing all authors as having something worthwhile to say, and as people whose position as someone who has made it into print gives them a certain authority, a more healthy position would be to view them as participants in a public exchange of views, whose contributions need to be evaluated against criteria such as relevance, coherence, clarity and strength of argument.

In building your own arguments or points of view, there are many ways in which you can make use of your reading. Too many students limit themselves to using authors who agree with their views to 'back up' what they are saying, as if they cannot refer to views they disagree with, or believe to be flawed.

Developing as an active reader

To make the best possible use of the time you spend reading, it is important that you learn to read actively, engaging with the meanings that authors are attempting to communicate, rather than allowing them to wash over you, as if you neither have any connection with them, nor any interest in anything other than the odd fact or argument to help you to impress your lecturer at the next tutorial or seminar, or that might come in useful in an essay or assignment.

Rather than merely following the words on the page with your eyes, perhaps hearing them sound in your head as you do so, you need consciously to make the effort to understand them – and to notice when you are failing to do so. Most students will confess to 'reading', at times, with little awareness of what they are reading about. And so we do not really want to inform you that to make good use of the time you spend reading, you must read with understanding, because you knew as much before you began reading this book. Rather, we want to draw your attention to the need to keep reminding yourself to read in such a way that you are actively pursuing meaning and understanding.

Make meaning as you read

If your reading is to be as useful as it might be, it will have to be not only about the attempt to take meaning from texts – by absorbing the information and points of view they present – but about making meaning in relation to them. Active reading involves the attempt to establish connections between the meanings that the author is trying to convey and what you already know. Attempting to bring all of your previous knowledge and experience to bear when you read:

- can help you to understand the author;
- can help you to remember what the author is communicating;
- may kindle your creativity and produce interesting (and perhaps even original) thoughts, as the ideas and facts and arguments that you are reading about collide with those you are already carrying around in your head.

We tend both to understand and remember things best when we can relate them to what we already know, when we can knit them together into a complex web of interconnections. One of the most important things you can do as a reader is thus to try to relate as much of what you read as possible to what you already know, so that important new knowledge and information, ways of thinking and arguing that you glean from texts, can become integrated with the vast range of things you already know. This is a good thing to bear in mind when you are taking notes about your reading.

Evaluate the author's success in communicating her ideas

As well as being about an attempt to understand what authors intended to convey, active reading also involves an attempt to evaluate how successful they are. As you read, ask yourself whether the author is clear. If she is, try to work out what has led to this clarity. Does it result from brevity or from a good choice of words, for example?

If an author is unclear, try to work out what she might do to make herself clearer.

- Is it her language that is unclear?
- Or has she failed to give you all the information you need?

Whenever you read you should evaluate the arguments – the reasoning and evidence – that authors give to support the points of view. Try to ensure that if you use what others have written in directly defending or building your own point of view, there is some real justification for doing so. The fact that you find an author's ideas attractive and feel inclined to agree with her does not mean that she has argued well. This might seem obvious, but more people than you might believe possible fail to notice the seductive way in which finding that an author goes along with one's own point of view can numb the ability to notice that she is arguing badly.

> If an author uses examples and illustrations, are they interesting and perti-nent? If she cites evidence, ask yourself whether it is good enough. Is it strong and to the point?

Sometimes authors cite as evidence, facts that are in themselves interesting and might have been strong evidence in favour of a variety of other conclusions, but are only marginally relevant to the argument they are attempting to present. Such evidence should not sway you, however interesting you find it in its own right. Consider, for example, an author who argued at the start of the year 2000 that the Labour Government was highly successful, because it had an overwhelming majority in the House of Commons. Although this argument might have had some attraction for those who had a vested interest in portraying the Labour regime as successful, it could not have been expected to persuade anyone with any power to reason, because the size of a government's majority in itself says nothing at all about how successful it is.

Engage with the author

Whenever you read academically, you should engage with the text and thus strike up some kind of relationship with its author. Mad though it might seem, you might try to imagine, as you read, that she is sitting beside you. What questions would you want to ask her? What feelings does her work evoke in you, that you feel it would be right to share? What suggestions would you like to make about ways of improving her text? What do you know that she might find useful in developing her ideas or stating them more clearly? Have you read anything that you think she should read? Why? All of these questions will help you, if necessary, to decide what to write about this author, should you use her work in an essay.

Decide on further reading

Active reading will always involve the attempt to decide whether you should read more in relation to your topic, and if so, what. You may decide that you need to read more to allow you to understand some point or argument that the author is making. Sometimes this might involve reading sources to which she refers, but sometimes and perhaps especially when you are reading books, you may find yourself wanting to read other parts of the same book; or to re-read what you have already read, more methodically. In some instances, you will want to pursue further evidence to support or substantiate a claim made by an author; in others, you might want, in addition, to check her use of sources.

For some people, the idea of having to revisit passages that they read hours or even days earlier will suggest failure – as if they didn't do a good enough job first time round. They are mistaken. Academic reading is difficult and it will hardly ever be possible to grasp the whole meaning of a text in one reading. Moving backwards and forwards through a text is part of the process of reading actively, especially when you find yourself wanting to check again on what an author has said earlier. The author may even suggest that this will be helpful, for example, by writing, 'I want now to make use of an argument I developed earlier …', or 'Towards the end of this article, I will make use of this idea in addressing …'.

Approach the text with questions

Before beginning to read any text, try to be clear in your mind about what you hope to get from it:

- What do I hope to gain from reading this text?
- What questions can it help me to answer?
- How much time do I intend to spend reading it?
- Do I want to record what I find out and if so, how should I do it?

Your answers to these questions will depend partly on your reasons for reading and partly upon how familiar you are with the material. They should help to form the ways in which you read. For example, if the text is new to you, it will probably be best to begin in an exploratory way by undertaking a kind of reconnaissance mission. On the other hand, if it is a text you know already, you may be looking for particular bits of information and have a good idea where they are to be found.

Some students develop the unfortunate belief that whenever they read they should be trying, as far as possible, to remember everything that the author has written. Such students will often read as if they are compelled to read every word. Their vision focuses on individual ideas in a way that does not allow them to notice the grand scale of the entire forest of ideas.

In reading you have to be able to move in and out of various levels of focus. You need to be able not only to see the wood as a whole and its relationship to the intellectual landscape around it, but also to examine things at the level of the individual tree or argument, and even at the level of the individual bud or leaf – the ideas and premises, the facts and opinions – that go to make up whole arguments, theses, theories and world views.

1.5

SQ3R: Survey, Question, Read, Recite, Review

We have been discussing some informal ways of making your reading more effective by changing the ways you read and perhaps, more importantly, the ways you think about reading. We hope you will try to utilize some of these. If, however, you would rather adopt a more systematic approach, you might find the technique known as 'SQ3R' or 'Survey, Question, Read, Recite, Review' (Beard, 1990) useful in gathering information from the texts you read. It has five stages.

SQ3R: The five stages	
Survey	Survey the text to get an overall grasp of what it is about, and decide whether it is worth reading in more detail.
Question	Next, think carefully about what you hope to get from this text. What do you want to know and where in the text might you find it?
Read	Squeeze as much useful information as you can out of the text. This will probably include skimming, scanning and detailed reading.
Recite	Now try to recall what you have learned, reciting or listing it to yourself, whether by remembering inside your head, saying it out loud, or writing notes on a fresh piece of paper or computer file.
Review	Finally, review what you have done and what you should do next. Is there, for example, any further reading you should do?

Putting SQ3R to use

Let us consider how you might apply SQ3R, using as an example, a simple task based on a book for older children, *Aborigines* by Virginia Luling (1982).

As part of a study skills module you have been asked to write a short essay about Aboriginal marriage customs, including who can marry whom. Frustratingly, you are only permitted to make use of one source, Luling's book *Aborigines*.

A quick **survey** of the book will not reveal anything obvious. Nor will the table of contents reveal explicit references to marriage. However, there is a chapter about 'Childhood' and one on 'Later Life', and since you are likely to get married after childhood, you might infer that the chapter on later life seems promising. And indeed, if you were to turn to it, you would find that there is quite a lot of information about Aboriginal marriage, although it is not as helpful as you might have hoped. Since none of the other content headings seem to be any more promising, you might need to ask yourself:

Where else might I find the information that I want?

You will now be in the **question** phase of the exercise. Other than the table of contents, the other major section of the book that is likely to give you clues about where you might find the information you want is the index, which will be towards the end of the book. A quick flick through will tell you that marriage is referred to on pages 22, 23 and 30. On page 30 you will find the chapter entitled 'Later Life', to which you have already referred. However, on page 22 you will find a chapter entitled 'An Ordered World', which explains in some detail the clan and moiety system in Aboriginal society. This chapter will give you the information you want, including information about which people are allowed to marry each other; you will need to **read** it in detail.

After reading and making notes on the chapter about 'Later Life' you will wish to **recite** what you have learned, to check that you have really answered your question. Finally, you can **review** the whole process, including the difficulties of locating the information that you wanted. You might reflect, for example, that it was a pity that the chapter on 'An Ordered World' had not been entitled something like 'Marriage Customs', because that would have made your task much simpler. On the other hand, you cannot reasonably expect an author's priorities in the organizing of her book to coincide exactly with your own. Virginia Luling was not just concerned with marriage, but with broader issues about how Aborigine society is organized, and to entitle the chapter 'Marriage Customs' or something like that would not have captured her intentions properly. However, reflecting on these things as you review what you have had to do to harvest the information you needed from Luling's text might well help you to realize just how valuable a good index can be, since it reflects far more accurately the range of concerns addressed in a book than the table of contents, which, quite rightly, reflects the author's organizational priorities.

When you first start to use SQ3R you will probably find it helpful to do so with a partner or even as part of a small group, so that you gain more confidence by having other points of view to set against your own. However, as you grow more experienced in this approach, you will probably begin to use it without thinking, as it becomes one of your reading habits or disciplines.

Give SQ3R a try

It would be a really good idea to try SQ3R for yourself as soon as possible, remembering that it will yield the best results if you use it flexibly. Give yourself permission to use it in whatever ways you find best. Although the stages are clearly laid out, the sky won't fall in if you deviate from them a little, for example, by allowing yourself the freedom to return to an earlier stage if that would be helpful. Having reached the recite stage, for instance, you might realize that you didn't undertake sufficiently detailed reading of a section of a chapter with what looked to be a strong argument that could be helpful to you in building the case you want to present in your essay. If that happens, just go back and read it again.

Task 10: Trying out SQ3R

Imagine that as part of a study skills development module your tutor has asked you to utilize SQ3R in finding out what you can about what Fairbairn and Winch (2011) have to say about common problems in the ways that people construct written arguments, in *Reading, Writing and Reasoning* – the book you are reading at the moment. She has pointed out that problems in reasoning are common, not just in student essays, but also in some professional academic work. She has drawn your attention, in particular, to the use of methods of persuasion that rely on non-rational means, rather than on cogent argument, and asks you to find out what you can about this.

Use what you have learned about SQ3R to address your tutor's task:

What is meant by the term 'non-rational means of persuasion'?

[Our response appears on page 247]

Remember that the first stage of SQ3R merely involves **surveying** the text to get a general idea of what it is about, in order to decide how helpful it might be for your purposes – skimming and scanning the text for relevant words, phrases or headings. Try to avoid being drawn too quickly into detailed reading, no matter how interesting the text seems; and try to be as methodical as you can, using the structural features of the text, including the contents list, index, summaries of chapters and so on. In a way, the survey stage of SQ3R is rather like making a reconnaissance flight over the territory the book covers, allowing you to map the conceptual landscape and to spot particular locations that merit closer attention. Having done this you are then in a position, at the **question** stage, to prepare yourself to visit these locations in a productive way, by thinking carefully about what you want to get from them, and formulating questions with which to approach them. What do you want to know? You are likely, even before the survey stage, to have had some ideas about the questions you wanted to ask of the text, but having gained a basic understanding of it, you will now be able to develop the questions by which you will interrogate it, in more detail.

It is because your time for reading is limited that preparing the way by surveying the text carefully, and thinking in detail about what you want to get from it, is worthwhile. Doing so means that when, in the next phase, you turn to detailed **reading**, your time is more likely to be well spent. However, it is important that at this stage you should take just as much care as you did earlier, adopting appropriate reading strategies and reading in different ways. Some of the time you will be scanning for information; sometimes you will skim sections and at other times you will slow right down, reading slowly and carefully to allow you to absorb factual information and to understand detailed arguments. You may want to take notes as you read, but you may feel that it is better to leave note-taking until the next stage, when you have more idea of what it is that you wish to take notes about.

Often you will need to read and re-read a passage several times until you are satisfied that you understand it and all its implications. Re-reading a passage should only very rarely be about simply reading it for a second or third time. It is much more likely that you will do so with different questions in mind than those with which you approached it on the first occasion – filling in gaps, making sure that you understood things correctly, checking details. In addition, during the second and subsequent readings you are likely to want to focus on sections that you found particularly difficult during the first reading as, in a sense, you become more of an expert on its subject matter.

Once you have systematically read the text and harvested everything you can from it, it is as well to take a rest, before moving on the next stage, when you reflect about what you have learned – to literally recall it and **recite** it to yourself, asking whether you have found answers to the questions with which you approached it. At this stage, even if you took notes while you were reading, you should certainly be taking notes, perhaps reorganizing and extending notes you took earlier. Finally, you should **review** what you have done, looking over the text again, to make sure that you haven't missed anything important. Have you found what you wanted? Make sure that you have gleaned everything you can from this text that will help to answer the questions you set at the beginning. Now look to the future. What should you do next? Is there more reading to be done? For example, have you come across references in this text that it will be worth exploring? You should also, at this stage, think about whether there is now any more reading you should do, or anything else you might now do to take your understanding further, such as discussing what you have found with friends or your lecturer.

1.6

Taking notes about what you have read

As a student you will be expected to remember, organize and make use of enormous amounts of information, most of which will probably come from your reading. Some will be the kind of information that we commonly refer to as 'knowledge', implying that there is a certain definiteness about it, or that it makes so much sense that people accept it as true. Other information that you will be expected to acquire and use will not be knowledge. Rather, it will take the form of opinions and points of view. When you take notes, you will have to find ways of distinguishing between these different kinds of information.

Why take notes while reading?

The range of reasons that people have (or think they have) for writing notes is huge. For example, you may make notes:

- to help you to remember the main points in the text/to jog your memory later;
- to give you ready access to particular facts and arguments in an easier form;
- to link new knowledge to what you already know;
- to help you to understand what an author is saying;
- to make a record of points that you might want to use in an essay.

Sometimes books or articles will strike you as so important, or so interesting, that they will stick in your memory without recording them. However, it is probably always best to work on the assumption that unless you record what you have read, you are going to forget it, or that even if you remember it, you are likely to forget that you do. Memory is a complex business. We do not usually remember the two times table when we are driving down the road, or a poem that we committed to memory as children when we are watching television. And unless we do some work in securing its memory, we may not remember what we have learned from a text.

Note-taking can help you to focus on what you read, but it can only do so if you remain aware of what you are taking notes about and why. As with all other aspects of reading, the most important thing about note-taking is that you should engage your brain: mindless note-taking is generally bad note-taking. Be discriminating, whatever style of note-taking you favour. Try to ensure that the notes you make will help you to recall not only the information the author is seeking to convey and her views, but your reactions to what she has to say. Reading actively, always attempting to relate what you read to what you know, will help you to avoid the possibility of becoming a mindless note-taker.

How do you take notes?

There are huge variations in the ways in which people write notes. Think a little about how you take notes when you are reading. Then reflect on the questions below.

- Do you take notes as you read, or do you read first and return to take notes during a second or even third reading? Do you perhaps take brief notes as you read and fill them out later?

- Do you ever take notes with the book or other text closed, then check what you have written by re-reading relevant passages?

- What form do your textual notes take? Are they different from your notes on lectures?

- Do you take linear notes – like a condensed version of the original? Do you write them in your own words? Or do you copy bits of what the author has said? Do you ensure that you distinguish her words and your own? How?

- Do you make pictorial/diagrammatic notes, using, for example 'web diagrams' or 'mind maps'?

- Do you record key words?

- Do you re-work your notes later? For example, do you transfer key words and main ideas to index cards or to computer files?

However you take notes, do make sure that you maintain an accurate biblio-graphical record of each source, including the pages on which quotations are to be found. How do you do it: in a big notebook, on index cards, using a computer database?

Make sure that your notes are clear and contain enough to be worthwhile. In particular, ensure that you maintain a full bibliographic record for all sources you have consulted and might use in the future.

Don't waste time taking notes about things that you already know.

The best place to keep notes is somewhere safe, where you can find them and access them easily, but where it is virtually impossible for them to get lost.

A computer file, or a series of files in a folder, is probably the simplest and best place to store your notes from your reading, but having a regularly updated printed version is a good idea. (And for goodness sake, make sure you have at least two electronic copies.)

Make sure that the files that contain your notes are labelled clearly, in a way that will allow you to remember what they contain, then organize them in a folder or series of folders in a way that allows you to access them easily. This has the advantage that when you come to write your essay, you can copy notes directly into the text, where they can be worked on.

Always make notes in your own words. If you handwrite them while you are reading a book or other source, transfer them to your computer right away, or as soon as possible. Remember that the longer you leave it, the more likely it is that you will lose them.

Make sure any handwritten notes are clear enough for you to be able to read them when you look at them in the absence of the relevant source. This is important, because writing notes is a good way of coming to understand the text, seeing what is essential and expressing that in your own words.

Take notes in your own words and avoid copying out large chunks of text.

Suggesting that you should make notes using your own words does not mean that you should not transcribe direct quotations from the text. However, you should take care if you do, to ensure that it is clear which words are yours and which come from someone else and label them clearly at the time. Don't risk doing this later, when you may have forgotten.

Only where you feel that a quotation is particularly apt or where it expresses an idea so clearly that you could not put it better yourself, even in note form, should you quote verbatim.

Never write in books owned by other people, or by libraries.

Don't write in books you own, without thinking very carefully about it. A book is a very cumbersome place in which to store notes, and in any case you might live to regret it.

If you decide that annotating important passages will help you to remember what you thought about them, in the future, beware of the temptation to clutter your books with your immediate reactions, especially if you disagree strongly with the author.

Part 2

Writing as a student

In Part 1, we discussed the importance of reading, both as a way of gathering information and knowledge, and of helping you to develop your own ideas by interacting with those of others. In Part 2, we turn to the skills and disciplines that are necessary for academic writing. Although our intention is to meet the needs of both undergraduates and postgraduates, much of what we have to say, especially about the writing process, will also be relevant for professional academics. In addition, although our focus is academic writing, much of what we say is relevant for those who engage in careful writing of any kind.

We begin with the need to think carefully about the writing tasks you are set as a student. For the sake of simplicity, we sometimes use the word 'essay' in a generic way to refer to any writing required of students, including scientific reports, evaluations of practice placements, proposals for research or other practical projects, and dissertations or theses.

People approach writing in different ways and it is important that you should find an approach that suits you – your personality, your lifestyle and the kind of writing that you are required to undertake.

We consider different approaches and look at some ways in which you can try to ensure that your written work is as good as it can be, including the development of a style that communicates clearly and simply. We address the need to strive for clarity when you are writing about complex ideas, and to take care over basics such as punctuation, spelling and grammar. Finally, we offer a detailed guide to the conventions of citation and referencing, which set academic writing apart from other kinds of writing, and discuss ways in which the need for citation can help you to develop the text of your essays.

2.1

The purpose of essays and other written tasks

Academic writing is different from other kinds of writing in a number of ways. Chief among these is the requirement to acknowledge the influence of others, using conventions of citation and referencing, which we discuss in 2.4. Other differences concern, for example, purpose and style. It is important to reflect on these, to avoid making the effort involved in writing essays and assignments, only to discover that your hard work is rewarded by a poor mark, because you have failed to establish the right register.

Task 11: What distinguishes one form of writing from another?

What do the following forms of writing aim to communicate? What differences in approach and in style might you expect to find between them?

- A poem
- A scientific report
- An article in a serious (broadsheet) newspaper
- A field guide to British birds
- A blog
- A novel
- An email to a colleague
- A message on a social networking site
- An essay written as part of an undergraduate degree

- Details from an estate agent about a house for sale

- An illustrated biography of a famous painter

- An article in a tabloid newspaper

- A letter of application for a job

In identifying the differences you should focus on style, layout and language, as well as content and the reasons the author has for writing. For example, ask yourself whether you would expect the language used to be:

- Easy or difficult?

- Formal or informal?

- Longwinded or succinct?

- Serious or light-hearted?

[Our response appears on page 248]

Many students in the early part of their course have the impression that the purpose of essays and assignments is simply to show how much they know. As a result their written work is packed full of ideas and facts that they have harvested from lectures, books, web pages and academic articles. Sometimes they even develop the misguided idea that the primary purpose of essays is to persuade someone else that they are in possession of specific knowledge. In extreme cases this leads to a kind of 'Guess what she's thinking' attitude to essay writing, which depends on the belief that their lecturer already knows the answer, and that all they have to do is to guess what she's thinking and then write it down. Do you ever entertain this idea?

In most instances, the idea that all that is required of a student essay is that it should demonstrate knowledge is incorrect.

Most essays require students to show that they have thought carefully about the topic or question, and have something coherent to say about it. To do this successfully they will have to develop the ability to organize and structure ideas in engaging and well-argued prose. Unfortunately, even when they realize that there is more to writing an essay than cramming it with information, or trying to ensure that the information it contains matches up with what their lecturer wants to hear, many students fail to write well-structured and persuasive essays.

Sometimes, of course, demonstrating that one possesses particular knowledge is a large part of the task. This is perhaps most likely in the sciences and on courses designed to prepare students for professional practice in, for example, health care, where specified curricular knowledge may be laid down by an outside professional body as part of an accreditation process. However, even when you are expected to demonstrate particular knowledge, you should beware of simply regurgitating notes, whether from lectures and tutorials, from books, articles or other sources. This mistake is not uncommon, particularly during exams, when information that has been 'crammed in' to your brain may have a tendency to burst out onto the page in any old order, whether or not it is relevant to the question.

Expectations in different areas of academic study vary enormously. For example, students writing in history or philosophy will usually have to demonstrate skill in handling concepts and in critiquing and constructing arguments. In contrast, a report of a project in a science or social science might be expected to include tables of results, statistical analyses and a discussion of the implications of findings and conclusions.

Variations exist not only between the expectations that are placed on students writing in different disciplines, but also in the nature of the writing required in different academic contexts. What is expected of an essay written as one of a pair, during a two-hour examination, will be different from what is expected of a 3000-word coursework essay on the same topic, written over an extended period. In each case, it would be reasonable for the examiner to expect a coherent attempt to address the question or topic. However, the level of argument and use of relevant literature that would be expected would differ. And although in an exam you will not normally be expected to give detailed references to sources, this will be expected in coursework.

> Whenever you write as a student, whether you are writing an essay, a dissertation or a short answer in an exam, remember that the way in which you organize and structure your work is crucially important if you want to help your reader to understand what you are saying.

One thing that all essays have in common is that they have word limits. You should pay close attention to these, both because they can be helpful in developing the discipline you need to ensure that you keep your essay focused, and because depending on your institution, you may be severely penalized if you go more than a few words over the limit you are given.

Word limits and the responsibilities of the author

No matter what you are writing, you should be careful not to squander the words you have available. Students at the beginning of their course, who are not used to writing anything other than relatively short essays, often think that writing 3000 or even 2000 words is almost impossible. In reality, an essay of 2000–3000 words is quite short, and in most cases the really difficult problem you will encounter is not finding enough words to fill your essay, but in deciding what you should cut out, to get it down to size. Try to develop the discipline of getting rid of anything that is not essential to your answer. This will involve learning to spot irrelevancies.

> If a word or sentence doesn't add something important, cut it out, even if you think it sounds nice.

When you have a limited number of words available it is likely that as well as cutting out material that is at best only marginally relevant, you will find it necessary to omit much that is relevant. Part of the skill in writing essays is in deciding what is essential and what is not from the relevant material you have at hand. To stay within word limits you will often have to assume that certain ideas and arguments are familiar to your readers. However, you must remember that part of your task will often be to show that you understand ideas and arguments to which you have been introduced in classes.

> To decide which ideas you can use without explanation and which you must explain, you will have to think carefully about the main point of the question or task.

Some questions more than others will be a test of what you know. Some will be more of a test of your ability to think through a problem for yourself. All will be a test of your ability to select appropriate material and to make decisions about what is centrally important in presenting a case.

Be especially careful if you are set an assignment with a larger word limit than usual. Too often students regard longer word limits as an excuse for relaxing the need to make every word and every sentence count for something. As a result, they may ramble on about very little, wasting words and their readers' time with facts or opinions that are only relevant in a tangential way, and even with material that is irrelevant, and serves only to fill space. Writing takes not only skill but discipline, and one of the most important disciplines you should strive to develop relates to the attempt to make every word earn its keep.

> Pay attention to word limits and do not exceed them by making sure that every word, every sentence and every paragraph in your essays pays its way.

Once they get further into their courses, students often worry that within the word limits that are put upon essays they cannot say everything that they think is important. This is understandable; most people who write professionally have the same difficulty. But it is part of growing up as a writer that you have to learn to take responsibility for what you leave in and what you leave out of your written work. Of course, in marking work at both undergraduate and postgraduate level, lecturers may write things of this kind in the margin:

> This is good as far as it goes, but I would have liked to have seen more discussion of the theory that underpins the approaches that you outline really quite well.

> You should have pursued this point in more depth.

> More about the causes of world poverty, including the purchasing strategies of major retailers, would have been helpful.

Comments of this kind can be upsetting if the additional material your lecturer would have liked was in your essay until you cut it out to get it down to the word limit. However, there is little you can do about it, other than ensuring, next time, that you write in a way that convinces her that you have missed particular points out because you believe others to be more important, rather than through ignorance or lack of thought. You can do this, for example, by briefly mentioning ideas you are not going to address in detail, before focusing on the ones that you judge to be more important.

Different types of essay

The purposes of essays vary. Some give you the opportunity to demonstrate how much you have learned. Others are intended to find out how well you can think. All offer you the opportunity to show that you are aware, to some extent, of what others have written and that you have thought about what they have said.

Always make sure that you understand what you are being asked to do, checking, if necessary, with the person who set the question or task.

Direct questions

Many essays are written in response to questions, for example:

- How did the British Government try to rally public support for the war effort during the Second World War?

- What sources of energy are available, other than those that are locked inside fossil fuels?

Questions of this kind seem simply to invite you to reveal the knowledge you have stored away. They do not demand much evidence of thought, although you would probably score even better marks if you showed that you had done some thinking. For example, in relation to the first question, it would almost certainly be worth introducing your awareness that some tactics, such as encouraging people to 'dig for victory', were more successful than others. Of course, not all essay questions are quite so straightforward. Consider, for example, the following questions, which would involve students drawing on the same bank of knowledge as the previous two:

- How successful was the British Government in rallying public support for the war effort during the Second World War?

- Which potential alternatives to the energy that we currently source by consuming fossil fuels are the most promising for the future?

Constructing an adequate answer to these questions would involve demonstrating the ability to make judgements, and to make use of your knowledge to justify your point of view. For example, in relation to the first, you would not only have to describe some of the tactics the government adopted, but also offer arguments for concluding that some were more successful than others. And in relation to the second, as well as demonstrating knowledge of different alternative energy sources, you would have to offer an account of the advantages and disadvantages of each, and come to a reasoned view about which are most promising.

Instructions rather than questions

Although we often refer to all essays as if they are written as answers to questions, in reality, of course, many are written in response to an instruction rather than a question, for example:

- Compare the traditional music of Scotland with that of Ireland.

- Discuss the mental health of the leader of a political party of your choice, as evidenced by party policy and media reports.

- Give an account of the synthetic production of living organisms, beginning with raw materials found in the average student's fridge.

In working on essays of this kind, you may find it helpful to think about how the topic might be translated into a question. Doing so will often help you to develop an individual slant or viewpoint from which to approach the topic.

Task 12: Turning essay topics into questions

Consider the essay topics listed above and, in relation to each, try to devise a question that would help you to address the topic.

[Our response appears on page 249]

Describing, discussing, critically evaluating and comparing

Instructions for essays often expect students to describe, discuss, critically evaluate or compare phenomena, ideas, people or events. Consider, for example, the following:

Description

- Describe Darwin's theory of evolution.
- Describe the ways in which behavioural psychology has been used in schools.
- Describe the causes of the Second World War.

Discussion

- Discuss the view that Darwin's evolutionary theory led to a revolution in nineteenth-century thought.
- Discuss the view that the influence of behavioural psychology is to be seen in every well-ordered school.
- Discuss the causes of the Second World War.

Critical evaluation

- Critically evaluate the claim that Darwin's theory of evolution can fully explain how the flora and fauna of the earth attained their present forms.
- Critically evaluate the claim that behavioural psychology can explain more than 75 per cent of human behaviour.
- Critically evaluate Mead's account of the causes of the Second World War.

Comparison

- Compare Darwin's description of the origin of species with that given in the Old Testament.

- Compare and contrast the behaviourist account of the development of morality with the psychodynamic account.

- Compare Mead's account of the causes of the Second World War with that given by D. G. Jones.

Description

Descriptive essays are probably the simplest form of essay. Bear in mind, however, that description is not always a simple matter, since you will sometimes have to decide between several contrasting accounts of, for example, a state of affairs, theory or event.

Discussion

Essays that ask for discussion will usually take more thought than descriptive ones. For example, if you were asked to 'Discuss the causes of the Second World War', you would probably feel compelled to discuss the strengths and weaknesses of the various possible accounts, and might even give reasons for accepting or rejecting them.

Critical evaluation

In an evaluative essay you will be expected to demonstrate the ability to make judgements between alternatives, and to develop commitment to a point of view, which you support with argument and/or evidence.

Comparison

Comparison can take place at the level of description, discussion or critical evaluation, depending on what you are asked to compare, and will often contain elements of all three. For example, in comparing two contrasting plays by the same writer you might simply 'describe' the ways in which their plots unfold, their relationship to each other and to the rest of a playwright's work, whereas in comparing two theories about the origin of the universe, you might 'evaluate' the support for each and conclude that one had more going for it than the other.

Our attempt to categorize essay questions and topics in terms of description, discussion, evaluation and comparison reflects the way in which essay-type tasks are often formulated or worded. However, as we have already implied, the expectations in each case are, in truth, less distinct and there is often a degree of overlap. So, for example, many questions that are framed in terms of 'description' will give you the opportunity to do more than simply describe an event, situation, theory or state of affairs, as if there is only one way of doing so. Indeed, a satisfactory answer to some such questions will involve showing awareness of alternative descriptions, and giving reasons for accepting one rather than others. For example, the essay titles 'Describe the origins of the universe' and 'Describe the way in which children develop language' each demand a discussion and evaluation of competing theories.

> Whenever you are writing an essay or assignment, think carefully about what a particular question or task is getting at – at what it might be trying to get you to do, both before you begin work, and then at various points during the writing process.

In deciding which approach to adopt in writing an essay you should remember that your lecturers' expectations will often relate partly to the knowledge and skills they can expect you to have acquired during your course, through private study as well as through classes. As a result, it is important, when you are writing, to be conscious of the ways in which you have been taught. For example, while an essay that asked for a comparison between contrasting accounts of economic development in post-colonial Ghana could be dealt with purely descriptively, it could also be dealt with more analytically. It would therefore be important for students to ensure that they approached such an essay in ways that matched the expectations of their tutor. If, for example, she had taught in such a way that comparison always involved the evaluation of evidence and the attempt to decide which of two or more possibilities was more likely, it would make sense to approach the task in this way.

> In general, you are likely to impress your readers more, and therefore to gain higher marks, if you demonstrate the ability to critique and evaluate alternative points of view, and the evidence in their favour.

Task 13: Description, discussion, evaluation or comparison?

Read each of the questions that follow and decide whether it invites description, discussion, evaluation or comparison, or some combination of these.

1 Is the building of structures such as the Great Wall of China and Hadrian's Wall a sign of weakness or of strength?

2 Does research on the exposure of organic materials to light have any practical application?

3 How does Shakespeare introduce us to the complexities of the character of Hamlet, Prince of Denmark?

4   Would a society in which it was traditional to eat one's dead, rather than, for example, burying or cremating them, be for that reason alone, an immoral one?

5   What impact did the terrorist attacks of 9/11 in New York and 7/7 in London have on the identity of British Muslims?

6   How may the landscape of South West Scotland be explained by reference to the geology of the area?

7   How valid is the view that the central character of the twentieth century is to be located in the acts of human depravity that it hosted, rather than in the technological advances to which it gave birth?

[Our response appears on page 249]

2.2

The writing process

Having said a little about some of the different kinds of essays you might be expected to write as part of your course, we turn now to the process of writing, because it is undoubtedly the case that by becoming more aware of different ways of approaching writing tasks, you will be able to improve both your writing and your life.

Engaging your reader

Whatever approach to writing you adopt, it is important to remember that your first paragraph introduces those who are reading it not only to your topic, but to you as a writer. You should aim in this first encounter with your reader to engage and interest (even excite) her and thus to convince her that it will be worthwhile reading further. When she gets to the end of your concluding paragraph, she should feel that the time she has devoted to your work was time well spent. If you achieve this you are likely to attain a good grade whether or not what you have written agrees with the reader's own views.

> Your job is to interest your reader and convince her not only that you know something but also that you have thought about the topic.

Some tutors may be impressed if you show how much you remember of your lectures and how much you have read. All will be impressed if you show you have thought about these things and how they relate to your topic.

Getting around to writing

More than anything else, what is important if you have an essay to write is that you should write. This might sound obvious, but it is important. As authors we are only too aware that the main problem faced by most people who have to write (including us and including you) is the temptation to put off doing so until the time is 'right'. It never is, at least for most people, because there is always something else that needs to be done, that can seduce us into thinking that it is more urgent than our writing, however important. That is why writing often gets left to the last minute, so that there isn't enough time to write as well as we would ideally wish to write.

Task 14: Excuses for not getting round to writing

We are all able to come up with reasons for not getting round to the important writing tasks in which we have to engage, and most authors we know frequently use such reasons as excuses for avoiding writing tasks. We list below a few examples of popular excuses for avoiding essay writing. Add your own favourites to our list, and then try to be aware of occasions when you try to use them, and avoid doing so.

I've got too much other stuff on at the moment to be able to concentrate on this as well.

I don't really understand the question, so there's no point starting until I've managed to sort that out … and my tutor never answers my emails.

I want to get all the reading I need to do for this essay done first and I haven't really got the time to do that at the moment.

I can't decide which of the topics for this essay I want to do, because I haven't managed to get hold of any of the recommended readings.

Writing for five minutes

The most significant hurdle in writing, as with many other tasks – academic or otherwise – is getting started. One way round this problem is to set yourself a really manageable target, one that will take you some way towards the moment when you decide that your essay or other assignment is ready for submission. The task should be one that will help you to move towards completion of your work, but so small that it is hardly conceivable that you could fail to succeed, no matter how tired, depressed, lonely, hassled or bored you feel. The next day, or the next time you come to this piece of writing, you will have made a start, and you will already have a draft, however short and however bad. And since short drafts can always be made longer and bad ones improved, the next stage should follow more easily.

The trick in utilizing this tactic is in inventing tasks that genuinely take you some way towards completion of the writing you have to do, but are so small that failure is pretty well impossible. Task 15 invites you to try out an approach of this kind, which can be used in relation to any topic. One of us has used it very successfully with school pupils of all ages, as well as with students and other inexperienced writers, inside and outside academia (Canter and Fairbairn, 2006; Fairbairn and Fairbairn, 2005). It involves writing for a very short time – only five minutes, but it has strict rules about how you should proceed. Have a look at the rules in the box below, then try the task that follows.

Rules for 'Writing for five minutes'

Write for no less and definitely no more than five minutes. This will necessitate a decent clock or a watch with a second hand.

Once you start writing you must not stop until five minutes have passed.

You must not think about what to write before writing it.

If you run out of things to say, rewrite the last word over and over again until you come up with something else to write (if you want you can substitute your name, or your favourite swear word).

You must not allow yourself to be distracted into thinking about the words you use; just write the words that come, uninvited, into your head as you are writing.

You must not stop to think about punctuation or spelling.

You must not allow yourself to worry about whether what you are writing is making sense.

You must not allow thoughts about whether what you are writing will impress your readers to come between you and your writing.

You must not allow yourself to worry about how you might justify what you are saying.

Task 15: Writing for five minutes

Even if, like most people, you usually write on a computer, we suggest that you undertake this exercise using pen and paper, because doing so will be helpful.

We want you to write for five minutes on one of the following topics:

- What I did last weekend.

- What I want to do next weekend.

- My best holiday ever.

- My worst holiday ever.

- Any other topic you'd prefer to write about, so long as it has nothing to do with your course.

Before you begin writing you should make sure that you won't be disturbed and that you are able to time yourself accurately – the best thing is a watch or clock with a second hand, or the stopwatch on your mobile.

Make sure, also, that you have a fresh page to write on and more pages that you can use if necessary, and make sure your pen is writing OK.

Write the title of the piece at the top of the page.

Make sure you recall the rules for five minutes writing, by re-reading the box.

Write for five minutes on your chosen topic, making sure that you obey the rules.

When you've finished, count the number of words you've written and write the total at the end of your text.

If you feel the need, you might want to read what you've written to see whether it makes any sense at all, but don't feel you have to do this.

Most people are astonished at how much they manage to write in only five minutes, and those who read what they have written are usually surprised to discover that they have written something of value. Often they will find that at least some of what they have written reads pretty well; often they are surprised to discover that what they have written makes sense, even though while they were writing they had no idea what they were going to say before the words poured out of their pen onto the page. Sometimes they even find that they have written things that they had never thought of before, or have written about them in unexpected ways, almost as if someone else was writing and not them.

The hardest part of writing for most people is the production of text. Becoming a writer of any kind involves developing the discipline and stamina that are necessary if you are to make the best use of the opportunities that you have for doing so. Inexperienced authors often think that it is only possible to write if they have a decent chunk of time in which to settle into writing. Writing for five minutes can persuade them that this is not true.

One reason that writing is so hard for people is that they often get so hung up about getting things right before they write them down, that they end up writing nothing. That is why we offer the following advice to everyone we are helping to develop as a writer:

Don't get it right, get it written[1].

Becoming a writer involves learning that it is better to write something that is not good enough, than to put off writing until you have time to write something better. Once you have written something, even if it is not good enough (and a first draft rarely will be), you can then work on it to make it better, gradually sculpting it into the shape that you want.

Task 16: Write for five minutes a day

After introducing people to the idea of writing for five minutes, we suggest that they should try to repeat this task on a daily basis for a week or two, writing each day about a different topic of their choice. And that is what we want to suggest that you should do.

It does not matter when you do it – whether, for example, you do it at the same time each day, or just when you can find the time. What is important is that you do the writing task seriously each day, and that you obey the rules carefully.

The topic is not important, although we suggest that at least initially you should write about topics that are unrelated to your academic work. So, for example, you could write for five minutes about:

- What I have done since I got up this morning.
- My favourite place on earth.
- My favourite person (on earth).
- What I'd most like to be doing right now instead of writing this.
- My favourite walk.
- The most enjoyable thing I have ever done.
- My favourite novel (or movie).

After a week or so of writing for five minutes a day, change to writing about more serious things, including your academic work.

Writing regularly for five minutes is a good way of developing both the stamina and the discipline that are necessary if you are to become a writer who is both willing and able to endure the slog of producing text, even on days when you don't feel like writing (and there will be many of those).

---

[1] This is such sensible advice that we feel sure it must have an owner. Unfortunately, we have no idea who first said it, because it is not something we can remember reading or hearing. Nonetheless, we acknowledge her or him, whoever she or he is.

We are not suggesting that you should undertake five minutes of writing a day in addition to all the other work that you have to do. On the contrary, after the initial week or so, you will probably find it helpful to begin using your daily five minutes of writing to write about something that you want to write about anyway. For example, you might use it to write some notes about a recent lecture or tutorial. Or you might use it to begin drafting an essay. If you decide to do this you might, for example, find it helpful (at least initially) to begin your five minutes of writing with the words, 'In this essay I …'. Even more usefully, you might find that later on in the process of writing an essay, the discipline of writing for five minutes is helpful in getting started on a particular aspect of your topic that you are finding difficult.

> Never use 'five minutes of writing' as a time for editing or redrafting.

This approach to writing in a disciplined way is intended for the production of text, not for its improvement, for getting it right.

A final word about 'writing for five minutes'

When we introduced the idea of 'five minutes of writing', we said that you should use paper and pen or pencil. However, if as we suggest, you begin to adopt it as a regular part of your approach to writing, you should change to writing on a computer after a week or two, or as soon as you have got used to the idea of writing in accordance with the 'rules'.

Getting started on an essay or other writing task

In five minutes' writing or typing, most people should be able to write 100–200 words, enough text for a short draft of an essay, and so you might decide to apply the discipline of writing for five minutes in this way. However, if that is too difficult, we suggest that you set yourself an even smaller task, say to write three sentences about what you want to say. They might focus on a number of areas:

- What you are going to address in this essay.
- One interesting fact about the topic/one thing someone else has said about it.
- One idea you want to explore.

If you get really excited, you might add a fourth sentence about:

- One problem you have in thinking about this topic.

The object is to ensure that you make progress, however limited. If you adopt this approach to getting started, the next time you approach a writing task with which you have found difficulty, you will have three or four sentences with which to work, rather than a blank sheet of paper or an empty computer file. The next step might be to imagine the questions that someone to whom your topic is completely new might ask, before writing what you think would be sufficient to ensure that the next person who reads your text won't have to ask these questions again.

As an alternative to writing three sentences at your first sitting, you might prefer to begin by writing a list of keywords or short phrases that you might want to include in your essay – rather like a shopping list, that you play around with – arranging and re-arranging them, adding ideas and explanations about their place in the essay that you imagine writing, before turning your list into as many sentences as it takes to say something about each idea you have listed, in a way that begins to address the question or topic you have been set.

For the next few days you should set yourself a short time each day to work on your developing text, adding more details and thinking about the order of your material; we find that tasks like this are often best accomplished if you reward yourself for your diligence, while undertaking them, with a decent coffee and a cake, preferably somewhere away from distractions – maybe at an art gallery or coffee shop where you are unlikely to meet friends.

Approaches to writing

Sometimes students claim that for them the best approach to writing an essay is to read around their topic, looking for inspiration and gathering information and possible references, before planning carefully, and writing an initial draft, with all the necessary references ready to hand. For some people, this is undoubtedly a good way to proceed. However, it is as well to be aware of a couple of problems to which it can lead.

The first arises for students who unwisely allow themselves to become focused on the idea that if they read enough, the answer to the question set or the right way of addressing the topic set will somehow become obvious, as if it is located somewhere in the sources they consult, just waiting to be found. In most instances, this is a foolish way to think. One problem to which this leads is that such students often become focused on the idea that particular sources are the ones that they 'must have' before they can even start writing their essay. And since, not surprisingly, such sources are usually the ones that have already been taken out on loan, they will often put off starting work while they wait for that precious source to become available, so that in the end it becomes like the 'Holy Grail' for them[2]. As a result, it is common for such students to put off working on their essay until so late in the day that in the end they have to rush it, knowing as they do that the mark they might have got had they started earlier is now beyond their reach.

The second problem arises for students who are lucky enough to find lots of material that seems relevant or possibly relevant to their essay – they begin reading; they read and they read and they read, until reading takes over, and they find it difficult to stop. As a result, it becomes increasingly difficult for them to get round to writing. What is more, once they do stop, they find that they have accumulated so much information that it is difficult to decide where to begin, and even to decide what to say. In other words, their heads and their notes have become so full of other people's ideas that they find it difficult to begin to work out their own point of view, and hence to begin the process of communicating that to others through their essay.

> It is no good reading enormous amounts of background material, making copious notes, and being so overwhelmed by what might be said that it becomes impossible to decide what should be said.

Think, plan, write and revise (but not necessarily in that order)

Students are often advised that when they are writing an essay, they should:

Think, plan, write and revise.

In a way this is sound advice, because all of these activities are necessary for successful writing. However, it is important to realize that most people will move between them as they write. For example, they might think about what they want to say and sketch out a plan of how to say it, before they begin to work on the first draft of an essay. However, as they write, they might realize that their material will communicate more clearly if they re-order it, and think of other ideas that they want to add. As a result, they might amend their plan before carrying on writing.

---

[2] The 'Holy Grail', which figures in the legend of King Arthur, was the mythical vessel used by Christ during the last supper, celebrated in the Christian sacrament of holy communion. To 'search for the Holy Grail' is to seek for an unfindable treasure.

Some writers find that a rigid step-by-step approach suits them best and 'Think, plan, write and revise', in that order.

Others find that a more flexible approach in which they move freely between thinking, planning, writing and revising suits them better.

Two contrasting approaches

We want now to introduce you to two approaches to writing that lie at opposite ends of a continuum.

i. The first is highly structured, involves the development of detailed plans, and stresses the need to know, beforehand, pretty much what you want to say.

ii. The second puts more stress on the gradual development of text in an apparently spontaneous way. It does not rely, at least initially, on planning and involves writing without thinking too much about what you want to say, before you begin.

Most authors, whether in the academic world or elsewhere, and whether students or professionals, would recognize in our characterizations of these approaches, at least the general pattern of the ways they approach writing; and most, if asked, would be able to say whether they were more inclined to planning or spontaneity.

For most writers, writing is a process in which they move between thinking, planning, writing and revising (although not necessarily in that order), gradually developing a coherent way of presenting their views.

i   A highly structured approach to writing

If you decide to use a structured approach to writing, you may find it helpful to prepare an outline before writing a first draft. This will help to ensure that you cover all relevant points and avoid repetition. Preparing an outline should also help you to work out the best order for the ideas and information you want to include in your essay.

In preparing an outline, consider carefully what you want to say:

- How should you best introduce it?
- How will you conclude?
- What are the central points of your argument?

You may find the following plan helpful in developing your first draft.

Writing your first draft: a highly structured approach

Decide what you want to say

List the main points you want to include in your essay. Paradoxically, you should think, right at the beginning, about what you wish to conclude, since this will influence what you decide to include in the main body of your essay.

Get your points in order

Work out the most helpful order for presenting your main points, that is, an order in which ideas and arguments flow naturally from one another.

Arguments and evidence

Sketch out any arguments that you intend to use and evidence you intend to employ in arguing for your conclusions.

Decide on examples and illustrations

Identify examples and illustrations that will help to develop and support the point of view or conclusions for which you argue. Never choose them simply because they are interesting or important for some other reason.

Make a skeleton of your essay

Include a note of examples, illustrations and key references you expect to use.

Decide on references

Make sure that you either have access to all sources you want to cite, or have accurate notes and full bibliographical details.

Check your plan for coherence

Check that the ideas you want to present follow on from one another coherently and that they really do lead to your conclusion. If they don't, add linking ideas.

Write a sketch of your introduction[3]

Write a draft introduction that aims to engage your readers by giving a 'trailer' for what is to come. Avoid the temptation to present a long-winded plan of what you intend to do in the essay.

---

[3] It will often be best to write the final version of your introduction last after you have finished the main text, because by then you know what you are introducing.

If you have to say what you're going to do, do it clearly and simply; don't make a meal of it.

Write a draft of the remainder of the essay
Using the structure you have developed and the examples and references you have decided on, write an initial draft of your essay.

Write the conclusion
At this point, you may wish to emphasize some points, recapitulate on the main threads in your argument, or indicate areas into which you have not entered, because to do so would have taken too much space. Make sure that your conclusion doesn't waste space or your reader's time by simply repeating what is said elsewhere.

A less rigid approach

An alternative to a highly structured approach to writing is to find ways of allowing your essay to plan itself, as the ideas for it gradually emerge over a period of writing and rewriting. This might sound like a crazy idea, but it makes a certain amount of sense, at least to those who write in this way, including one of the present authors, who finds himself disabled if he tries to plan too much, too early. Like others who favour this general approach, he likes to begin work on writing projects by writing freely, allowing ideas to pour out spontaneously. Oddly enough, although the writing is spontaneous, because beforehand he has not thought in any detail about what he wishes to write, he often structures such sessions quite tightly, for example:

- By allowing himself only five minutes to write down his initial thoughts.

- By deciding that he is going to write one page that contains three paragraphs, each on a different aspect of the paper he thinks he is going to write.

- By deciding to begin by writing the conclusion to an article he hasn't yet written.

After his period of writing, however short, and however spontaneous or structured he has made it, he will end up with a piece of text – a first draft, that he can begin to shape. At times, as he is writing, he finds that a plan begins to form in his mind. If it does, he may decide after he has finished writing to record it, but it will in any case be in his mind as he re-reads his embryonic draft and begins to develop it.

Many authors who prefer this kind of approach to the creation of text recognize that it has something in common with other creative pursuits. Once they have a rough draft they are able to gradually develop the text – adding a bit here, taking away a bit there, and perhaps changing the order of ideas, as it begins to exert its authority and make it clear how it wants to be organized and arranged. The creation of a first draft will usually generate tasks that need to be undertaken, for example:

- Checking a reference, or a hastily transcribed quotation.
- Looking for support for an idea or argument.
- Researching relevant facts.
- Checking whether his recall about what an author has written is accurate.

If you decide to adopt or even just to try out this approach, you will probably find it useful to edit successive drafts on printed copies. Some people think that printing too early in the process of writing is wasteful of resources. However, the cost is often easy to justify when set against the time and effort that can be saved, because spotting mistakes and making sensible decisions about changes is easier when working on paper than when working on screen. For those for whom the cost to the planet is even more important than financial cost, and cost in terms of their own time and energy, it is worth noting the environmental saving that can be made by:

- Always single spacing, until you print your final copy.
- Printing double sided, whenever possible.
- Always printing successive drafts 'two-up', so that two printed pages appear side by side, like this.

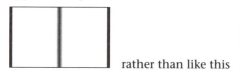 rather than like this

Most printers allow you to do this. Printing 'two-up' like this has the added advantage that it makes it easier to see how chunks of text relate to one another and hence to make decisions about rearranging and restructuring text.

Check your essay is fit for purpose

Make sure that you present your ideas in a coherent way, remembering that your reader was not present at their birth. It is your job, as an author, to explain why you came to embrace these ideas and how you think they hang together.

Whether you work to a rigid plan, or choose to allow your ideas to evolve more organically, remember that you are responsible for ensuring that you have said everything that is necessary to answer the question, or address the topic. This will include, for example, making sure that any illustrations and examples are appropriate and effective, and that your introduction and conclusion do their job well. In both approaches, you should check, at different stages, that each word, each sentence and each paragraph plays an important part in your essay.

A spectrum of approaches

Between the highly structured and more spontaneous approaches to writing we have outlined, there lies a continuum of possibilities. For example, you may write some notes before attempting a relatively spontaneous first draft. Alternatively, you may begin by writing the first thoughts that come to mind on a topic, then use these to help you to formulate a detailed plan. Or you may carefully plan some sections of your work, but work on the introduction and conclusion more spontaneously.

One of us adopts a more structured approach to writing and likes to plan in detail, before setting out to write the bulk of the text, while as we have already said, the other favours a more relaxed and apparently more spontaneous approach. In the early stage of each edition of this book, the latter encountered a certain amount of difficulty in producing first drafts. It took him some time to realize that this was because of the rigorous planning that had gone into setting out not only the content, but also the expected shape of the book. Rather than being helpful, he found that this constrained his ability to write. Eventually he began writing about the ideas he had for the book more spontaneously, as a way of getting past his writer's block. When he did, he found that his ability to write came back.

If at any time the approach you are using does not seem to be helping you to write, try something else. If writing in a rigorously structured way doesn't work, try writing about the aspect of your topic with which you are having difficulty in a more spontaneous way. On the other hand, if usually you write spontaneously but this is not working, try writing some notes about what you want to say and organizing these into a possible plan for your essay, or some smaller section of it.

We do not wish to advocate either a more or a less structured approach as being the best one. What is important for you, as it is for us, is that you find an approach that suits you. It is probably worth trying a variety of approaches and finding what works best. It may be that you will find more and less methodical approaches useful on different occasions.

> Thought, planning and revision are always important if you hope to write well, whether you plan rigorously before you begin to write, or rather lay your plans as you progress with your writing tasks.

Whatever approach you adopt it is as well to keep these questions in mind as you write:

- What am I trying to communicate?
- Where and how should I begin?
- Where and how should I end?

> In relation to each page and each paragraph you write, ask yourself: 'How does this help to answer the question I am addressing or to fulfil the task set?' If the section in question does not obviously add anything, omit it.

One of the worst pitfalls for any writer in attaining clarity and directness is the temptation to retain material that is irrelevant or only marginally relevant to the topic. Aim, when you are revising drafts of your essays, to cut out material that does not help to answer the question, even when it is of interest to you, or when you find that you have expressed yourself in a way that you find pleasing. One consolation to keep in mind as you remove material, is that however interesting, removing it will probably improve your text. Another is that good ideas can often be used in other places.

> For any piece of academic writing, always create a separate file or files into which you save text that you reject, because for the purpose in hand, it is superfluous or only tangentially relevant. For many academics, such 'dump-files' are important seed-beds for further work.

Drafting and revising

Successful academic writing involves putting words together in coherent and convincing arguments in favour of conclusions or points of view. The best academic writing does all this in an engaging style that is both easy to read and communicates clearly. Very few people, if any, are capable of writing like this at one sitting. Most take many drafts to move from the bare bones of an idea about what they want to say, to a completed text that says it in a way that others can understand, and with which they will want to engage.

Sorting out what you have to say

Always think carefully about what you want to say when you write. And always check that what you write says what you intended it to say. Ideally, you should be checking like this throughout the writing process, going over each draft to ensure that it not only says what you think it does, but says it clearly.

> Before you write anything as a student, you should take care to work out what it is that you want to say. Failing to do so may result in your writing something that says very little, takes too long to say what you want to say, or says it in a way that is unappealing and difficult to understand.

Writing is difficult, even if words come easily to you; or at least it is difficult if you want to write well (and we hope you do). It involves more mental and physical effort than speaking, which probably explains why people are often reluctant to rewrite what they have written. However, if you are to write as well as you can, it is important that you should develop a disciplined approach to drafting and revising your written work. Although we still come across students who seem to believe that it is possible to do all the reading and then write their essays the day before submission, most now realize that an essay will always be best if it goes through a number of drafts, as it is gradually honed into its final shape, before checking it for mistakes prior to submission. You will probably still find that you go through at least three or four drafts (perhaps many more) before you arrive at an essay with which you feel pleased, because it is as good as you can make it.

Getting started with your first draft

As you read successive drafts you will spot places where you have made mistakes, like having misspelled or even omitted a word; or where you have failed to acknowledge the source of an idea, or to give an appropriate reference. You will probably also spot places where you can extend your argument by including examples, or offering an explanation of an idea. It is helpful to record some notes about what needs to be done, in the form of a series of instructions or suggestions to yourself, or of questions that you think need to be answered. You could do this in several ways:

- In a notebook.

- In a clearly labelled and easily accessible computer file.

- By writing inside your developing text.

Which of these you choose to do is up to you. The important thing is that you should find a way of organizing such notes and of keeping yourself up-to-date, so that you always know both what you have done and what you still have to do.

Depending on the amount of time you have available and the complexity of the issues that you identify in your draft, it will often be even more helpful if you make an immediate attempt to amend your essay, taking account of the concerns you have noted. In doing so, you might be clarifying points; extending the text; removing irrelevant material; restructuring a sentence or argument, or inserting a new illustration.

If you include notes to yourself within the text, you may find it helpful to do so using a contrasting font or color. Consider, for example, this snippet from an anthropology student's draft of an essay about approaches to social research. Faye's comments are rendered in **bold** (in the original they were rendered in red, using the same font)

> Geertz **(ref?)** discussed the idea that an ethnographer's 'truths' are interpre-tations, since the data upon which they are based are also interpretations. **(Link this to the question)** This demonstrates the limitation inherent in the human viewpoint, that it is impossible to be wholly objective, because we all have past experiences that influence **both** what we set out to discover and what we 'see'. Observation is never neutral. **(give some examples here – brief and to the point)**:

By careful reading of this draft of a single paragraph of her essay, Faye has pinpointed a number of simple ways to improve it. Importantly, she has reminded herself about the need to locate the reference for Geertz. However, she has also pinpointed a couple of places where she can extend her essay, for example, by making a direct link to the question she is attempting to answer. This is good, because it lets her tutor know that she is focusing on the task he set. However, in terms of the development of her text it is less significant than the idea of including some illustrative examples, because doing that will help Faye to show that she understands the point about personal history influencing not only the questions we ask as researchers, but also the ways that we perceive things, even when we are attempting to maintain objectivity.

Task 17: What is Julia planning to do in her next draft?

Read the short passage that follows, which comes from an early draft of an undergraduate dissertation by Julia, a student on a BA in Peace and Development. Look at the points she has made in editing her work and try to list the changes she is suggesting to herself, and the ways you think they might improve her text.

> In my research about Indonesia's development, I intend to use a case study approach **(refer to Silverman, I think it's 2005 – and full ref in ref list)** Doing so will allow my investigation to retain the holistic and meaningful characteristics of real life events. **(say what I mean by this)** as I develop detailed understanding of what is happening **in** Indonesia's complex circumstances (Moore, 2000 – **say what Moore says!**) However, I will have to take great care in designing case studies to overcome the criticisms to which this method is often subjected. – **(List some of these criticisms and say where they come from – for example, Yin, 1994)**

[Our response appears on page 250]

Get a friend to check your work for you

Getting someone who is unfamiliar with your work to read it will give you an indication of how successful you have been in communicating what you wanted to communicate. This person should be someone who knows you well enough to be frank without giving offence. Of course, it is easier to suggest that you should find someone you trust sufficiently to allow them to be frank in sharing their opinion, than it is to actually find such a person, but it is worth the effort.

In general, we find that if another person thinks what we have written is unclear, it is nearly always worthwhile rewriting in an effort to make things clearer.

If your friend asks questions like, 'What exactly is the point you're trying to make?', don't argue. Work out what you're trying to say and then try using new words to make the point; it's likely that in the earlier version you were being longwinded.

> Whenever you've written something try to get a friend to read it and then attempt to summarize what you've tried to say. If she can't understand what it is you are attempting to communicate, rewrite as much as is necessary to make your meaning clear to her.

If there is no-one you can ask to check your work for you, imagine the task of telling a friend the main points in your argument. This will help you to structure your writing and to decide upon content because it will allow you to pinpoint the key elements in your argument and to clarify the best order in which to present them.

> In structure, as in choice of words and phrases, it is better to be simple rather than complex, short rather than long.

Being your own severest critic

If there is no-one to whom you feel you can turn for an objective and supportive view, you will have to make doubly sure when you are reading your own work that you do so in a way that allows you to achieve something akin to objectivity.

> When you are reading and revising drafts, you should always attempt to be your own worst (and hence best) critic.

Try to enter dramatically into reading your own work as if you are someone else. Familiarity with your work might mean that you are tempted to skip over some sections, because you know them so well. However, if you are going to write well you need to learn to read your own work as if it was written by someone else, and then to be honest in appraising it.

Don't get too attached to your words

Don't develop too much attachment to the words you have written. Just because they have come out of your head does not make them somehow sacred, no matter how much you like them; how interesting the point they make; how well they make that point, or even (and actually, especially) how nice they sound. They are there to be used if they do the job you intend them to; and they are there to be discarded if they do not.

> Don't be afraid to cut out text, if you realize, part of the way through writing an essay, that it is not important, even if you like it.

In the case of an essay or other assignment, you must make sure that they help you to address the question.

If words you have written don't add anything useful to what you want to communicate, cut them out, however fine and intelligent and impressive they sound. Don't become too attached to them.

Copyediting and proofreading

In drafting and revising successive versions of your work you will have to learn to read it in at least two ways, which are broadly speaking the same as the styles of reading undertaken in copyediting and proofreading in the publishing world.

Copyediting

Copyediting involves reading your work (as if you have never read it before) at the level of content, looking for places where it is unclear, badly phrased, or repetitive.

Ask yourself:

- Do I make all the points I intended to make? And do I make them as succinctly and clearly as I could?
- Rather than merely saying what I believe, have I justified my reasons for believing it?
- Have I fulfilled promises? For example, if I have written, 'I will argue that ...', have I really offered an argument, that is, given reasons and justifications for my views?
- If I have said that I will enter into more detail about a point later in my essay, have I actually done so?
- Have I addressed all the issues that I claimed I would address and given all the arguments that I claim to have given?
- Have I done everything I say I did, and addressed everything I claim to have addressed? For example, if in my conclusion I have written 'I compared x and y ...', did I actually offer a comparison, rather than describing both x and y and allowing my readers to make the comparison themselves?
- If I have employed phrases like 'It follows from this that ...' or 'This leads me into a discussion of ...' and so on, do they fulfil a useful function? In other words, does whatever I claim follows from an earlier point or argument really follow from it?

Proofreading

Proofreading involves reading your work with an eye on more technical and presentational aspects. Is it well presented? Are there errors in spelling, punctuation, grammar and so on? Are the words that appear the ones the author intended to use, or have typos resulted in her using words she didn't want to use, thus changing her meaning, or removing it entirely? Sometimes when we are writing, especially if we are working fast, the wrong word leaps onto the page or onto the screen, without us having any idea at all how it could have done so.

For example, when one of us was working on the book *Becoming an Author: Advice for academics and other professionals* (Canter and Fairbairn, 2006) he began a new section on first, second and third person writing, with the sentence:

> There is a great deal of disagreement about whether academic discourse is best carried out in the first or the third question.

He had intended to talk about the 'third person', and the fact that this sentence survived a number of drafts shows how easy it is for even the most experienced of proofreaders to make silly mistakes.

As in copyediting, if you are to be successful in proofreading your own work, you will have to develop the ability to read it as if you were not its author.

> If you are to be a good proofreader you will have to learn to read important text (because your essay is important) without paying too much attention to the meaning it is intended to convey.

If, while proofreading, you allow yourself to get drawn into the meaning of your words, it is too easy to be seduced into going to sleep 'on the job', so that the text passes in front of your eyes, but your brain does not engage with it, even at the level of technical correctness.

To avoid the pitfalls that can arise from being seduced into sleeping as you try to proofread, you might find it useful to:

- Use a ruler or blank sheet of paper to focus your attention on one line at a time, a little like you perhaps did when you were first learning to read.

- Read your text out loud, including references and punctuation marks. Apart from anything else, this will help you to identify sentences that are too long.

Task 18: Mistakes in proofreading and copyediting

Have a look at the following snippets of text, the first from a news item about an incident on Mount Everest, the second drawn from a student's self-assessment of his developing study skills, and the third from a web page advertising a hotel with some remarkable features. Each has some mistakes a copyeditor or proofreader should have picked up. See if you can spot them:

i   However, he was very much alive though in a poor way, when Mazur and his team came across him, sitting on the edge of a cornice, minus oxygen mask, snow gobbles and gloves, as they climbed towards the summit.

ii The proof reading exercise was a challenge and meant that I had to re-read the passage several times and even made some mistakes. It was food that i did this exercise as it showed that very often you need to read a piece of work more than once to make sure that it correct.

iii This friendly, independent, two star hotel is located 15 minutes' walk from the city's main attractions. We have 45 bedrooms all with small en-suite shower rooms, a breakfast room and continental style brassiere serving snacks and beverages.

[Our response appears on page 250]

Copyediting and proofreading: the overlaps

Although we have made it sound as if copyediting and proofreading are two distinct processes, in reality they often overlap and you will often find yourself proofreading and copyediting at the same time. There is nothing wrong with this. However, it is vital that you should separate out these functions when you are proofreading a final draft, because in trying to give birth to a piece of writing it is very tempting to make last-minute alterations to style and content. This can be disastrous, unless, after making your changes, you undertake a final proofread to check that it is 'clean' and free as far as possible of technical and stylistic errors.

Making the best use of your computer for writing

Most people write using a computer, and it is very likely that you have been doing this for so long that you can't imagine writing in any other way. In spite of this, and in spite of the fact that they make writing much easier in all kinds of ways, many people do not use computers to their best advantage.

Writing effectively requires technical skill to allow you to make changes to text, move it about, delete it or save it; add footnotes; create tables of contents; organize references; print your text or send it electronically to others who can comment on it and return it to you quick as a flash. This is probably why many people view the computer primarily as a way of presenting text, rather than using it as a literary tool to help them to develop it so that it communicates as clearly and engagingly as possible. If you are going to make the best use of this wonderful technology, it is important that you should learn to use your computer in this way.

Rather than just being a way of writing down, storing and then printing off copies of your essays and other assignments, if you give it the chance, your computer will allow you to explore ideas on screen in a living medium, in which you can manipulate your work: adding, changing and taking away text; trying new forms of words through which to convey your meanings; structuring and restructuring what you have written, while preserving older attempts to say the same things in different ways. Conceived like this, writing on a computer is not simply about the physical production and reproduction of text, but about the literary process of creating. It involves laying down an embryonic version of an imagined text, and then interrogating it to determine what needs to be done to enable it to say what you want it to say, as clearly as possible. For some authors, the literary function of the computer is even more significant than this, because it is the means by which they first establish what they want to say, and even what they believe.

Making it your ambition to extend your knowledge of how your computer works, and how to get the best out of it as a writer, will pay dividends in terms of time and the ease with which you can get your essays written. However, it need not mean that you have to set out to become an expert, only that you should try to learn the simplest ways of doing as many as possible of the things that you need to do as a writer, including:

- Navigating round your text using your mouse or touch pad, and keyboard
- Increasing the size of type on screen
- Selecting text
- Copying, deleting and saving text
- Cutting and pasting text
- *Italicizing*, **bolding** or (very occasionally) <u>underlining</u> text
- Organizing your files in folders
- Setting tabs
- Indenting text

- Using bullet points and numbering

- Selecting fonts

- Setting the width of your page

- Justifying text

- Undoing typing

- Wordcounting

- Checking spelling

- Consulting the Thesaurus

- Printing

- Creating a new file or opening another file, while keeping the present one open.

These are basic operations that anyone using a computer for writing must learn, and you may think that we are being a bit patronizing in even mentioning them, because you can already do most or even all of them. However, in our experience many people, including many undergraduate students, are unaware of some of the ways that it is possible to do these things, including the use of keystrokes (combinations of keys) that are quicker than using a key pad or mouse to work with icons and menus.

The best way to develop your skills in writing on a computer is to ask your friends how they do the things you need to do. Get them to show you – slowly, and one step at a time – whatever skill you want to learn; practise doing it yourself, and then write a detailed description of what you have to do in an easily accessible file on your computer or laptop, in which you keep notes on the new skills you learn.

Learn keystrokes as an alternative to accessing on-screen menus with mouse or key pad

It is, for example, a good deal quicker to save a file by holding down the 'control' key (or the 'command' key on a Mac) and typing 's', than to select the **'disk' icon** or to use the drop down 'file' menu, using a mouse or touch pad. And while it is possible to render highlighted text as **bold**, *italics* or underlined text using another pull-down menu or by clicking on the relevant icon, doing so by holding down the control/command key and typing a 'b', 'i' or 'u' respectively is easier.

Attending to the appearance of your work

Your job in writing for others is to communicate meaning, and you are likely to be most successful in this if you think carefully not only about the things you say and the way you say them, but also about what your work looks like.

> For most academic purposes, the best presentation is usually the simplest.

You must think carefully about the font and print styles you use, and also about how you lay text out on the page. For example, should you present some points in the form of lists? And should listed points be numbered? Should you perhaps utilize features of your computer, such as:

- bullet points?

Problems with layout arise at both the aesthetic level and at the intellectual level. You should thus make the effort necessary, both to present your ideas in the right order and in chunks (paragraphs) that help a reader to follow your argument, and to make sure that its visual impact does not detract from its meaning.

> In setting out your work, make sure that the layout is as simple and easy to follow as possible. Doing so will help you to communicate your ideas better.

Depending on your institution, or even on your particular faculty or department, you may be expected to adopt a clearly set down 'house style' for the submission of essays, which may dictate font and font size, as well as settings for margins. In such cases, your job is to follow the instructions you are given. If you are not given directions about these things, you will have to make your own decisions. In that case, your work will benefit from attention to detail in formatting. We would suggest choosing a simple font that is pleasant to look at, easy to read and relatively 'serious' in appearance.

Of the 'serif' fonts, 'Times New Roman' is probably the most common in academic work, but many people find 'Garamond', which is very commonly used in books, easier to read and thus use it as their font of preference. Among the 'sans serif' fonts, 'Arial', a traditional font, is still very common, but again, many people use 'Calibri', which they find more aesthetic and easier to read.

Avoid the overuse of variations in font size. Preferably, stick to one font size throughout. For most fonts, 12 point or perhaps 11 point will produce a result that is readable and sits well on the page.

Be sparing in your use of alternative print styles. The simplest visual impact is best, and in general this is obtained by using ordinary type most of the time, with occasional use of *italics* or **bold** type and very occasional use of underlined type.

Housekeeping: keeping your files in order

In addition to developing skills that will allow you to make the best use of your computer for writing, it is important that you should develop good 'housekeeping' practices, both so that you always have access to files in which you are storing your work and so that you do not risk losing them.

Organize your files

Establish a system of folders and files on your computer for storing your work. For example, if you were studying Archaeology and Anthropology you might have a folder called 'UniWORK' inside which you have two folders called 'Archaeology' and 'Anthropology'. The 'Archaeology' folder might contain folders called 'Lecture Notes', 'Copied Articles', 'Essay Work', 'Fieldwork' and 'Dissertation Ideas', each of which has further sub-folders.

Save regularly

Develop the habit of saving your work regularly – say, every few minutes, while you are writing. Doing this can help you avoid the trauma of losing your work if your computer 'crashes'. (Disasters of this kind do happen, and they can happen to anyone; they will happen to you.)

> Save your files regularly.

Back up your files regularly

An astonishing number of people do not take the trouble to back up their files regularly. Even more surprisingly, many students seem to favor carrying their work around with them on a memory stick, almost as if they are tempting fate to do its worst; and it sometimes does. If you recognize yourself in either of these descriptions, we strongly urge you to change your ways.

> Develop the habit of making back-up copies of all of your important files on a regular basis so that, in the event of a disaster – a hard drive that loses its

mind and your work; a laptop that is stolen from your room, or infected by a virus that attacks your files – you have a recent version from which you can rebuild your work. Although doing so can be time-consuming, try also to develop the discipline of printing and storing labelled and dated copies, as a kind of insurance against disaster.

Store back-up copies of your work in a different location from the one where you usually save it, for example, on an external hard drive, or on another computer, preferably somewhere that is as safe as it can be, from the attentions of thieves and the possibility of damage. Better still, try to make more than one back-up copy.

Give your files names that help you to recall what they contain and try to maintain a record of which name you have given to which piece of work. If you hold on to several versions of the same material – for example, older and later drafts of the same essay – find ways of distinguishing them and remembering how they relate to one another. One way of doing this would be to add the dates they were made to the file names.

Establish a system of folders in which you catalogue your files, collecting related files together – say a folder for 'lecture notes', one for 'notes on reading' and one for 'essay work'.

Never rely solely on a USB stick, either as the place on which you store 'work in progress' or as a place to keep back-up copies; otherwise you risk disaster.

Never risk storing the main copy of a piece of work anywhere (like the university system, or a friend's computer) that is controlled by someone who might delete your work by mistake.

If, for any reason, you have important material on a USB stick – say, if you have been working away from home and have chosen to transport it in this way, rather than emailing it to yourself (the safest option) – never remove the USB from a computer without going through the 'remove safely' procedure. It really is true that if you do not remove a USB stick 'safely' you can wipe everything.

2.3

Getting your writing right: punctuation, spelling and grammar

Perhaps as a result of the ways in which they were taught in school, where creativity may have been prioritized over accuracy in the use of language, many students have problems with the basic skills of writing: punctuation, spelling and grammar. Not only that, but some view these technical aspects of writing as less important than the ideas they are used to express. In one way this makes sense, because the point of writing is to communicate ideas, rather than to demonstrate skill in the use of the conventions of spelling, punctuation and grammar. However, there are good reasons for ensuring that you can spell and punctuate well and have a grasp of at least some of the rudiments of grammar. For one thing, poor spelling, unhelpful punctuation and ungrammatical writing are likely to cause a bad impression, not only on your teachers, but in the future on prospective employers. And perhaps even more importantly, unless you have a reasonable mastery of these technical skills, you will be less able to express your ideas successfully, because, as we shall argue, errors in punctuation, spelling and grammar can all interfere with the attempt to communicate.

Punctuation

Punctuation is useful. For one thing, punctuation marks such as full stops, commas and exclamation marks help readers to understand meanings in written texts that in speech would be conveyed by tone of voice, by gesture, by pausing or by stressing particular words or syllables.

Punctuation helps us to structure what we write. It holds our words and ideas together and keeps them in order, so that the meanings we want to convey are clear. Poor punctuation has the opposite effect.

Used badly punctuation can make your writing difficult to read and may cloud or even alter your intended meanings, especially where it is overused. Try to heed some wise advice of Shoosmith (1928), who wrote that, 'stops being of the nature of a disagreeable necessity, should be used as little as possible'. When checking your work before submitting it, ask yourself whether each punctuation mark you have used is performing a useful function; if it isn't, get rid of it.

Punctuation can help you to communicate both accurately and elegantly and it is important that you learn to use it appropriately if you want to write well as a student. In a book of this size, we cannot begin to do justice to all of the issues raised by punctuation. However, in the next few pages we provide a simple guide to the following:

full stop [.]

capital [upper-case] letters

question mark [?]

exclamation mark [!]

comma [,]

semi-colon [;]

colon [:]

apostrophe [']

inverted commas [" "] & [' ']

hyphen [-]

parentheses [()]

dash [–]

You should know how to use these punctuation marks. However, it is important to realize that although there are many conventions, punctuation has very few absolute rules, other than the rule, with which you are no doubt familiar, about sentences always beginning with a capital letter and ending with a full stop (.), a question mark (?) or an exclamation mark (!).

To some extent, the way in which you punctuate is a matter of personal taste and there is often more than one correct way of punctuating a sentence.

The most important thing to bear in mind as you write is that the way in which you punctuate should help readers to gain your intended meaning.

The full stop (.)

The main use of the full stop is to mark the end of a sentence, except where a question mark or exclamation mark is used:

- This sentence is short. So is this one. This one is longer and more complicated, but it ends in the same way as the shorter ones that came before it, with a full stop.

- It is because it brings sentences to an end that the full stop is called the full stop.

- The full stop is the strongest mark of punctuation.

- Another name for the full stop is the 'period'.

- If a sentence ends with a question mark or an exclamation mark, or with a title or abbreviation that contains its own punctuation, there is no need for a full stop.

In addition, the full stop is used in the construction of some abbreviations, especially when they are shortened forms of words such as Rev. (Reverend), Prof. (Professor) and Oct. (October) that do not end in the same letter as the whole word. On the other hand, abbreviations like Mr (Mister) and Dr (Doctor) that do end in the same letter as the full word are usually written without a full stop.

> Strictly speaking, Rev., Prof. and Oct. are abbreviations, whereas Mr and Dr are contractions, because they result from leaving out the middle of the word they signify.

In the past, the full stop had much more work to do, because of its use in abbreviations of different kinds, and it is as well to note that it is much less commonly used now than in the past. For example, it used to have a use in writing acronyms – the words that are produced by stringing together the first letters of names such as the North Atlantic Treaty Organization (NATO); the General Medical Council (GMC) or the Royal Society of Arts (RSA); and of other features of modern life, such as the Anti-Social Behaviour Order (ASBO); Acquired Immune Deficiency Syndrome (AIDS) or Random-access Memory (RAM). However, it is now more common to write acronyms without full stops.

It is also common to omit full stops from abbreviated forms of names that cannot function as a word, but must rather be pronounced as a string of letters, such as BBC (British Broadcasting Corporation); USA (United States of

America) and RAC (Royal Automobile Club); which are usually referred to as 'initialisms' or 'alphabetisms'. Full stops are more often retained in abbreviations that include lower-case letters, such as M.Ed. (Master of Education) and Ph.D. (Doctor of Philosophy), although this is not always the case.

'Capital' or 'upper-case' letters (A, B, C etc.)

Capital letters should be used sparingly. However, there are some places in written English where they are essential:

i. The pronoun 'I' is always a capital 'I' and never a lower case 'i'. This is especially important when informality in communication is encouraged by the overwhelming influence of texting and other, similar forms of instantaneous written 'conversations'. So, for example, you should never write something of the kind:

    When our Dean sent round a notice looking for help with new students at Freshers' Week, i volunteered.

> **REMEMBER:** The first person singular pronoun 'I' is always a capital 'I' and never a lower case 'i'.

ii. Sentences in the English language always begin with a 'capital' letter (A, B, C, D, etc.). This should be second nature to anyone who gains good enough grades in school to enter university as an undergraduate. Unfortunately, from time to time we come across students' work that seems to suggest that, perhaps as the result of the informality in texting, they have forgotten both this and the fact that the pronoun ('I' is always a capital 'I' and never a lower case 'i'.

iii. As well as appearing at the beginning of sentences, initial capital letters are used in a number of situations, including:

  • The names of people and organizations, for example, Donald Cameron and the Bank of Toytown.

  • The days of the week and months of the year (Friday and Saturday; April and October).

  • The names of places, including continents, countries, islands and states; regions, towns and villages; local areas within towns and so on (e.g. Africa, Sierra Leone, Iowa and California; Yorkshire, New York, Dunscore and Walberswick; South Woodford and Oxgangs).

  • Adjectives that derive from the names of countries and other places, such as German, Scottish, Appalachian, Mancunian, Glaswegian and Lilliputian.

- The names of religions, for example, Islam, Judaism, Christianity, Buddhism and Hinduism.

- The names of religious festivals and holy days, such as Easter, Ramadan, Divali and Purim, and the names of important events, religious books and certain important figures (e.g. the Last Supper; the Qu'ran; the Torah; the New Testament, and the Prophet).

- Distinctive historical periods, such as the Bronze Age, Middle Ages and the Industrial Revolution.

- In referring to an individual using their title, for example, President Obama, Queen Elizabeth II, the Archbishop of York and the Chief Rabbi.

Although this list may look fairly straightforward, there are some complications to look out for.

Words like 'queen' and 'bishop' are only written using capital letters when they are part of a person's title, otherwise they are common nouns and do not need a capital letter.

God is usually only given a capital when we are referring to the one God, not to a collection of gods.

Finally, as we have seen, capitals are used in many abbreviations. However, others, including 'ibid', 'op cit' and 'eg', are written using only lower-case letters.

The question mark (?)

The question mark is used instead of a full stop at the end of sentences in which a direct question is asked.

What time is it?

What is the sound of one hand clapping?

Do you love me?

Where's the cat?

Questions can be asked in complete sentences, as illustrated by these examples. On the other hand they can be just one word.

Who? What? Why? Where? When? How?

Note that in a sentence like 'He asked what time it was' in which a question is referred to, but not asked, a question mark is not required.

John asked what time it was.

Homer asked what the sound of one hand clapping was.

She asked whether he loved her.

Jeremy asked where the cat was.

> Always end a direct question with a question mark (?) but never use a question mark for indirect speech.

The exclamation mark (!)

The exclamation mark is most often used to emphasize a point. For example, the owner of a quarry, conscious that he did not want trespassers putting their lives at risk, might erect signs alongside his boundary fence warning 'DANGER! KEEP OUT!' And the authors of a guide to student writing who wanted to illustrate the use of exclamation marks might write, 'You should not use an exclamation mark except when you wish to emphasize a point!'

Exclamation marks can be useful in, for example, personal letters, emails or texts, and they are used, at times, to mark surprise, joy or humour. Consider, for example, the sentences 'What a beautiful day!' and 'A fsh!', which is the punchline for the joke, 'What do you call a fish with no eye?'

> In general, when you are writing essays and other assignments, it is best to avoid exclamation marks and instead to emphasize points by the careful use of emphatic language.

The comma (,)

The comma helps to make the structure and meaning of sentences clear by, for example, showing which words and ideas belong together, and which do not. It should be used carefully, because its overuse can lead to a lack of clarity. It has a number of distinct uses:

- To mark a pause much briefer than that indicated by the full stop, question mark or exclamation mark.
- To separate distinct parts of a sentence.
- To separate the elements of a list.

Pauses

It is difficult to give clear guidance about the use of commas to indicate pauses, because to some extent this depends upon the way in which a writer would read a sentence out loud. However, in general a comma should be used to indicate a pause only where this is not obvious from the sense of the words, or where its use actually changes the sense of the words.

Separating parts of a sentence

The insertion of commas to separate the parts (clauses) of a sentence can change the meaning of the sentence dramatically. Consider, for example, the following two sentences, which contain the same words but convey different meanings:

> The ambulance drivers in London who were the first to strike are the most anxious to begin work again.

> The ambulance drivers in London, who were the first to strike, are the most anxious to begin work again.

The first sentence implies that the first ambulance drivers in London to come out on strike were the most anxious to return to work. By contrast, the second, which uses a pair of commas round the phrase 'who were the first to strike', suggests both that ambulance drivers in London began striking first, and that they were the most anxious of all ambulance drivers to return to work. It could be replaced with:

> The ambulance drivers in London were the first to strike, and they are the most anxious to begin work again.

Separating the elements of a list

Probably the most simple use of the comma is in separating the elements of a list.

> Lots of flowers appear in spring including snowdrops, crocuses, daffodils and primroses.
>
> The main devices for indicating pauses in writing are the full stop, comma, semi-colon, colon, question mark and exclamation mark.
>
> During her gap year Laura travelled to many countries, including Germany, France, Switzerland, Italy and Slovenia.

Note, however, that as in these examples the last two members of a list are usually separated by the conjunction 'and' rather than by a comma.

The omission of a comma in a list can change the meaning considerably, as in the following sentence in which the writer reports on what sounds like an interesting culinary experience:

> For dinner we had smoked salmon sorbet, roast beef with Yorkshire pudding, bakewell tart and coffee.

Inserting the missing comma makes the menu more understandable:

> For dinner we had smoked salmon, sorbet, roast beef with Yorkshire pudding, bakewell tart and coffee.

The semi-colon (;)

The semi-colon is used instead of the comma to separate the elements of a list, in several different situations, including occasions when the use of a comma might cause confusion. In the following two examples, confusion would have been caused by the use of commas to separate the elements of the lists, because those elements in themselves consist of lists separated by commas.

> The modern symphony orchestra consists of several groups of related instruments, including violins, violas, cellos and basses in the strings; flutes, clarinets, oboes and bassoons in the woodwind; and trumpets, horns, trombones and tubas in the brass.
>
> John's cottage had a wonderful alpine garden with saxifrages, thyme, sedum and candytuft; a herbaceous border with hostas, aquilegias, delphiniums and astilbes; a hothouse in which he grew flowering plants and produce such as tomatoes and grapes; and a well-stocked kitchen garden with vegetables and soft fruit.

Semi-colons are also often used in lists, made up of items that contain the conjunction 'and' – as in 'Tom and Jerry', 'gin and tonic' and 'fish and chips'.

> The menu, which consisted of rather greasy foods, included fish and chips; chicken and chips; sausage and chips; spam and chips; and bacon and chips.

Finally, the semi-colon may be used instead of the comma to avoid confusion in the presentation of a list made up of elements that are themselves rather long.

> In St Renan market we saw a fishmonger selling live crabs and lobsters that were moving around in a tank; a blond boy playing Breton music on a beautiful old violin; an elderly woman selling eggs and bunches of fresh herbs from a basket by her feet; and a young man on a unicycle, whose juggling with knives was spellbinding.

The other main use of the semi-colon is to link two closely related ideas that might otherwise stand independently, thus emphasizing the link between them. In such circumstances, the semi-colon acts as a kind of pivot between the two ideas:

> Jessica always left the light on at night; otherwise she found she couldn't sleep.
>
> In a book of this size we cannot begin to do justice to the issues raised by punctuation; for that you should consult a reliable text.
>
> Both trailers and reminders should be short and serve a useful purpose; they should not be simple repetitions of what is said elsewhere.
>
> 'Apologies' can be little more than words; unless they are accompanied by the right intentions and feelings, they mean little.

The colon (:)

The colon has several uses. For example, it is often used to introduce material that is block indented[4] or set out from the rest of the text, including quotations that run to several lines. You will find examples throughout this book. It may also be used to introduce a list:

> Pineapple surprise uses only a few ingredients: one medium pineapple; three tablespoons of Greek yoghurt; one fresh egg; one tablespoon of honey, and a few freshly toasted slivers of almond.

The colon is also used in sentences in which the second half explains, amplifies or summarizes the first.

> Writing a good essay takes several things: understanding of the ideas it contains; the ability to write clearly and engagingly, and most of all a lot of hard work.
>
> There were two reasons for his success: his innate talent as a storyteller and the effort he put into researching the material for his novels.

---

[4] 'Block indented' means that the entire section of text is indented at both sides, thus making it stand out from the body of the text in which it appears.

> After a period of silence, the old man shared his secret: he was the last in a long line of Marslings who came to Earth when their planet dried up 100,000 Earth years ago.

The apostrophe (')

The apostrophe has two uses – to indicate possession and to denote contractions.

Possession

In the case of singular nouns, proper names, and plural nouns that do not end in 's', possession is usually indicated by adding an apostrophe plus an 's' (often referred to as an 'apostrophe s'). Thus, for example, we would write about the city's limits, the car's wheels and Tom's car, and refer to women's or children's rights.

In the case of singular nouns such as grass and glass, that end in 's', possession is indicated by adding an apostrophe s, if in saying the word you would normally pronounce an extra 's' sound. Thus, for example, we would refer to the grass's bright green colour and to the glass's sparkle. The same is true in the case of proper names like James and Harris, which end in 's'; so, for example, we might refer to James's drums and to Harris's books. However, in such circumstances, some people prefer to use only an apostrophe and would thus refer to James' drums and to Harris' books. Either is acceptable.

In the case of plural nouns that end in 's', it is customary only to add the apostrophe and thus we would refer to the ladies' handbags. The apostrophe is also used by itself where a word or proper name already contains two 's' sounds; thus we might refer to Moses' wife and to a thesis' contents, rather than to Moses's wife and a thesis's contents.

In the case of multiple-noun possessives, you should add the apostrophe to the last noun, referring, for example, to Fortnum and Mason's delicatessen, and in the case of compound nouns it is added to the last word, as in brother-in-law's.

> Note the difference between brother-in-law's, which assigns possession of something to a brother-in-law as in 'My brother-in-law's car is a Porsche', and 'brothers-in-law', which is the plural of 'brother-in-law'.

Contractions

The use of the apostrophe to denote contractions (where two words are collapsed into one) is most common in colloquial English and is best avoided when you are writing as a student, unless you are reporting direct speech or writing fictionally. The apostrophe takes the place of an omitted letter or letters in words like:

don't (do not)

couldn't (could not)

can't (cannot)

it's (it is)

The apostrophe is also used in the common contraction of 'two of the clock' to 'two o'clock', and in contracting dates as, for example in, the summer of '76 or the winter of '89.

Never use an apostrophe in the attempt to form a plural

In spite of what many people seem to believe, the apostrophe is not used in forming plurals. For example, the plural of cat is cats not cat's; the plural of profit is profits and not profit's, and despite what many vegetable stall holders seem to think, the plurals of carrot, cauliflower and orange, are not carrot's, cauliflower's and orange's, but carrots, cauliflowers and oranges.

Its or it's?

Perhaps the most frequent mistake that native English speakers make in writing their language is mixing up the spelling of two words that sound the same, although they mean entirely different things and look different. These two words are:

its and it's

The first – its, is a personal pronoun like his, hers, ours, yours and theirs, and like them, it does not include an apostrophe; the second – it's, is a contraction or shortened form of the words 'it is'. It is important to get the spelling of these two words right, because spelling them wrongly will make it look as if you do not understand the difference between them, and on paper, at any rate, it will make you look as if you are using the wrong word.

Getting its and it's right

Perhaps the easiest way to be sure that you have spelled these two words correctly, is to try substituting the words 'it is' for the its or it's in your phrase or sentence, to see if the phrase or sentence still makes sense. If it does, then the word you should be using is the contraction it's. If, on the other hand, it doesn't, the word you want is its.

Try it out with these two sentences, in both of which we have used it's, in one instance correctly and in the other mistakenly:

It's better to be safe than sorry.

The dog hid it's bone in the garden.

Substituting 'it is' in each case yields:

It is better to be safe than sorry.

[*This makes sense, and hence the use of it's was correct*]

The dog hid it is bone in the garden.

[*This does not make sense, and hence the use of it's was incorrect*]

Task 19: It's or its?

Read the sentences below and every time either its or it's appears, decide whether it is correct or incorrect. Note those that are correct and those that are incorrect.

The mechanic who examined my car told me that its radiator needed to be replaced.

It's important to get punctuation right, otherwise its likely that those who read your essay will get its meaning wrong.

The comma should be used carefully, because it's overuse can lead to a lack of clarity.

The Royal Bank, which was rescued by the government after coming near to financial ruin, has awarded all of it's senior staff large bonuses.

It's only rice pudding, but I like it.

Its not right that we have to wait so long for the train.

It's a shame that so many people find problems with the use of the apostrophe.

In writing the possessive pronoun it's, its important never to use an apostrophe.

[Our response appears on page 250]

REMEMBER: An intelligent dog hides its bone in the garden, because it's better to be safe than sorry.

Inverted commas (also known as 'speech marks' or 'quotation marks')

Inverted commas (' ' or " ") fulfil several functions. Perhaps the most important is their use to indicate direct speech, which is why they are often known as 'speech marks' or 'quotation marks'.

The witness said, 'I saw the thief running into the pub, your honour.'

As he rushed into the room, John looked round and asked 'What time is it?'

'This', said the teacher, 'is the correct way to use inverted commas.'

Inverted commas are also used to indicate that one is quoting directly from something another person has said or has written. In this case, immediately after the quotation, you should insert the page(s) in the source from which it came, in brackets.

March (1983) who studied weaving, writing and gender among the Tamang of Nepal, argued that 'Weaving, especially the weaving of women's skirts, is a vital symbol of the Tamang women's world, marking Tamang women in several important ways' (p. 730).

Kennicutt et al. (2003) believe that 'In contrast to the study of the formation of individual stars, which has advanced dramatically over the past two decades, our theoretical understanding of star formation on galactic scales remains relatively immature' (p. 929).

Other uses of inverted commas

Sometimes inverted commas are used to indicate that one is referring to a term, rather than using it.

In this paper, we ask what individuals and societies mean by the term 'reconciliation', and how that affects what they expect from the reconciliation process.

They are also used when a technical term is introduced for the first time:

> It is important to distinguish between two senses of equality, which Dworkin (1975) refers to as 'equal treatment' and as 'treatment as an equal'.
>
> Later, we shall turn to a consideration of acts of suicide and apparent acts of suicide that do not lead to death and of the terms that are used to label them, including 'non-fatal suicide', 'gestured suicide' and 'cosmic roulette' as well as 'attempted suicide' and 'failed suicide'.

Another legitimate use of inverted commas is to indicate unease about using a term. For example, someone who doesn't subscribe to the view that madness is the result of illness might signal this to her readers by placing the term 'mental illness' inside inverted commas. And a bioethicist discussing the claim that it can be morally right to kill some people, might refer to 'non-voluntary euthanasia' to underscore his view that arranged death should only be referred to as euthanasia if it is initiated by those who are to die.

The legitimate use of inverted commas described in the previous paragraph must be distinguished from an apparently similar, but different use, which is illegitimate and should be avoided. It is the habit, developed by some students, of putting inverted commas round any word with which they feel uncomfortable, to indicate their uncertainty or nervousness about using it. In this context inverted commas are often known as 'scare quotes'. Consider, for example, the student who wrote:

> ... the theory is structured on a 'model', as with many theories of economics, and within the 'model' assumptions are established.

This student seems to be wary of referring to a way of thinking about economics as a model. Avoid such uses of inverted commas, by making sure that you only use terms about which you feel confident.

> Never place inverted commas round a word as a way of indicating your uncertainty about whether it is the correct word to use. Instead, use a word that you understand, or rewrite your sentence so that its use becomes redundant.

Single (' ') or double (" ") speech marks?

Opinions about whether one should use single or double speech marks have changed over the years. To some extent this decision is a matter of taste, and even publishers adopt different conventions. The main thing is that you should aim for consistency. However, since, in the UK and in many other places, there is a marked preference for single speech marks to indicate both direct speech and quoted passages, we suggest that unless you are given clear guidelines by your teachers, you should, in most circumstances, use single quotation marks (' '). The exception to this rule is situations where to do so would cause confusion. This might, for example, occur when direct speech, signalled by the use of speech marks, is used within a quoted passage, and also when a quoted passage itself contains a quotation. In each case, the use of both single and double speech marks is necessary to avoid confusion.

Wittgenstein (1958) raised the problem of ostensive definition in a memorable way in the *Blue and Brown Books*: 'The questions "What is length?", "What is meaning?", "What is the number one?" etc., produce in us a mental cramp. We feel that we can't do anything in reply to them and yet ought to point to something' (p. 3).

Smith (2007) argues that 'There is almost certainly no end to the universe, and so Carper (2005) is probably right to claim that "Provided we do not come across some impediment to our progress, of which there might be many, if we travel out from our planet in any direction at all, we really will keep traveling forever." (p. 1135) Of course, none of us will be around to know it' (p. 45).

The hyphen (-)

The hyphen is used to link together the elements of compound words such as son-in-law, water-wheel, half-witted, best-seller, short-sighted, blue-eyed and empty-headed. Many words that were once hyphenated are now accepted as one word, including, for example, nightdress, inkwell and haystack; if you are unsure whether a hyphen is necessary, you should consult a reliable and up-to-date dictionary such as *The Shorter Oxford English Dictionary* (2007).

The hyphen may also be used in words such as re-cover and re-sign where without the hyphen an entirely different meaning would be conveyed. A footballer who re-signs has not resigned (indicated his decision to leave his club). And a person who recovers his Victorian chaise longue after it is stolen may or may not have it re-covered (that is, have the fabric replaced). The omission of a hyphen can have some amusing results, as in the newspaper headline 'Man eating tiger escapes from safari park', which conveys something different when it includes a hyphen in 'man-eating', letting us know who was eating whom, and incidentally, who or what was escaping.

Brackets ( )

Brackets have several functions, many of which relate to the organization or layout of text, including their use in presenting Harvard style citations within the text (see pages 123–132).

Among the more literary uses of brackets, the most important is probably their use to interject an aside from the main train of thought, which might otherwise have formed the basis of another sentence. Consider, for example, this sentence from an essay about euthanasia:

> This alternative would have the benefit over the last, that doctors would not put (and could not be accused of putting) ideas into the heads of those who were satisfied with their lives.

Sometimes brackets are referred to as 'parentheses', although strictly speaking a parenthesis is an aside that may be indicated using brackets, dashes or commas.

> Never use brackets to inject a humorous remark into your essays, which is most often inappropriate in academic writing, certainly at undergraduate level.

The dash

The dash (–) is a useful punctuation mark, although some people disapprove of its use. It can be used either singly – like this, or in pairs. Used singly, it sometimes replaces a colon in introducing a list. Used in pairs, it sometimes has a function similar to that performed by brackets in indicating an aside, although brackets are usually used to mark a stronger division from the main thrust of a sentence than dashes, which are more often used to emphasize a point than they are to interject a separate idea.

> My favourite food is fish – cod, tuna, halibut, haddock and sole.
>
> The microwave – whether you like it or not – is now a standard feature of most well-equipped kitchens.

Punctuation can change meaning

As we have already illustrated with reference to the use of the comma (page 88) and the importance of a hyphen if we are to know who is eating whom, in the sentence about a 'man-eating tiger' (page 97), the way in which we punctuate can change the meanings we convey. It is therefore important to exercise great care in punctuating your work.

Consider the following string of words:

The teacher said the girl is very silly

The meaning of this group of words is entirely different depending on the punctuation:

'The teacher', said the girl, 'is very silly'.

The teacher said, 'The girl is very silly.'

Or consider the following:

When we arrived at the restaurant we met Alex and his brother Sam joined us later.

As it stands this sentence implies that the speaker and his companions met Alex at the restaurant and that they were joined later by Alex's brother who is called Sam. Adding a semi-colon completely changes the sense:

When we arrived at the restaurant we met Alex and his brother; Sam joined us later.

Here we learn that when they arrived at the restaurant the speaker and his companions met Alex and his brother, and that Sam joined them later.

> Check that by adding or omitting punctuation marks, you have not changed the meaning of any sections of your text.

Paragraphing

Punctuation is not just about commas, full stops, apostrophes and other, similar signs. How we organize our writing – in sentences, paragraphs and larger sections and blocks of text – is also important.

Arranging your writing in paragraphs breaks it into manageable chunks. More importantly, it helps to make the structure of an argument or discussion clear, because a new paragraph usually signals a change in direction such as the entry of an important new idea or argument. Each paragraph can usefully be thought of as a container for a separate point in a topic or argument; when you move off in a new direction or introduce a new thought or idea, you should start a new paragraph.

Many people, including students, are uncertain about how long the paragraphs they write should be. There are no rules; in a way the length of paragraphs is a matter of personal choice, provided that the way in which you structure your writing helps to communicate your meaning. However, you should avoid very long paragraphs, particularly when you are writing something quite short like an essay, because long paragraphs can make your work difficult to read. At the same time, be aware that if you find yourself using lots of short paragraphs, it is likely that your writing style is rather stilted, with ideas coming out in bite-sized chunks, when it might be more helpful, and certainly more fluent, to allow some of them to develop at a more leisurely pace.

Make sure that your paragraphs are neither too long, nor too short.

If you find yourself beginning paragraphs with words like 'Therefore', 'However' and Furthermore', it is probable that you are inserting a break where there should not be one, since these words imply a close link to what has gone before.

Spelling

Unlike, for example, French, Welsh and Polish, the English language is not straightforwardly phonetic. As a result, it contains many irregular spellings. Not only can some sounds be represented by different combinations of letters, but some combinations of letters represent very different sounds, depending on the word in which they appear. Think, for example, how 'shoe', 'clue', 'new', 'through' and 'loo' each uses different letters to represent the sound 'oo', and of the difference between the way that the letters 'ough' sound in the words 'cough', 'rough', 'though', 'through', 'plough' and 'bought'.

Given the inconsistent nature of the way in which the letters of our alphabet are combined to make up words, it is not surprising that many people writing in English have problems with spelling, including many students.

Poor spelling creates a bad impression, and is likely to lead to lower marks for essays. That is why we want to urge you to devote some energy to ensuring that the work you submit has as few spelling errors as possible. Even if you disagree with our emphasis on the importance of spelling, you may want to reflect on the aggravating effect that poor spelling might have on your lecturers and the detrimental effects that could have on your marks.

Think about your spelling

How good (or how bad) a speller are you?

How aware are you of thinking about spelling, as you write?

If you are aware that you have problems in spelling particular words, have you developed any ways of getting past them?

Do you have strategies for remembering the spellings of words with which you have difficulty?

How do you know how to spell words, and how do you go about learning new spellings?

Are you to some extent reliant on rules of spelling that your teachers taught you in junior school?

Do you rely on your visual memory of the way a word looks, or on your ability to break it up into its various sounds?

Do you have an 'inner voice' that recites the spelling of words to you in the voice that you used when you were a child, memorizing groups of spellings for homework?

Do you 'sound' certain words inside your head as you write them, in special ways that are suggestive of their spellings, perhaps sounding the silent 'k' in 'knight' or 'knot', or saying the word 'yacht' in such a way that the 'ch' sounds like it does when a Scotsman says the word 'loch' or a German says the German word 'acht'?

What steps, if any, do you take to try to ensure that your work is as free of spelling mistakes as possible, before submission?

If you are dyslexic, do you think that your dyslexia makes spelling more or less of an issue for you than it is for others who are not dyslexic? Have you developed any strategies to help you to produce work with as few mistakes as possible, including engaging help with proofreading?

Attending to the ways you speak

If you want to spell well it is important to attend to the way you speak, because the ways we pronounce words when we speak them can lead to errors. For example, problems can arise from the continued use of infantile versions of words such as 'fing' for 'thing', which is surprisingly common as, in some parts of England, is the use of 'kekkle' for 'kettle', both of which we have seen rendered in print, by students. Or consider the honours year student, training to be a primary school teacher, who wrote:

A teacher might not of been aware that he was indoctrinating ...

There are, of course, many variations on this mistake, including 'might of', 'could of' 'will of' being used instead of 'might have', 'could have' and 'will have'. You might refuse to believe that anyone studying for a degree could use expressions of this kind in their writing, but you would be wrong. Many years ago one of us had a colleague who had amusing oddnesses in the way she spoke. One of these was that whenever she used the word 'specific' it would come out of her mouth as 'pacific'; the same was true of a family of related words. So, for example, she might say that she had 'Pacifically asked George not to be so noisy.' She had clearly not rid herself of a mistake she had lived with since childhood and did not realize she was making it. The fact that she wrote the word 'pacific' in place of 'specific' was not so amusing.

The examples we have given so far are about eccentricities in the ways individuals speak, even though they might be shared by many people. However, it is important, also, to note more commonplace examples of the ways that words are spoken that lead to misspellings. Some of these arise when people omit the sounds of particular letters as they say certain words. Think, for example, of the word 'boundary', which is often pronounced so that the 'a' sound before the 'r' is lost, leading to the misspelling 'boundry'; the word 'inventory', which is often pronounced so that the 'o' sound is missing, which can lead to the misspelling 'inventry', and of the mispronunciation of 'itinerary' as 'itinery' and its resultant misspelling. Other misspellings arise when people habitually insert superfluous sounds into words; one example of this is the insertion of an 'r' sound when they say the word 'drawing', leading to the misspelling 'drawring'. Finally, problems arise when people get the sounds in a word muddled, so that they have all the right sounds, but not in the right order. For example, many people say, and as a result write, 'jewlery' rather than 'jewelry' in American English, or 'jewellery' in UK English, and some people say and as a result write 'nucular' rather than nuclear.

> Watch out for spelling errors in your work that you make because of the ways you pronounce words.

Homophones

Some of the most common spelling mistakes arise from confusions between words that sound the same but are spelled differently and mean different things. A mistake with such a word can thus mean that you seem to be saying one thing when actually you intend to say another. The fact that words such as these sound the same can lead to confusions in spelling, although a little thought should help you to avoid this. Words that sound the same or nearly the same, but have different meanings, are called 'homophones'. There are hundreds in the English language, including, for example:

accept, except	canvas, canvass
advice, advise	complement, compliment
bare, bear	counsellor, councillor

descent, dissent

discreet, discrete

elicit, illicit

emigrate, immigrate

emigrant, immigrant

insight, incite

lose, loose

maybe, may be

pole, poll

practice, practise

premier, premiere

principal, principle

prise, prize

sight, site, cite

some time, sometime

stationary, stationery

their, there, they're

threw, through

weather, whether

whose, who's

your, you're

Of course, pronunciation varies from community to community, and even from family to family so that, for example, whereas few Scots people could find themselves pronouncing 'where' and 'were' so that they sound the same, many English people would speak these words in exactly the same way, and the same is true, for example, of 'weather' and 'whether', and for 'Wales' and 'whales'. And so some of the words we list will be homophones for some people and not for others.

Task 20: What homophones catch you out?

Read the list of homophones we have given above and make a note of any that you think you confuse or might confuse (there will be some).

When you are writing on a computer, you will probably find that mistakes with spelling creep into your work simply because you are typing so fast that your fingers are more or less doing the thinking. Strictly speaking, of course, such mistakes are 'typos', rather than spelling errors. For example, one of us frequently finds that he has typed 'peron' instead of 'person'; 'hostipal' instead of 'hospital', and 'reducation' instead of 'reduction'.

Many spelling errors that result from typing faster than we can think involve the mixing up of homophones, so that, for example, you might write 'there' when you meant to write 'their', or 'two' when you meant to write 'to' or even 'too'. Such mistakes are commonplace, even among those who would not make such mistakes if they were working more slowly. However, mistakes such as these may remain in your final draft, unless you develop the habit of reading your work carefully for spelling mistakes. Even the best work can retain residual 'typos' if we do not proofread carefully enough.

> There is no excuse for carelessness, and if you submit work that has not been checked rigorously, you should not expect a comforting response to the plea that really you know how to spell these words and that they're only there because you didn't have time to check your essay through before submission.

Improving your spelling

If you know that you frequently make spelling mistakes, are convinced by what we have said about its importance, and want both to make a good impression and to gain good marks, you will want to make some attempt to improve your spelling. The first step to take is to identify the words with which you have difficulty.

Task 21: Make a list of problem words

Make a list of words whose spelling causes you problems. For most people, even if they are excellent spellers, there will be some such words. Having identified these words, try to take whatever steps you can to ensure that you can spell them correctly in the future. For example, you might make a note of them on a credit card sized piece of card that you keep in your wallet or purse, or decide to check the spellings in a dictionary whenever you use those words. Or you might find a way to recall the spelling; that is why, for example, one of us always recites the words 'One **c**ollar and two **s**ocks', when writing the word 'ne**c**e**ss**ary'.

You can readily find out about strategies you could adopt in attempting to improve your spelling in books such as *Spelling it Out* (Pratley, 1988), *Spelling Made Easy* (Dykes and Thomas, 1989) and *The Usborne Book of Better English* (Gee and Watson, 1990) and so we do not intend to offer a comprehensive overview of such strategies here, although we shall say something about some that you might consider adopting.

> Try to devise ways of reminding yourself how to spell words with which you have difficulty, similar to 'one collar and two socks' for the spelling of 'necessary', recording them both in a portable notebook and in an easily accessible file on the desktop of your computer.

Print out a list of words with which you know you have difficulty, and post them in a place that means you can't avoid seeing them from time to time, say next to the bathroom mirror.

Write any words you frequently spell wrongly into a small notebook, or on a credit card sized piece of card, along with any spelling rules you learn; by checking whenever you use them, you should be able to avoid errors in their use, and after a while you may find that you remember the spellings without having to do so.

Develop your visual memory of words with which you have problems using a technique called 'Look, Cover, Write, Check', which involves looking closely at a word you want to learn to spell, covering it with your hand, writing it down and then checking to see whether you got it right, at which point you should attend to any mistakes in your first attempt.

Develop your aural memory by listening carefully to how words sound, attending in particular to consonant clusters in the middle of words like 'switching', or break long words down into syllables, both to remember the spellings of those you use commonly, and to attempt unknown spellings.

Prefixes and suffixes

A more formal approach that you might adopt in the attempt to improve your spelling would involve becoming more familiar with the way that the English language works, including learning about prefixes and suffixes and the ways in which they modify other words.

Adding the prefix 'anti' to simpler words yields, for example, antifreeze, anticlimax, antithesis, antiseptic, antifreeze and anticlockwise.

Adding the prefix 'dis' to simpler words yields, for example, disarm, disengage, disappear, discord, discomfort, discover, disprove, disapprove and discontinue.

Adding the prefix 'un' to simpler words yields, for example, unacceptable, unpredictable, unhappy, unsophisticated, unopened, unattractive and undiscovered.

Adding the suffix 'less' to simpler words yields, for example, heartless, careless, bottomless, meaningless, mindless, tasteless, pointless, restless, speechless and powerless.

Adding the suffix 'ly' to simpler words yields, for example, currently, highly, certainly, greatly, equally, honestly, deceitfully and seemingly.

Adding the suffix 'ful' to simpler words yields, for example, boastful, hateful, restful, tearful, tasteful, mindful, fearful, hopeful, disgraceful and spiteful.

Some English words have both a prefix and a suffix and some have more than one prefix or suffix:

unutterably includes both the prefix 'un' and the suffix 'ably'

disinterestedly includes both the prefix 'dis' and the suffix 'ly'

unmissable includes both the prefix 'un' and the suffix 'able'

inequality includes both the prefix 'in' and the suffix 'ity'

tastelessness includes two suffixes: 'less' and 'ness'

reinvigorate includes two prefixes: 're' and 'in' and the suffix 'ate'

disgracefully includes the prefix 'dis' and two suffixes: 'ful' and 'ly'

Some English words, when combined with prefixes and suffixes, produce whole families of words, which have similarities in their spellings. Consider, for example, how, by adding and taking away prefixes and suffixes which themselves have regular spellings, the words 'grace', 'taste', 'equal' and 'sign' give birth to many others with related meanings:

grace – graceful, gracious, graceless, gracefully, gracefulness, disgrace, disgraceful, disgraced and disgracefully

taste – tasteful, tasteless, distaste, distasteful, tasty, taster

sign – signal, signature, signatory, ensign, insignia, resign, re-sign, consign, assign, assignation and signet ring

equal – equals, equality, inequality, unequal, unequally, equalize, equalled, equalizing, equalizer

Rules of spelling and their exceptions

The prospect of studying the ways in which English words build through the addition of suffixes and prefixes, and thus relate together in families sharing common roots, is perhaps a little daunting if you have no reason for doing so other than improving your spelling. However, there are other strategies that are open to you. One of these is to learn some spelling rules. Among these are, for example, rules about the ways that plurals are formed.

> The plural of most nouns in English is formed by simply adding an 's', so that, for example, 'noun' gives us 'nouns', 'tiger' yields 'tigers' and 'wardrobe' yields 'wardrobes'.
>
> The plural of English nouns that end in 's', 'sh', 'x' or 'ss', is formed by adding 'es', which, among other things, makes it possible to say the resultant plurals, so that 'gas' yields 'gases', 'wish' yields 'wishes', 'fox' yields 'foxes' and 'glass' yields 'glasses'.

These are useful rules, as is the rule about the changes that the addition of a 'magic e' – which you probably learned about in school – makes to vowel sounds in words such as man, win and nod, which together with the other examples we give below, end up with longer vowel sounds:

cap (cape)	cod (code)	cut (cute)
mad (made)	pet (Pete)	win (wine)
man (mane)	slop (slope)	pop (Pope)
nod (node)	Tim (time)	pip (pipe)

Unfortunately, many of the rules for English spelling have important exceptions; such is the inconsistency in our use of the phonic system. Consider, for example, the rule that most children learn to help them to spell words that contain the 'ee' sound, made either with 'ei' or 'ie':

'i' before 'e' except after 'c'.

Although helpful, this rule has notable exceptions, including:

'caffeine', 'weird', 'seize', 'protein' and 'seizure'.

Don't rely on spellcheckers

When writing on a computer you have ready access to spellchecking, which can be very useful as one way of detecting spelling mistakes in written work. However, you must never rely on your computer's spellchecker to locate all the mistakes you might have made in writing your essay, because it will not pick them all up. One reason for this is that in general spellcheckers will not spot misspellings if what you have written is in itself an acceptable word in the English language.

For example, it will pass over situations in which you have substituted a correctly spelled homophone for the word you intended to use (and we all do this from time to time, especially when we are writing quickly). For example, if you were to write that 'The principle of the school was their when the boy fell threw the skylight after his assent of the flagpole', all of the spellcheckers we know would suggest that you had made no mistakes in spelling, whereas we can detect four. And if you where to right this sentence, nun of the spellcheckers that we no wood be able to spot that their are as many as ate mistakes.

Although spellcheckers can be useful, using them does not guarantee that you will end up with an essay or assignment with acceptable spelling, and so after you have decided that your text is finished at the level of content, it is always as well to check it carefully for spelling mistakes, before deciding that it is finished.

In addition, unless your spellchecker is working in UK English, rather than US English mode, relying on it to improve the spelling of your work may result in it taking on North American spellings when you might prefer to stick with the British versions of words such as color, valor, gray, program, counselor, jewelry, favorite, humor and thru. Of course, if you are reading this in North America or learned to speak English in a place where American English is the norm, rather than UK English, you may prefer American forms of English spelling; indeed, if you are studying outside the UK you may well be required to use them.

Task 22: Spotting spelling errors

How many spelling problems can you spot in the following sentences? How many of them would have fought their way past your spellchecker? How many are the result of the substitution of homophones?

   i.   The opinion pole showed that the principle reason for the Prime Minister's fall in popularity is the belief that taxis are fair two high.
   ii. The interviewer tried to brooch the subject as sensitively as possible, but inn the end she just said it in a straightforward way.
   iii. The decent to the bottom of the cliff was dangerous and Dawn bagged Eric too take grate care.
   iv. When she fell of the sea saw, Majorie landed on her write hand and as a result was unable to right four too months.

[Our response appears on page 251]

Improving your spelling: helpful hints

To reduce the likelihood of spelling errors occurring in your essays, always get a friend to read your work with the intention of pointing out spelling errors, and even places where she is unsure whether you have spelled a word correctly. She is likely to do so better than you, because she is less likely than you are to be so familiar with the text that she manages to skip gaily past obvious errors.

- Listen carefully to how words are sounded; break long words down into syllables.
- Learn some common rules of spelling.
- Learn or devise ways of remembering spellings with which you have difficulty.
- Maintain both an easily accessible computer file and a small notebook, in which you store away the spellings of words you frequently misspell.
- Learn common homophones and their meanings.
- Use 'Look, Cover, Write, Check' to develop your visual memory of words.
- Learn about prefixes and suffixes and the work that they do.
- Use the meanings of words to remember spelling.
- Use a dictionary to check words with which you have problems.

Grammar

Most people who are reasonably competent readers and writers have an implicit understanding of grammar – a set of rules that govern the way our language works. Whether or not you can recall anything at all about the grammar you learned at school, other than the fact that it has something to do with 'nouns' and 'verbs', 'adjectives', 'prepositions' and 'conjunctions', you are one of these people, and your understanding of how words 'hang together' will help you, most of the time, to construct sentences that make sense. However, like most people, you will sometimes write nonsense, because you fail to follow the rules and because you fail to notice, in checking your work, that you have done so.

Often when you are writing, you may think that what you have written must make sense, because you know what it means. However, this is not necessarily true; sometimes, poor grammar will render what you have written unintelligible. As a result, even if you have good ideas, an essay may gain a poor mark, because you have been unclear in stating them. And even when your tutor can guess at your meaning, she is unlikely to be pleased by having had to make the effort to decipher ungrammatical English.

> You cannot expect your work to be marked on the basis of what your lecturers think you probably meant. Their job is to mark what you have written, not what they think you might have meant by what you have written.

In this section, although we do not intend to offer a comprehensive overview of grammar, we want to help you to avoid some of the most common grammatical errors.

Avoiding grammatical errors

You should be able to avoid many common grammatical errors, simply by reading your work carefully and thinking about the way in which you construct sentences.

Attend to sentence structure

Make sure that your sentences contain a main verb.

Make sure that verbs and nouns or pronouns agree; that is, that plural nouns or pronouns have a plural verb and that singular nouns and pronouns have singular verbs.

Ensure that tenses of verbs are consistent; that is, make sure that if you are writing about something in the past, you use past-tense forms of verbs, and take similar care when you are talking about the present and the future.

Make sure that no significant words are missing.

Make sure that your sentences contain a main verb

To make sense, most sentences need a main verb. Consider, for example, the following:

John comes home tomorrow.

John is coming home tomorrow.

John will come home tomorrow.

These are all grammatically acceptable sentences. Their meanings are clear. In each case omitting the verb ('comes', 'is coming' or 'will come') would leave us with a collection of words that would be unacceptable in Standard English:

John home tomorrow

> Check each sentence in your essays and assignments to make sure that they make sense and have a main verb.

Make sure that verbs and nouns or pronouns agree

To be acceptable in Standard English, verbs must agree with nouns or pronouns, that is, plural nouns or pronouns must have a plural verb, and singular nouns or pronouns must have singular verbs. Consider, for example, the following:

The geese on the Solway coast look wonderful, but they make a dreadful racket.

Every year a blackbird lays her eggs in a nest in the hawthorn hedge.

In the first example, the plural noun 'geese' is matched by the plural verb 'look', while the plural pronoun 'they' is matched by the plural verb 'make'. In the second example, the singular noun 'blackbird' and the singular pronoun 'her' are both matched by the singular verb 'lays'.

Now look at the two examples below, which are unacceptable:

They all runs to school.

John walk to the park.

In the first of these two simple sentences a plural pronoun, 'they', is mistakenly used with the singular verb 'runs', while in the second, the plural verb 'walk' is wrong, because 'John' is singular. To render these sentences acceptable we would have to change them thus:

They all run to school.

John walks to the park.

> Check each sentence in your essays and assignments to make sure that verbs agree with nouns and pronouns.

Ensure that tenses of verbs are consistent

The 'tense' of a verb lets you know when actions take place: in the present, in the past or in the future. To be acceptable in Standard English, the tense of verbs in a sentence must be consistent. Consider, for example:

On Saturday morning we went to the Bistro on the High Street where we had freshly squeezed orange juice, bagels and scrambled eggs with smoked salmon.

Thomas and Sam are really enjoying living in Eastbourne, where they are establishing themselves on the local music scene.

Although he likes most fish, our cat, Jackson has a definite preference for haddock over either hake or halibut.

The tense of the verbs in each of these examples is consistent. But now consider the following:

We came home and then we have our tea.

This simple sentence is unacceptable, because the verb 'came' is past tense, while 'have' indicates action in either the present or the future. To make it work as Standard English we would have to change one or other of the verbs. For example, we could change it to read either:

We came home and then we had our tea

or

We come home and then we have our tea.

Check each sentence in your essays and assignments to make sure that the tenses of verbs used are consistent.

Make sure that you do not omit significant words

The importance of ensuring that you have not accidentally missed out a word may seem obvious, but the omission of words is a frequent problem in student assignments, which can change the meaning of sentences, and even render them meaningless. For example, as it stands, the sentence, 'Students should strive ensure that the sentences write make sense', is nonsensical, because two important words have been omitted. Adding these words, we get:

Students should strive **to** ensure that the sentences **they** write make sense.

The mistake of omitting words can arise easily if you are careless in developing an essay from notes. Consider, for example:

Bernstein's theory of codes unpopular nowadays.

Manhattan Project scientists relieved to discover after first nuclear bomb test that only 1 in 3 million chance of igniting atmosphere.

Wiącek argues narrative research methods more ethical in research with deaf blind people, because more respectful.

Wittgenstein says meaning of word in use.

These would be fine in notes taken during lectures, because they would remind you of something that was said; some fact or piece of information; some idea you wanted to pursue further, or something you wanted to think about. However, since to work as 'stand alone' statements, they need to have verbs and other words added; they would be unlikely to endear you to your tutor if they appeared like this in an essay. Here they are again, with missing words inserted:

Bernstein's theory of codes is unpopular nowadays.

Manhattan Project scientists were relieved to discover after the first nuclear bomb test that it had had only a 1 in 3 million chance of igniting the atmosphere.

Wiącek argues that narrative research methods are more ethical than others in research with deaf blind people, because they are more respectful.

Wittgenstein says that the meaning of a word is in its use.

Omitting words is a very easy mistake to make when you are writing quickly and the only real way to avoid it is by re-reading what you have written word by word, out loud if you can, and avoiding the temptation to skip-read.

> Check each sentence your essays to make that no significant words missing. (Did you notice the missing words in this sentence?)

Task 23: Practise proofreading

Read the following examples and spot places where:

- A main verb is missing.
- Verbs do not agree with nouns or pronouns.
- There is inconsistency in tense.
- Important words are omitted.

How much time students spend using mobiles? Researchers at the University of Billericay conducted experiment about mobile among students. Nocci and Ohtou (2003) reporting that on average students uses cameras on mobiles ten times a week. They also find that mobile use increase with the age students, until a final year student spend up to two hours day, speaking to friends, texting and access the internet.

Writing are difficult. It involve more mental and physical effort than speaking, which probably explains why people is often reluctant to rewrite what they written.

This year was the 200th anniversary of birth of the Polish composer Chopin. He has been credit with the production of many essentially romantic master-pieces. His compositional style portray miniature approach to piano playing, which many commentators thinks has done little to further appreciation of the instrument. Nevertheless many people in homeland regards him as a national hero.

The use of citation to indicate the relationship of one's work to what others wrote, is one of characteristics that distinguished academic writing from other species of writing, including fiction and intelligent journalism. It is expect of all academic authors, whether they is first year undergraduate students, lecturers, or professors.

[Our response appears on page 251]

The technical vocabulary of grammar

In writing about sentence structure, we have used some technical words: 'noun', 'pronoun', 'verb', 'tense', 'plural' and 'singular'. If you do not understand these words, what we have said above will not make much sense to you; you will probably fail to understand grammatical points in feedback from your lecturers, and you will have little chance of understanding anything at all in more formal discussions of grammar. If you did not learn these terms at school, or have forgotten what you once knew, we suggest that you look through a simple guide to English grammar, noting down the words with which you are unfamiliar, along with points that you think will help you to improve your work. *The Usborne Book of Better English* by Gee and Watson (1990) is a good and simple introduction, but if you want to refer to a more advanced text, we would recommend *Rediscover Grammar* by Crystal (2004).

Don't rely on a grammar checker

If you frequently receive feedback about grammatical errors, you should make the effort to remedy them. If you don't understand what your tutor has said in her feedback, ask her to explain what she means, especially if she writes vague remarks on your assignments like, 'This isn't a sentence'; 'This is ungrammatical' or even, 'There are many grammatical problems in this essay'. Although it is not the responsibility of a lecturer in, say, history, psychology or peace studies, to teach you to write acceptable English, it is reasonable for you to expect that she should give feedback that identifies problems clearly, so that you at least know what it is that you need to sort out. If you are fortunate, you might even find that she is willing to give you a little additional help in coming to understand the problems to which she is drawing your attention.

Don't feel shy about asking your friends and classmates for help in understanding grammatical problems. And, if necessary, consult one of the texts that we have referred to above. Whatever you do, don't assume that a grammar checker on a computer will sort out your problems in this area. Grammar checkers tend to be vague in the advice they provide for remedying problems, and in any case they allow many grammatical problems to pass by, unnoticed. Here, by way of illustration, is an example of the kind of ungrammatical writing that can get past the grammar checker of a sophisticated word-processing package. It comes from a student essay about teaching English in primary schools and we have borrowed it from a discussion about the ineptitude of grammar checkers, in a book about computing and calculating:

> The teacher's role in the teaching of reading not only providing a variety of experiences but to provide a balanced programme of instruction. The teacher's role is therefore to be a guide to the child and aim to ensure pleasure, understanding, appreciation of organisation and recognising letters are successfully accomplished. (Solomon and Winch, 1994, p. 136)

Can you spot any errors in the above passage? The grammar checker used by Solomon and Winch failed to do so. However, we can see several. Here is the passage after necessary changes have been made:

> The teacher's role in the teaching of reading is not only to provide a variety of experiences but to provide a balanced programme of instruction. The teacher's role is therefore to be a guide to the child and to aim to ensure that pleasure, understanding, appreciation of organisation, and the recognition of letters are successfully accomplished.

First, we substituted 'is to provide' for 'providing' in the first sentence (in technical terms, we substituted the present tense for a participle). Next, we inserted a couple of words that she had omitted from the second sentence: 'to', which needed to be inserted before 'aim to ensure ...', and 'that', which needed to be added before 'pleasure'. Finally, we substituted 'the recognition of' for 'recognising' in the last line. Even with these changes the passage is not particularly elegant, and unfortunately even after these changes, we are not quite sure what the author is getting at, because we do not understand what she means by 'appreciation of organisation', unless she is referring to the need for writers to appreciate the importance of organisation and structure in written work.

Interestingly, when we invited our grammar checker to look the original passage over for us in January 2010, its report on the first sentence read 'Fragment: consider revising', but gave no opinion about how we might do so, while the second sentence was passed over with no comment. Even more interesting is that back in the mid-1990s, an earlier version of the same grammar checker seemed to think that there were more problems, and proffered the following advice:

First sentence: This does not seem to be a complete sentence.

Second sentence (in relation to the last clause, i.e. 'are successfully accomplished'): This main clause may contain a verb in the passive voice.

The first of these points was (and still is) at best an unhelpful partial truth, since it gave no clues about what the first sentence is, if it is not a complete sentence; the second makes no sense at all. In any case, neither comment is of any practical help since no suggestions are given about what one might do to correct the possible errors pinpointed.

Don't rely on a grammar checker to spot your mistakes in the use of English.

2.4

Getting your writing right: citation and referencing

In writing as a student you will be expected not only to demonstrate knowledge and thought, but to support the views you express, by presenting well-worked-out arguments in their favour, and by 'citing' what other people have said or done. As we shall demonstrate, these two kinds of support will often come together, as you adopt a critical stance in relation to authors whose work you cite, in order to develop arguments in favour of your own point of view. Developing your understanding of citation will help you to become a better writer.

> Good academic writers write in a style that ensures that their arguments and ideas 'hang together' in a way that flows, and is easy for their readers to understand. Used carefully and sensibly, citation can help you to write like this.

What is 'citation' or 'referencing'?

The practice of 'citing' or 'referring to' what others have written should allow anyone who reads your work to locate the sources that have influenced you. All academic authors, whether they are first-year undergraduate students, lecturers or professors, have to engage in it, and it is one of the distinguishing features of academic writing. It involves drawing attention in your text to what the authors in question have done, concluded or argued and then, in a separate 'reference list', giving full bibliographical details for the source cited, which will allow your readers to follow up what you have said. That is why you must be careful to ensure that whenever you read something that you might draw on in your work, you record details like author, date, source, publisher and so on. It is also why, if you have not already done so, you should learn how to present this information in a way that is both clear and consistent.

> The use of citation to indicate the relationship of your work to what others have written is probably the key characteristic that distinguishes academic writing from other species of writing, including fiction and intelligent journalism.

Who and what do I have to cite?

You should 'cite' or 'refer to' the authors of all texts, including articles and books, that influence what you write, ideally in a way that informs readers about how they have influenced you. For example, you should do so if, in your essay, you make use of factual information that you obtained by reading what they have written. So, for instance, if you had read Mithen's book *The Prehistory of the Mind: A Search for the Origins of Art, Religion and Science*, and wanted to refer to what he says about the use of tools among chimpanzees, you might write:

> Mithen (1996) points out that while the chimpanzees of the Tai forest in West Africa use sticks to extract bone marrow, they do not go ant fishing.

Even more importantly, perhaps, you should cite any author whose ideas or arguments have influenced the development of your own point of view.

Most of the sources you use as a student will probably be textual – academic books, journal articles and web pages; government documents; legal reports, newspaper articles and unpublished conference papers. However, depending on your subject, you may also want to refer to sources of other kinds that have influenced you. For example, in some subjects it may at times be appropriate to cite TV programmes, movies or CDs. Finally, you should alsorefer to lectures, or to 'personal communications' such as conversations with friends or colleagues, during which you have been given useful information, heard interesting ideas or perhaps received helpful criticism of your own ideas.

> Your use of citation is likely to have a significant influence over the marks you receive as a student, because it is one of the elements of your written work

that your teachers will use in assessing what you have learned, and how well you can think.

The purpose of academic citation and referencing

Many students develop the unfortunate idea that the main point of citation in academic writing is to make their work look scholarly, and to convince their teachers that they have read something. As a result, rather than viewing it as integral to the task of writing academically about anything, they come to view it as an added burden when they are writing essays and other assignments.

Reasons for citation

- To acknowledge the source of information that you have used.

- To contextualize your work by relating it to what others think and to what they have done.

- To acknowledge that an author or source has influenced your work – your research, ideas, arguments and point of view – and to show the extent and nature of that influence.

These three are centrally important for all academic authors, students and teachers alike. However, as a student there are other reasons for citation that are worth noting:

- To demonstrate to your teachers that you have been reading round your topic, that you understand what you have read, and that you are able to use it in developing your own ideas.

- To facilitate the development of your essay, by providing ideas, arguments, points of view and factual information around which you can develop your own position.

Providing evidence of the work you have done in trying to understand your topic is a legitimate reason for citation in student work. However, you should avoid the temptation to allow it to overtake other reasons for citation; and you should avoid the temptation to which it sometimes leads, to rely too much on simply reporting what others have written, rather than making use of what they have written to develop your own point of view or argument.

When should you refer to what others have written?

As we argued in Part 1, academic reading is, or at any rate should be, a critical pursuit, in the sense that it should involve interrogating the author via her text, assessing what she writes for coherence and clarity as well as for the strength of her arguments and for the relevance and strength of the examples, illustrations and evidence she uses. Reading in this way helps to build knowledge and understanding; it helps to form our interests, at the same time as developing our views and the arguments that are necessary to support them. It is an important part of the process of academic writing, whether at undergraduate, postgraduate or professional level.

Reading a lot isn't good in itself. What is good is reading in depth, coming to understand what authors say and then being able to use what they say to build your own understanding, arguments and points of view.

You may cite an author because what he has written agrees with your point of view; indeed, many students develop the misguided idea that the purpose of citation is to 'back-up' what they are writing by showing that others agree with them.

'Backing up your ideas' by reference to others who agree with you is one function of citation. However, to be really effective as an author, you will have to do more than merely point to some 'authority' who shares your view, or from whom your view derives.

When, in the course of your reading, you come across arguments that support or help to shape your own point of view, you will often be able to cite them directly. However, rather than simply pointing out that other people share your view or part of it, you should always attempt to show why their position is attractive and their arguments strong. The fact that someone else, however eminent, agrees with your position, is never a reason for blindly accepting what they say as evidence in your favour.

Rather than simply pointing out that others share your point of view, or say things that support it, always give reasons for accepting what they say.

Citation allows you to demonstrate that you can think critically about what others have said. This will involve doing more than simply harvesting ideas, arguments and evidence from what they have written, that support your own point of view. In addition, you will, at times, have to show that you are able to pinpoint, and comment constructively about, flaws in their reasoning.

> It is possible to use the arguments of others in arguing in favour of your own point of view even when they disagree with you.

Demonstrating what is mistaken or inadequate about points of view that differ from or oppose your own can be useful in persuading others of the attractiveness of your position. However, you should try always to be respectful of the authors whose work you read, even when you think they are mistaken. Presenting an author's views as favourably as possible and then demonstrating what is inadequate about them is more impressive than simply attacking their arguments without explanation.

> You are likely to make even more impact if, before critiquing an author's ideas, you first state her position or argument as fairly and as accurately as possible.

Doing so will make your argument all the more powerful, because it demonstrates mastery of the position you intend to attack, and thus strengthens your claim to be able to pinpoint its weaknesses. After presenting the argument or position you wish to attack as sympathetically as you can, showing how the various steps follow from one another, and contribute (or are thought by the author to contribute) to the conclusion reached, you should point out flaws in her line of reasoning. For example, you should draw attention to places where the various steps do not follow from one another and perhaps, to mistakes in facts or understanding that lead you to reject it. Having drawn attention to the weaknesses in her position you should then attempt to show how your position can help to overcome them. This is a more sophisticated use of citation than merely pointing to people who share your point of view, and one that is likely to gain you brownie points, because it gives evidence that you can think arguments through. As you read, you should thus note weaknesses in the arguments that authors present, and consider whether and how they might be made stronger.

Less obvious, perhaps, is that it can be helpful to adopt a critical stance in relation to the arguments and evidence employed by those whose conclusions mirror your own, or whose conclusions you find attractive.

> Demonstrating a willingness to critique those whose views you share will make your citation of places where you think they are right even stronger. (Can you see why?)

Citation and referencing: the practicalities

There are a number of different approaches to citation and referencing, among which the most common are the so-called 'numerical' system and a number of variations on what is known as the 'author–date' system.

Whoever we are, we will be expected to adopt specific conventions in our writing by those we are writing for. For example, researchers writing for academic journals have to tailor their citation and referencing to the requirements of the particular journal to which they intend submitting their work; and students will have to do whatever is required by their teacher or institution. Unfortunately, in our experience, the requirements for citation and referencing presented by institutions, journals and publishers sometimes contain inconsistent information; and whereas some are rather vague, others are so detailed that they cause confusion. That is why we decided that in this book we would offer a simple guide to the Harvard system, because it is very easy to understand and has much in common with other author–date approaches, which are nowadays more popular than numerical systems. However, after our detailed discussion of Harvard we also provide an overview of numerical referencing, since you will probably come across academic sources that employ it, and thus need to know how it works (see pages 149–151). If your course requires you to use numerical citation, our overview will be helpful but please, in addition, read what we have to say about using the Harvard system on pages 122–148, because much of what we have to say will be helpful to you.

There is a huge divergence of views about the minutiae of citation and referencing. However, we suggest strongly that unless you are already competent in using some approach consistently, you should work your way carefully through pages 122–148 of this book, in which we set out a simple and consistent guide to Harvard style citation. Please think carefully about this, because in our experience, many students who claim to have such competence actually do not. Although your time is limited, undertaking the tasks and exercises that we provide will help you to think about and practise citation and referencing using Harvard. Having internalized the approach we suggest, you should find it easy to adapt your practice to meet other expectations that you may come across, including variations of the Harvard and other systems.

Citation using the Harvard System: a guide

Although it can seem a little confusing at first, Harvard is easy to use, both as a writer and as a reader. As a writer, it is a simple way of presenting information about the sources with which you have engaged; as a reader, it enables you to follow up sources referred to in the books and articles you read. It involves two essential steps:

i Citation within the text

ii Presenting full bibliographical references in an alphabetical reference list.

We begin, on pages 122–23, with a detailed discussion of citation within the text; then, on pages 132–42, we turn to detailed guidance about how to write full references to a range of different types of source that you might wish to cite. We have chosen to limit our ambitions to some of the more common sources, both because to offer detailed guidance about writing full references in relation to a wider range of sources could take up a whole book in itself, and more importantly, because doing so would risk confusing our readers. This is what many guides to citation and referencing available on university and college websites across the world do, and we think that is a pity.

i Citation within the text

Whenever you use or draw attention to something another person has written or spoken about, you indicate this within your text, by mentioning their name and the year in which the source was published (or, in the case of unpublished material, the date from which it originates). If you are citing a source with up to three authors, citations within the text should include all of their names, provided that this does not interfere with the flow of your essay, for example:

Davies and Jarvis (2007) draw attention to evidence that supports the belief that the internal combustion engine was first imagined by Da Vinci.

Morris, Fraser and Wilkinson (1998) argued that in the age of globalization, all children should pursue not one, but two modern foreign languages to GCSE.

However, where there are more than three authors, you should use the abbreviation 'et al' to indicate 'this author and others', for example:

Webb et al (2010) argue that there is a great lack of clarity in the way that the term 'reconciliation' is used, in discussions of post conflict reconstruction.

Textual references can take a number of different forms. For example:

Ignatieff (1996) distinguishes between truths told for the purpose of reconciliation, and truth told for its own sake.

Sympathy is an emotive response. Tschudin (1986) points out that it means 'suffering with, feeling the same suffering'.

A recent study (Hardy et al., 1998) compares psychoanalysts' accounts of the therapeutic process, with those of their patients.

A number of authors have argued that fewer people would die in motorway accidents if the maximum speed was raised to 80 mph (see for example, Erikson, 2005; Jeffries, 2006 and Bates, 2008).

Customer compatibility management emphasises the controllability of customer to customer interaction in the higher education environment (MacMinn, 1996).

Successful decision making is a characteristic of the professional, and the ways in which decisions are reached arguably allow us to pinpoint expertise (Chi et al, 1988; Eraut, 1994).

In citation within the text, where the author's name occurs naturally in what you are writing, as it does in the case of the references to Ignatieff and Tschudin above, the year of publication is given in brackets and, for reasons that we share below, we favour this form of citation. However, in many areas of academic life, it is much more common to find that authors' names are isolated from the text and bracketed off, almost as though they don't really have anything to do with the ideas being discussed. The references given above, to 'Mac Minn, 1996'; 'Chi et al, 1988' and 'Eraut, 1994', are of this kind. They tell us nothing at all about what the authors cited believe or say, or have done. Rather we are left to guess whether, for example, 'Chi et al and Eraut' offer empirical research evidence for the idea that professionals are characterized by successful decision making; argue that this is the case, or merely believe it. We are also left wondering whether in the source cited, MacMinn is creating the concept of 'Customer compatibility management' or merely telling us how it is used in a higher education context.

By contrast, the references to Ignatieff and Tschudin do tell us a little about these authors – that Ignatieff thinks there is a difference between the two species of truth to which he refers, and that Tschudin not only thinks she knows what sympathy is, but is prepared to share her view with us. Finally, although the reference to 'Erikson, 2005; Jeffries, 2006 and Bates, 2008' looks superficially similar to the vague references to Chi et al and Eraut, it is different, because unlike them, it does tell us something about these authors – that they have each *argued* that increasing the speed limit would reduce the number of motorway accidents.

If you cite more than one source published by an author in the same year, these are usually distinguished by adding lower-case letters (a, b, c, etc.) after the year and inside the brackets. For example, you might refer to Timmis (2005a) and then, later in the same essay, to Timmis (2005b).

Where there are two or more authors the surnames of each author are given; where there are more than three the surname of the first author is given, followed by 'et al', short for *et alia* (which is Latin for 'and others')[5].

In the case of anonymous works, 'Anon.' is used in place of the author's name.

Comparing different forms of Harvard citation within the text

As you read academic and professional articles, books and so on, you will come across citations in different forms. Many will look like this:

Apes can be taught to use sign language, so they should be given the same rights as humans (Williams, 1990).

Although they are extremely common, citations of this kind are rather vague. They give us no indication about why the cited author is being cited. To work that out we would have to look up the source for ourselves.

You will also come across citations in this form:

Williams (1990) argues that since apes can be taught to use sign language, they should be given the same rights as humans.

Citations in this second form are more helpful. This one hints at what Williams believes and outlines her argument. Of course, from what is said we cannot assess whether this argument is strong or well founded; however, it does, at least, tell us that she has 'argued'. By contrast, although the first citation to Williams said similar things, it gives us no clues about why Williams was being cited.

Citation is nearly always strongest when authors include the names of those to whom they wish to refer, in their text, as in the second of the two references to Williams (1990) and those to Ignatieff (1966) and Tschudin (1986). Including the name of the author or authors in the text is helpful, because doing so means that you have to say something about them – about, for example, what they have done, argue or believe. This is a good way of

---

[5] Note, however, that in a reference list the names of all authors in a publication should be given, no matter how many there are. In some of the physical sciences and in medical research, for example, where it is common to have multiple authored articles, simply writing out the list of names can at times be a major undertaking, as illustrated by one of the examples of full references to journal articles we give on page 00, which has 21 authors. The largest number of authors that we know of being listed for a single article is 144, who were listed as authors of the article 'The Sloan Digital Sky Survey' (York et al, 2000).

developing your text, as well as of making it easier to follow and helping to ensure that there really is a reason for making the reference in the first place.

You may find yourself wanting to reject our advice about trying, whenever possible, to include the names of authors you are citing in the text of your essays, because you have noticed, as we have already pointed out, that lots of academic writing uses citations in which cited authors' names simply appear, with the date of publication, at the end of a sentence. If you do, it is important to realize that this response commits you to being the kind of academic writer who leaves her readers to guess at the reason that she is citing the people that you are citing. Our first version of the Williams (1990) reference was one example. Here is another, in which two references are given:

> There is a great deal of disagreement about the best way of addressing the problems of bullying in the workplace (Biggs, 1998; Cunningham, 1987).

Note that we have no way of telling which side of the fence Biggs and Cunningham sit on, from this citation. It tells us nothing about whether they are participants in the debate about how best to address workplace bullying, or have perhaps simply written about the disagreement that is mentioned. Imagine how much more helpful and informative it would have been if the authors had, instead, written:

> People find it hard to agree about how best to address the problems of bullying in the workplace. For example, while Biggs (1998) argues that it is best to deal with complaints in a low-key way, bringing the individuals together in an informal discussion, Cunningham (1987) is less convinced. Although he agrees that, in mild cases, Biggs' approach will be helpful, Cunningham counsels caution where the person alleging the bullying shows signs of extreme distress.

Of course, this is much longer than the first, uninformative reference to the same sources. However, it is much more worthwhile, because it gives us real information about the two cited sources, which the author has used in such a way that as readers we gain the impression that he has read them in some detail. Whereas the author of the first example merely 'points at' his sources, the author of the second uses them to explore his topic. Importantly, doing so has helped him to develop his text.

Task 24: Which use of citation is most helpful?

Read the examples below, each of which contains two contrasting paragraphs. Decide in each case whether (a) or (b) uses citation in the most helpful way, and write a couple of sentences justifying your decision. Talk to at least two of the other members of your tutorial group about this and compare your answers.

Example 1

(a) At another level, problems of a psychological kind often occur in deaf-blind people. Majewski (1995) who carried out an international literature review, points, for example, to low quality of life, loneliness, little control of one's life, challenging behaviours, and depression.

(b) At another level, problems of a psychological kind often occur in deaf-blind people, including low quality of life; loneliness; little control of their life; challenging behaviours, or depression (Majewski, 1995).

Example 2

(a) Everyone knows that the sun rises in the East and sets in the West (Smith, 1994; Thompson, 1995; Behringer, 1996a; Cullen, 1997). This is one reason that house builders try to ensure that bedroom windows face East (Jones, 1996; Wittgenstein and Russell, 1994; Lessing, 2000). Psychological literature suggests that when house builders do not attend to the changes in mood that arise as a result of the orientation of homes, they contribute to a net decline in the health of the nation (North, 2006; Naesby, 2003; Davies, 2004).

(b) Several scientists claim to have demonstrated conclusively that the sun rises in the East and sets in the West, including Smith (1994) who filmed the sun rising and setting in fifteen locations across the world, over a six month period. However, his findings have been challenged by others, notably Thompson (1995), whose attempt to replicate Smith's work failed to record the sun's either rising or setting at all. Thompson's research has been severely criticised by Cullen (1997), who argues that it is deeply flawed, because he chose to conduct it in the North of Norway during July.

[Our response appears on page 251]

Citation is nearly always best when it is obvious why a source is being cited, because this demonstrates that you have read and understood it and have good reasons for your citation. Often this will involve saying a little about, for example, what the author has done or has found; argues or suggests; draws attention to, or has demonstrated. For example, if you wanted to discuss arguments about the intervention of one state in the affairs of another, which appeared in an article by Barker, published in 1998, you might begin by stating Barker's view, before moving on to briefly state the argument she offers in its favour:

Barker (1998) believes that at times the leaders of powerful nations should intervene in the internal affairs of less powerful nations. She argues that they should do so when there is clear evidence of extensive human rights abuse.

An even stronger way to use Barker might involve pointing out how her views differ from those of some other writers. For example, you might write:

Smith (1983) and Davies (1988) share the view that intervention in the internal affairs of another country can never be justified, simply because what is happening there seems unjust or unethical, even if intervening might prevent innocent suffering and facilitate changes that will benefit that country's citizens. By contrast, Barker (1998) believes that powerful nations should intervene in the affairs of other countries when human rights are being abused.

By comparing the views of authors like this, you can show, not only that you know what they believe, but that you are aware of alternative points of view.

Discussing an author's views and arguments and comparing them to those of others is good. However, in general, it is even better if you engage critically with what she has written, because the fact that she agrees with you is, in itself, not sufficient to support your view. That depends on how well she has reasoned, and on the strength of the evidence she presents in support of her beliefs. And so, for example, before you decide to cite an author who agrees with your point of view, or with some part of it, it is a good idea to make sure that you understand the reasons she presents, so that when you cite her you can say why you think her view is worthwhile. In Part 3, we discuss 'arguments from authority' in a bit more detail.

> The fact that some academic – even some very well-known academic – has put forward an idea or argument, does not make it correct.

If you were arguing in favour of a narrative approach to social research and had read Kearney's book, *On Stories: Thinking in Action*, you might use it to try to support your view, by writing:

Kearney (2002) argues for the importance of narrative in our lives.

This would be a step in the right direction, because it would demonstrate to your readers your awareness that Kearney not only believes in the importance of narrative, but offers arguments to support this belief. However, to be as helpful as possible in developing an argument, it would be best to go further by outlining and then critiquing Kearney's arguments and perhaps offering some original examples to illustrate the part that you think narrative plays in our everyday lives.

In the case of empirical work you might give a critical account of the work of researchers to whom you refer, although it is important to realize that by a 'critical account' we don't mean one that attempts to pull what someone has written or done to bits, but a careful account of both strengths and weaknesses in what they have said and done, and perhaps about how you think it might be improved.

> In most instances, referring to other people's work is a vacuous exercise if you do it for no other reason than to impress others with how much you have read or want people to think you have read.

Avoid using citation to give public displays, either of how clever you are (or want people to think you are) or of how much you have read. Doing so can lead to bad reading habits. For example, it can lead you to direct your reading towards the collection of 'trophies' that you can use to decorate your essays, rather than to engaging with ideas and arguments that you read about, in the hope that by learning something about the research others have carried out and the arguments they have presented, you can advance your own thinking and argument a little.

Task 25: What is the purpose of the citation?

Look at the following examples of citation and try to work out what the purpose of the citation is in each case. Try, in each case, to imagine what might come next.

- Is the citation informative?

- How much do we learn about the author cited?

- Does the writer critically engage with the author or authors she cites?

Davis (1977) has developed a model of global warming that acknowledges the impact of human actions, but has the potential to minimize the effects of the paralyzing culture of blame promulgated by many authors.

Citation analysis has interested information scientists, sociologists of science, and applied linguists (for useful overviews, see Bornmann and Daniel, 2008; Nicolaisen, 2007; Small, 1982; White, 2004).

Several researchers have concluded that though Jameson's approach to the assessment of empathy among torturers was interesting, the methodology used in his research on torture was flawed (see, for example, Dobson, 2001; Thomson and Weatherstone, 2003; Maitland, 2006).

Wing et al (2002) investigated the history of leek growing competitions in the North East of England.

Thomas (1983) argues that the research he compared, including that by Melia and Boyd (1974), Balls (1977), Fisher (1975), Dreyfus (1970), Otrebski and Wiącek (1969), Mair and Little (1985), Weitz (1986) and Cunningham and Jude (1971) all made use of the same observational techniques, and that each made the same errors.

Smith (1990) believes that since some apes can use sign language, they should be treated as if they have the same rights as humans.

McCormack (1986) carried out an interesting, but flawed study of the eating habits of gerbils in Saddleworth, from which he concluded that they have a preference for pecans over pine kernels.

Smail (1987) is sceptical of the way in which psychotherapists often regard what they do as having some kind of scientific justification. The reasons for this view are easier to accept than his somewhat demeaning contention that psychotherapy has something in common with prostitution.

Ignatieff (1996) distinguishes between truths told for the purpose of reconciliation, and truth told for its own sake.

Sympathy is an emotive response. Tschudin (1986) points out that it means 'suffering with, feeling the same suffering'.

[Our response appears on page 252]

Referring to authors whose work is cited by others, but which you have not directly consulted

In the course of your reading, you will come across references to sources in which the authors discuss ideas and arguments that are of interest to you, and this will often prove to be a productive source of ideas for new avenues of literary research. Whenever possible you should look such sources up, both to check what the author you are currently reading has said about them, and so that if you decide that what they have to say is important, you can cite them. However, it will sometimes be impossible to do so because, for example, your university library does not subscribe to a particular journal, or because all the copies of the book you want are out on loan. If this is the case, it is important to be aware that you cannot legitimately cite sources that you have not consulted. However, there is a way in which you can draw attention to important ideas that you have heard about second hand.

> The best way to use ideas that are cited by an author you have read, if you are unable to get hold of the original work, is to introduce those ideas by citing the author(s) whose work you have read, and discussing what they have to say about the source you have been unable to access.

For example, in an essay in which you examine the case for and against school uniform, you might write:

> Tompkins (1993) reports research by Wilson, suggesting that schools in which children wear a uniform tend to achieve more success in public examinations than schools that do not.

In this instance, even though the idea you wish to introduce into your essay is Wilson's, you are citing Tompkins, because you have not read Wilson directly and therefore are not in a position to cite him. And so it is Tompkins' work that you must cite, and his work to which you must give a full reference, not Wilson's.

Imagine that during your reading for an essay about conflict resolution, you came across the following sentence in an article by Alidu et al (2008):

> According to Osamba (2001) indigenous African people are inclined to adopt rituals that provide 'co-operative problem solving' techniques rather than the confrontational and power-bargaining practices often associated with Western reconciliation mechanisms.

The ideas that Alidu et al attribute to Osamba are interesting, and so you might decide that it would be helpful to mention them in constructing your own essay. However, you might have difficulty in locating the Osamba reference, which is from a little known journal; if so, you would have to cite Alidu et al, while acknowledging that the ideas they are discussing, are Osamba's. For example, you might write:

> In a challenging discussion of the nature of reconciliation, Alidu et al (2008) refer to Osamba, who discusses the use that indigenous African people make of 'co-operative problem solving techniques'.

As in the previous case, in this instance you would be citing not the person whose idea interests you, but the authors whose work has drawn that idea to your attention. And so, in this instance, you would give a full reference to Alidu et al, and not to Osamba.

> If you use ideas from an author that you know about only through reading about them in something written by another author, do not refer to them

directly, but instead cite the author you have read as a way of introducing the ideas you want to discuss, making sure that you attribute the ideas to the person to whom they belong, as in the following examples:

In arguing that narrative approaches to medical interviewing are not only more humane, but more efficient than the pseudo-scientific ways of interacting with patients taught in many medical schools, Clerk (2005) draws on Hudson's research about doctor–patient communication. Among other things, he focuses attention on Hudson's use of actors to play the part of patients in the teaching of interview skills.

Phillips (1993) draws attention to the importance for research on human resilience, of the work of a number of authors, whose accounts of their experience of situations of extreme terror, underpin much of the most productive work in the field. Among these, he draws special attention to Drury, whose story he relates in some detail. In 1971, Drury was captured by bandits, while trekking through Afghanistan.

According to Millett (1988) much of the most productive work on the classification of the unique grasses found in the isolated islands to the east of the Walgowrie peninsula, was carried out by Father Francis, who was a missionary there during the early twentieth century. Francis, who had no scientific training, apparently gathered more than 10,000 specimens, which he meticulously organised according to criteria that he himself devised.

Something to avoid: the patchwork approach

A surprisingly large number of students, even in the second and third year of a degree course, adopt a simplistic approach to using what they have learned from their reading. Rather than using sources, in a simple way, to 'back up' or support their developing position or argument, or in a more sophisticated way by offering a critique of what they have to say as a way of building their own point of view, they will often do little more than 'harvest' ideas from authors who have addressed their topic, merging them in a kind of Frankenstein's monster of an essay. Such essays are more like a collage made up of scraps torn out of texts written by others, than coherent discussions of a topic. They are usually made up of a mixture of direct quotations, and sections of work by others, which the student has subtly, and sometimes not so subtly, paraphrased into his 'own words'. Often there is little in such an essay to suggest that an author was present at its creation, because there is little evidence of a developed viewpoint, rather than an account of what others think.

Assignments that are little more than a patchwork or collage of snippets from the authors you have read will do little to persuade your lecturers that you can think.

A much more fruitful approach is to use ideas you gather from reading and engaging with books and other sources as scaffolding to support the development of your own arguments and points of view.

If you choose to adopt this approach, you must be careful to ensure that your accounts of others are accurate. However, what really matters is the views you use them to support. It involves critical judgement, because to switch metaphors for a moment, it involves both 'setting out your stall' – that is, making clear what you believe – and deciding what evidence from authors you have read can best be used in supporting your own developing arguments and points of view.

Writing full references and presenting them in an alphabetical list

For each source you cite, you should give a full 'reference' in an alphabetical list at the end of your text. Such a list is usually referred to as a 'reference list'. However, some people favour the expression 'bibliography', and it is thus possible that you may be asked to include a 'bibliography' rather than a 'reference list' with your essays and assignments. In either case, you will be doing exactly the same thing: giving details of the source in question that will allow readers to locate it.

Although most 'reference lists' or 'bibliographies' will contain the same information, you will find variations, especially in the way that this information is arranged, depending on the publisher. The general rule is that a full reference should contain enough information to allow others to locate the source in question, as in the following examples:

Adedeji, J.L. (2001) 'The Legacy of J.J. Rawlings in Ghanaian Politics, 1979–2000', *African Studies Quarterly* (internet) 5 (2). Available at http://www.web.africa.ufl.ed/asq/v5/v5i2a1.htm (Accessed 5 April 2010).

Fairbairn, G.J. and Fairbairn, S.A. (eds) (1988) *Ethical Issues in Caring*, Aldershot, Gower Publishing.

Mithen, S. (1996) *The Prehistory of the Mind: A Search for the Origins of Art, Religion and Science*, London, Thames and Hudson.

Schulz, B. (1989) 'Conflict resolution training programmes: implications for theory and research', *Negotiation Journal*, 5 (3) 301–309.

Winch, C. (2010) *Dimensions of Expertise*, London, Continuum.

Writing full references is a simple business, but we wish we had a pound for every student who seems to find it impossible to write them accurately and in a consistent way.

Our experience has led us to the incontrovertible truth that students who memorize a simple but consistent way of setting out and punctuating academic references, become academically stronger than those who do not, because the work they put into mastering this central, but often confusing feature of academic writing means that it eventually becomes 'second nature' to them. As a result, it becomes helpful for them as writers, rather than remaining as it is for many, a time-consuming piece of window dressing, aimed at little more than making their essays look 'academic'.

There are a number of different ways of presenting the information that you should include in full references, and endless variations in the ways that they may be punctuated. Not only do different academic publishers adopt different 'house styles' of punctuation and layout for references, but different universities also adopt different styles, and there may even be variations in the punctuation and layout required by the different faculties and schools in the same university. In addition, you may find that teachers in different subjects have divergent expectations about how you should write full references, and even that individual teachers in the same subject might have competing views about the 'correct' way to reference. That is why, unless you are already very sure of yourself in writing full references to most kinds of source, we suggest that you should try to internalize the simple approach to setting out full references in an alphabetical list, outlined below.

> By practising writing full references to different kinds of texts, using the examples we give as a guide, you will find, after a while, that writing references comes naturally to you.

You will also find that having become proficient in one simple and consistent layout and punctuational style for full references, it is relatively easy to adapt to any set of requirements you are given.

What information should be included in a reference list?

A full reference should give as much information as is necessary for a reader to locate the source referred to, although the information that is given will vary according to the source cited.

In this guide we do not intend to offer advice about how to write full references to every possible type of source to which you might want to refer. Rather, we focus on a few of the main ones:

- Authored books
- Edited books
- Chapters in edited books
- Articles in academic journals or periodicals (paper versions)

- Articles in academic journals or periodicals (electronic versions)
- Articles in newspapers and magazines (paper versions)
- Articles in newspapers and magazines (electronic versions)
- Websites
- Personal communications

Developing skill in writing full references for these sources will help you to internalize some general principles that can be applied elsewhere. One such principle is the use of italics to indicate the titles or names of freestanding sources, including books – for example, *The Rough Guide to Ethical Living* and *God and Human Dignity*; the titles of journals, newspapers and magazines – for example, *The Journal of Medical Ethics*; *The Sunday Times* and *The New Statesman*. This principle applies, also, when you are writing full references to other free standing documents, such as government reports, conference proceedings and holiday brochures, and also when you are citing, for example, television programmes, movies or CDs, say, the BBC TV series *The Story of the Guitar*, presented by Alan Yentob in 2009, the film *Mystic River*, directed by Clint Eastwood, or the CD *My Goal's Beyond*, by John McLaughlin.

Although you will come across many different styles of punctuation for full references in books and journals, it will be helpful in learning to use citation and referencing in a consistent way, to simply follow the punctuation that we specify, which is simple and easy to memorize. It is important, however, that we emphasize that we are not claiming that it is the only way to punctuate full references. However, we commend it to you, because it is simple, consistent and easy to learn.

Authored books

An authored book is one in which a single author (or group of authors) has written the entire text. In giving a reference for an authored book, you should include the following information:

- Surname(s) and initials of author or authors
- Year of publication, in brackets
- *Title of the book*, in italics
- Place (town) of publication
- Publisher

This information should be arranged as in the examples that follow. Please note the punctuation that is used to separate the elements of the references:

Authored books with one author

Crystal, D. (2002) *The English Language*, London, Penguin.

Glover, J. (2001) *Humanity: A Moral History of the Twentieth Century*, New Haven, London, Yale University Press.

Winch, C. (1998) *The Philosophy of Human Learning*, London, Routledge.

Authored books with more than one author

You should list the names of the authors, with their initials, in the order that they appear in the book.

Canter, D. and Fairbairn, G. (2006) *Becoming an Author: A Guide for Academics and Other Professionals*, Buckingham, Open University Press.

Harré, R. and Secord, P. (1973) *The Explanation of Social Behaviour*, Oxford, Basil Blackwell.

Edited books

References to edited books take the same form as references to authored books, but add (ed) or (eds) in brackets after the name(s) of the editor or editors. In other words, you should include the following information:

- Surname(s) and initials of editor or editors
- (ed) or (eds)
- Year of publication, in brackets
- *Title of the book*, in italics
- Place (town) of publication
- Publisher

This information should be arranged as in the examples that follow. Note that as with authored books with more than one author, the names of the editors of books with more than one editor, should be listed in the order that they appear in the book, and never in alphabetical order. Please note the punctuation that is used to separate the elements of the references.

Examples

Fairbairn, S.A. and Fairbairn, G.J. (eds) (1989) *Psychology, Ethics and Change*, London, Routledge and Kegan Paul.

Midlarsky, M. L. (ed) (1992) *The Internationalization of Communal Strife*, New York, Routledge.

Winch, C. and Heyting, F. (eds) (2005) *Critique and Conformity in Liberal Society* (also published as a special edition of the *Journal of Philosophy of Education,* 2004), Oxford, Blackwell.

Chapter in an edited book

If you cite a chapter in an edited book, your reference should include details of the chapter and its author or authors (in the order that they appear in the book) as well as details of the book and its editors:

- Surname(s) and initials of chapter author or authors
- Year of publication, in brackets
- 'Title of the chapter' (note the use of single quotation marks)
- in
- Surname(s) and initials of editor or editors
- (ed) or (eds)
- *Title of the book*, in italics
- Place (town) of publication
- Publisher

This information should be arranged as in the examples that follow. Please note the punctuation that is used to separate the elements of the references:

Examples

Smail, D. (1989) 'Psychotherapy: deliverance or disablement?', in Fairbairn, G. and Fairbairn, S. (eds) *Ethical Issues in Caring*, Aldershot, Gower.

Stafford, J.M. (1991) 'Love and Lust revisited: intentionality, homosexuality and moral education', in Almond, B. and Hill, D. (eds) *Applied Philosophy: Morals and Metaphysics in Contemporary Debate*, London, Routledge.

Winch, C. (1997) 'Authority in education', in Chadwick, R. (ed) *Encyclopaedia of Applied Ethics*, San Diego, CA, Academic Press.

Journal articles (paper versions)

When you cite an article in an academic or professional journal or periodical, you should begin with the following details:

- Surname(s) and initials of author or authors
- Year of publication, in brackets
- 'Title of the article' (note the use of single quotation marks)
- *Title of the Journal*, in italics

After this you should give details of:

- The volume of the journal
- The 'number' or 'part' of that volume in which the article appears
- The pages on which the article appears, including references

Academic and professional journals are usually published in annual volumes, although some have more than one volume in a year. Each volume is published as a series of separate issues, usually labelled as 'numbers' or 'parts'. Information about this should be given in the following way:

15 (3) 227–256

Here '15' tells us the volume of the journal; (3) the 'part' or 'number' in that volume, and 227–256 the pages on which the article appears.

Examples

In the following examples, note the punctuation that is used to separate the elements of the references:

Chandler, P., Robinson, W.P. and Hoyes, P. (1988) 'The level of linguistic knowledge and awareness amongst students training to be primary teachers', *Language and Education*, 2 (3) 161–174.

Fairbairn, G. (2009) 'Suicide, assisted suicide and euthanasia: when people choose to die, does it matter what we call it?', *Roczniki Psychologiczne* (the *Annals of Psychology*), 12 (1) 97–120.

Garvey, J. (2008) 'The wickedness of the long hot shower', *The Philosopher's Magazine*, 41 (2) 85.

Kennicutt, R.C. Jr., Armus, L., Bendo, G., Calzetti, D., Dale, D.A., Draine, B.T., Engelbracht, C.W., Gordon, K.D., Grauer, A.D., Helou, G., Hollenbach,

D.J., Jarrett, T.H., Kewley, L.J., Leitherer, C., Li, A., Malhotra, S., Regan, M.W., Rieke, G.H., Roussel, H., Smith, J.T., Thornley, M.D. and Walter, F. (2003) 'SINGS: The SIRTF Nearby Galaxies Survey', *Publications of the Astronomical Society of the Pacific*, 115, 928–952.

Winch, C. (1983) 'Education, literacy and the development of rationality', *Journal of Philosophy of Education,* 17 (2) 187–200.

Journal articles (internet versions)

When you cite an article in an internet version of an academic or professional journal or periodical, you should give the following details:

- Surname(s) and initials of author or authors

- Year of publication, in brackets

- 'Title of the article' (note the use of single quotation marks)

- *Title of the Journal*, in italics (internet)

After this you should give details of:

- The volume of the journal

- The 'number' or 'part' of that volume in which the article appears

- Pages on which the article appears (if available)

As is the case with paper versions of academic and professional journals, internet journals are usually published in annual volumes, with each volume published as a series of separate issues, usually labelled as 'numbers' or 'parts'. Information about this and about the pages on which the article appears should be given as a series of numerals, as in this example:

15 (3) 227–256

Finally, you should give details of the web site address/URL at which you accessed the article, and of the date on which you accessed it. For example:

Available at: http://www.ariadne.ac.uk/issue21/web-cache/ (Accessed 2 December 2004).

Examples

In the following examples, note the punctuation that is used to separate the elements of the references.

Boughton, J. M. (2002) 'The Bretton Woods proposal: an in depth look', *Political Science Quarterly* (internet) 42 (6). Available at: Blackwell Science Synergy http://www.pol.upenn/articles (Accessed 12 June 2005).

Hamill, C. (1999) 'Academic essay writing in the first person: a guide for undergraduates', *Nursing Standard* (internet) 13 (44) 38–40. Available at: http://libweb.anglia.ac.uk/ejournals/333 (Accessed 12 June 2005).

Keller, J. C. (2004) 'Parents provide doctors with insight on dying children', *Science and Theology News* (internet). Available at: http://www.stnews.org/ Research–337.htm (Accessed 17 September 2006).

Articles in newspapers and magazines (paper versions)

When you cite an article in a paper version of a newspaper or magazine you should give the following details

- Surname(s) and initials of author or authors

- Year of publication, in brackets

- 'Title of the article' (Note the use of single quotation marks)

- *Title of the newspaper or magazine*, in italics

- Number (if necessary)

- Day(s) and month

- Pages

Examples

Please note the punctuation that is used to separate the elements of these examples. Note also that in the reference to the *Tesco Magazine*, no day is given, because this magazine covers a period, rather than being published on a particular day.

Ayres, C. (2009) 'The Spector spectacle: lust, murder and shocking hair', *The Times (Times 2)*, 2–3, 15 April.

Clayman, M. (2008) 'It's easy being green', *Tesco Magazine*, September–October, 32–35.

Fairbairn, G.J. (1997) 'After-dinner indigestibles', *Times Higher Educational Supplement*, p12, 28 March.

Articles in newspapers and magazines (internet versions)

When you cite an article in an internet version of a newspaper or magazine you should give the following details:

- Surname(s) and initials of author or authors
- Year of publication, in brackets
- 'Title of the article' (note the use of single quotation marks)
- *Title of the newspaper or magazine*, in italics
- (internet)
- Additional date information
- The web site address/URL at which you accessed the article
- The date on which you accessed the article

Examples

Please note the punctuation that is used to separate the elements of these examples.

Chittenden, M., Rogers, L. and Smith, D. (2003) 'Focus: 'Targetitis ails NHS', *Times Online* (internet), 1 June. Available at: http://www.timesonline. co.uk/printFriendly/0,,11–1506–669.html (Accessed 17 March 2005).

Ginzburg, C. and Gundersen, T.R. (2003) 'On the dark side of history: Carlo Ginzburg talks to Trygve Riiser Gundersen', *Eurozine* (internet), 2 May. Available at: http://www.eurozine.com/articles/2003–07–11-ginzburg-en. html (Accessed 20 September 2007).

Websites

When you cite a website you should give as much of the following detail as possible:

- Name of author or authors, or name of source organization
- Year of publication, in brackets
- *Title of web document*
- (internet)
- (Date of last update, if available)

- The web site address/URL
- The date on which you accessed the site

Examples

Please note the punctuation that is used to separate the elements of these examples.

National Electronic Library for Health (2003) *Can walking make you slimmer and healthier?* (internet) (Updated 16 January, 2005). Available at: http://www.nhs.uk.hth.walking (Accessed 10 April 2005).

Council of Europe Directorate General of Human Rights, Equality Division (2006) *Convention on 'Action against trafficking in Human Beings'* (internet). Available at: www.coe.int/trafficking (Accessed on 8 May 2008).

Scottish Intercollegiate Guidelines (2001) *Hypertension in the elderly (SIGN publication 20)* (internet). Available at: http://www.sign.ac.uk/pdf/sign49.pdf (Accessed 17 March 2005).

Boots Group Plc. (2003) *Corporate social responsibility* (internet). Available at: http://www.BootsPlc.Com/Information/Info.Asp?Level1id=447&Level2id=0 (Accessed 23 July 2005).

Conference papers

Occasionally you may come across a paper from an academic or professional conference that you would like to cite, even though it has not yet been published. You may, for example, have had the opportunity to attend a conference or been given access to a copy of a paper that was presented at a conference by one of your teachers. This has the advantage that you may be referring to material that is very fresh and may, in some cases, even be at the 'cutting edge' of research in your area. It has the disadvantage, however, that the material has not yet undergone the quality control provided by 'peer review', by which the relevance, rigour and importance of academic articles are, at least to some extent, tested before they are accepted for publication.

If you do want to refer to a conference paper, you should write the full reference in a style that is very similar to references to journal articles, as shown in the examples that follow, which include references to unpublished conference papers as well as to conference papers that have been published on paper or electronically.

Unpublished conference papers

Alidu, S. (2008) 'The Ghana National Reconciliation Commission: reconciliation or cultural reconstruction?', paper presented at *The Culture of Reconstruction: Interdisciplinary Perspectives on the Aftermath of Crisis*, University of Cambridge (June).

Medina Bustos, A. (2007) 'Healing narratives: Curing through words', paper presented at *The Narrative Practitioner*, North East Wales Institute of Higher Education (June).

Conference papers that appear in published conference proceedings

Fairbairn, G.J. (1995) 'Suicidal acts and their meanings', in Barlow, V. (ed) (1995) *Depression and Self-Harm in Adolescence*, University of Sheffield.

Conference papers that appear in published conference proceedings: electronic

Fairbairn, G. (2004) 'Supporting students as developing writers', Australian Association for Research in Education Conference, Melbourne (2.12.04); http://www.aare.edu.au/04pap/fai04793.pdf. (Accessed 24 May 2009)

Unpublished dissertations and theses, presented for postgraduate degrees

Some of the best research is carried on as part of the work for a doctorate. Sometimes such research is published in the form of a series of articles, a book, or perhaps both. However, most doctoral theses end up gathering dust in a university library basement or are consigned to cyber space via electronic wizardry. However, if you find yourself wanting to cite a PhD thesis, or even a Masters level dissertation, you handle the full reference in a way that is similar to that for a book.

Examples

Fairbairn, G.J. (1980) *Morality, intention and the development of moral persons*, unpublished MEd Dissertation, University of Manchester.

Winch, C.A. (1981) *The Theory of Restricted and Elaborated Codes: a philosophical description and evaluation of the sociolinguistic thesis of Basil Bernstein*, unpublished PhD Thesis, University of Bradford.

Personal communications

The main reason for citation is that it enables you to contextualize your work, that is, to show how it relates to what other people have said; and where they have influenced you, it is about acknowledging that influence. Usually, this will involve giving references to books, articles, websites and so on that have influenced your ideas. However, you should also cite people who have influenced your work more directly and personally, through, for example, conversations, letters or emails. Unlike references to books, articles and so on, references to such communications are not usually about allowing readers to check what is said; rather, they are about maintaining academic values – in this case, courtesy to those who have personally influenced your thinking, honesty and the avoidance of plagiarism.

In some circumstances, as a matter of politeness, you may wish to ask the individual in question for permission to cite them. This might be the case, for example, if the communication in question included content that might cause that person embarrassment.

Examples

Rowley, D. (2008) Discussion of the importance for parents of adults with learning disabilities, of the question 'Who will love him and care for him/her after I've died?', *Personal communication* (9 September).

Webb, D. (2007) Discussion of the ethics of space, *Personal communication* (5 November).

Writing full references to other sources

In the last few pages we have given instructions about how to write full references to some of the main kinds of source that you may consult in writing your essays and other assignments. We do not intend to give a comprehensive guide to writing full references for the whole range of sources that academic authors may cite, including Government Reports, Acts of Parliament, Law Reports, email discussion lists, Company Reports, lecture handouts and other informal documents, because to do so would be to risk confusing you with too much information, as happens too often in guides to citation and referencing on university websites and elsewhere. Instead, we want to list the main points to which you should attend in constructing a full reference to any source, so that, if necessary, you can make a reasonable stab at writing a full reference for any source[6].

---

[6] If you find that you frequently wish to give references to a kind of source in relation to which we have not given detailed instructions, you may wish to consult one of the many guides to Harvard referencing that may be found on websites of universities and colleges all over the world, although please bear in mind the fact that these are often inconsistent.

Constructing a full reference list to a source: general rules

Be accurate and give as much information as you can, including the title of the *document* or *web document* in italics.

If there is one named author, give their name and initial(s).

If there is more than one author, give their names and initials in the order in which they appear in the source, even if there are a large number of authors, as happens frequently in some academic areas, including medicine and some physical sciences.

If there is a date of publication, give it.

Where possible, give the town of publication.

Give the name of the publisher.

For sources that are part of a larger whole, try to pinpoint them within that whole as accurately as possible, for example, by giving page numbers.

If the source has a number of subsections, for example, a government report with chapters, a CD with individual tracks, or a website with individual articles, use italics for *the larger source* (the name of a CD, say) and use single speech marks, 'like this' for the smaller item (an individual track on the CD – say, for the track 'Goodbye Pork Pie Hat' on the John McLaughlin CD *My Goal's Beyond*, to which we referred earlier).

Location and arrangement of full references

In the Harvard system of citation, full references to all sources cited are gathered in a list, which usually appears at the end of the article, chapter, essay or other assignment, book or other document.

Arrangement of references

Arrange references in strict alphabetical order of surnames and, if necessary, of first initial, for example:

Mitchell, C. (1992) 'External peace-making initiatives and intra-national conflict', in Midlarsky, M.L. (ed) *The Internationalization of Communal Strife*, New York, Routledge.

Mitchell, D. (1967) *Planting Patio Tubs for Colour*, Brechin, Hepworth & Co.

If you refer to more than one item an author has published, order them by year of publication, for example:

Fairbairn, G. (2002) 'Brain transplants and the orthodox view of person-hood', in Fisher, R., Primosic, D., Day, P. and Thompson, J. (eds) *Suffering, Death and Identity*, Amsterdam and New York, Rodopi Press.

Fairbairn, G. (2004) 'Developing academic storytelling'. Australian Association for Research in Education Conference, Melbourne (30.11.04); http://www.aare.edu.au/04pap/fai04793.pdf (Accessed 2 March 2009)

If you refer to two or more items an author published in the same year, distinguish them using letters, for example, Ledermann (1985a) and Ledermann (1985b) and list in alphabetical order of the letters:

Ledermann, E.K. (1985a) *Mental Health and Human Conscience: The True and the False Self*, Aylesbury, Gower.

Ledermann, E. K. (1985b) 'Mechanism and holism in physical medicine', *Explorations in Medicine*, I (1).

Task 26: Practise writing full references

Practise writing full references to sources of different kinds, first by copying out some examples from those we offer for each kind of source, on pages 134–144, and then by writing some full references to similar sources. Make sure as you do so that you include all the information we list, and copy the punctuation that we specify.
Pay particular attention to the following:

- Authored books
- Edited books
- Chapters in edited books
- Articles in paper versions of journals
- Articles in electronic versions of journals
- Websites

If you want to check that you really understand, try to explain to a friend how to write a full reference for each of the kinds of source for which we give detailed instructions.

A note on the punctuation and layout of full references

In the instructions we have given about writing full references we have used a very simple approach to punctuation, which we have also used throughout this book. As we said on page 135, unless you are already competent in writing full references, we suggest that you try to commit this simple approach to memory. If you do, it will help you to develop the consistency that is necessary for citation. However, it is important to note that we are not claiming that our style is the only correct way of punctuating references, only that it is simple and consistent and therefore easy to absorb. In our experience, this is helpful in getting the hang of referencing.

Cluttering your text: a danger to look out for in using Harvard style referencing

For all its convenience and ease of use the Harvard system can disrupt the flow of the text and you should therefore only use citation to show that you have evidence for what you are saying; to acknowledge that ideas you are using have come from other people, or where discussing other people's work can help you to build a case.

Do not throw in textual references just to show off how much you have read or are aware of.

Try to avoid this kind of thing, which is prevalent in some areas of academic writing:

The introduction of new management systems (Radcliffe and Riley, 1997; MacMinn and Collingbourne, 1999; Scrimshaw, 1998; Thomson et al., 2000) was thought by some people (de Pear, 2001; Langley and Smith, 2002; Maclean and Burrows, 2000; Wilton, 2003, 2005) to have caused more problems than it solved, because it moved the focus away from service delivery (Dowson, 2001; Smith and McDonald, 2000).

The overuse of citation, as illustrated by this example, can be irritating and confusing, especially when the reason for the multiple citations is unclear. Note how much easier it is to understand when the references are removed:

The introduction of new management systems was thought by some people to have caused more problems than it solved, because it moved the focus away from service delivery.

This example, we have to confess, is a bogus one that we made up to illustrate our view that citation can get in the way of communication at times. However, in the real world of academic writing things are just as bad, or perhaps even worse, as illustrated by this passage in a very interesting article by Etherington (2002):

> Narrative research (or inquiry as I prefer to call it) is a means by which we collect, analyse, and re-present people's stories as told by them. It is based on the worldview that people live storied lives and that we live in a storied world (Gergen and Gergen, 1986; Howard, 1991; Mair, 1989; Sarbin, 1986); that narrative represents, constitutes and shapes social reality (Bruner, 1987, 1990, 1991; Frank, 1995; Ochberg, 1994; Spence, 1982); that competing narratives represent different realities, not simply different perspectives on the same reality (Baldwin, 2001; Freeman, 1993; Gergen, 1994) and that telling and re-telling one's story helps a person create a sense of self (Burr, 1995; Cushman, 1995; Frank, 1995) and meaning (Bruner, 1990).

To be fair to Etherington, who is a narrative researcher of distinction, the remarkable second sentence in this passage is not typical of the article from which it is taken, which is well written, as indeed is this sentence if it is rewritten without the citations. Nonetheless, it is a very good illustration of the way in which over-citation can render otherwise well written, engaging and easily readable text much less 'user friendly' than it could be.

Other examples of the way in which citation can get in the way of the straightforward communication of ideas may be found in most academic disciplines. For example, we see it in a passage about the function of citation in academic writing by Harwood (2009) and in a passage from a paper about dwarf galaxies by Zucker et al. (2004):

> Although it is true that more recently informants have been consulted about their citing behaviour (e.g. Bonzi and Snyder, 1991; Brooks, 1985, 1986; Cano, 1989; Case and Higgins, 2000; Liu, 1993; Shadish et al., 1995; Snyder and Bonzi, 1998; Vinkler, 1987), as White and Wang (1997) point out, this body of research also suffers from obvious methodological weaknesses.

> There are many fewer dwarf galaxies than predicted by a direct scaling of the dark matter halo mass function … A number of theoretical explanations for this have been explored: feedback from supernovae leading to disruption of dwarf galaxies (e.g. Dekel & Silk 1986) or strong reduction of their luminous/dark matter ratio (e.g. Hayashi et al. 2003), reduced substructure in warm dark matter halos (e.g. Moore et al. 2000), enhanced satellite disruption and reionization (e.g. Bullock et al. 2001), or suppression of dwarf galaxy formation through photoionization (e.g. Somerville 2002).

The numerical system of citation and referencing

The numerical system differs from author–date referencing, of which Harvard is an example, in three main ways:

- In the way that material is cited in the text, where numbers rather than the author's name are used to identify the source.

- In the presentation of full references in numerical order, rather than in alphabetical order of authors, when they appear in a reference list at the end of the text. (Note, however, that sometimes in the numerical system, full references appear at the bottom of the page in which the citation in the text appears.)

- In the placing of the date of publication in the full reference, which in numerical citation usually comes at the end.

The numerical system of referencing: an overview

i   Sources are identified in the text, by inserting numbers, beginning with 1; these numbers correspond with the numbered references at the end of the text. These numbers are inserted in one of several ways:

> Is Malebranche really a 'disciple'[1] of Descartes?

> In a recent study, Jones (3) has shown that cats can talk.

> Linguistic imperialism is part of cultural imperialism [4].

> Thomas[2] offers very weak support for his outrageous views.

Of these, superscript numerals ('disciple'[1]) are the most common:

ii Full references are given either in a number list at the end of the text, or as numbered footnotes at the bottom of the page on which the citation is made.

iii As with the Harvard system, if the actual words used by another person are quoted, the page number on which they are to be found is provided in brackets, at the end of the quotation:

> Discussing a particularly poorly written passage, Orwell[5] writes, '… words and meaning have almost parted company. People who write in this manner usually have a general emotional meaning – they dislike one thing and want to express solidarity with another but they are not interested in the detail of what they are saying' (p164).

iv One potentially confusing feature of the numerical system is the fact that it often makes liberal use of the Latin abbreviations 'ibid' and 'op cit' to indicate that a reference is to a work already cited:

ibid is used to indicate that the current citation is to the same source as the previous one. (It is the abbreviation for the Latin *ibidem*, meaning 'in the same place'.)

op cit is used to indicate that the current reference is to a work already referred to. (It is the abbreviation for the Latin phrase *opere citato*, meaning 'in the cited work' or 'in the work [already] cited'.) When it is used, enough information should be included to allow the original reference to be identified.

Whereas 'ibid' refers the reader, quite helpfully, to the previous reference, 'op cit' might be referring to a reference much earlier in a list, sending the reader scurrying through the text to look for it. For example,

1. Rebus, J. *Fighting with Demons*, Edinburgh, Old Town Press (2001).

2. Rebus, J. ibid.

3. Tortellini, F. *Pasta and the Italian Baroque*, 2nd ed., Glyn Ceiriog, Dolan and Harris Ltd (1985).

4. Frances, D. 'Violence and intimidation in street-level drugs trading', in Vanhoutte, K. K. P. and Lang, M. (eds) *Bullying and the Abuse of Power: From Playground to international relations*, Oxford, Inter-Disciplinary Press (2010).

5. ibid.

6. Tortellini, F. op cit.

7. Loon, B. *Understanding Analog Electronics,* London, Poppleton Press (1998).

8. Bates, J. *Engineering Mathematics*, 3rd ed., Fourmerkland, Cairnview Press (2000).

9. Loon, B. op cit.

10. Jones, E. *Bullying in the Modern World*, New York, Arnold & Co. (1936).

11. ibid.

12. Rebus, J. op cit.

In reference 2, 'ibid' tells us that the author is citing the same text as he did in the one immediately before, in this case to Rebus (2001) and similarly, reference 5 and reference 11 use 'ibid' to point us back to the citations to

Frances (2010) and Jones (1936) respectively. Reference 6 uses 'op cit' to tell us that Tortellini was cited earlier and that the present citation is to the same source, and in references 9 and 12, 'op cit' directs us back to earlier citations to Loon and Rebus, respectively.

Location and arrangement of full references in the numerical system

In the numerical system of citation, full references and footnotes/endnotes are given in numerical order either at the foot of the page on which the citation appears, or at the end of the text. The format will vary, but the information provided will be very similar to the information we stipulate for each type of source in our guide to the Harvard system. One difference that we have already mentioned is that the date in numerical references usually goes at the end of the reference.

The numeric system is often combined with the use of notes in which the author makes explanatory asides that are not strictly essential to the main drift of her case, perhaps supplying additional information or anticipating an objection to something she has said.[7] Notes are indicated in the text in the same way as cited work – by the insertion of superscript or subscript numerals at an appropriate point, with the footnote appearing either at the foot of the relevant page or sometimes in a numbered list at the end of the text, when strictly speaking, rather than a footnote it is an 'endnote'.

How much reference should you make in your essays to what you have read

Some students develop the misguided notion that whether an author is an undergraduate student or a research professor, it is possible to assess how much he knows by looking at the number of sources he cites. But although some people – both students and professional academics – who cite a lot also know a lot, the density of citation in an academic text proves little in itself, because citing a source does not show that you understand it, or even that you have read it, because it is possible to insert a citation to a source that you have not read; some people undoubtedly do so.

---

[7] Although footnotes are unusual in a book of this kind, there are a number scattered throughout. This is one of them.

In general, you should only refer to another person's work if it has actually influenced your own, or if by doing so you can make points that help you to build up a case.

Referring to other people's work is a vacuous exercise if you do it for no other reason than to impress others with how much you have read.

Whenever you cite a source, make sure that it is clear, that you understand what the author says, and that what she says really is relevant to your discussion.

Try to avoid the temptation, to which many students succumb, to use ideas that you do not fully understand in your essay or assignment, because some writer whose name you wish to mention uses them. This is dangerous, as is any citation that is more about the attempt to impress people, and especially your lecturers, than it is about using an author's ideas, because it offers you the perfect opportunity to demonstrate what you don't know and understand, rather than what you do know and understand.

The only way to show that you have read a source to which you refer is to make sure that when you cite it, you do so in a way that demonstrates that you know and understand what the author has said, or done, or believes.

Being clear about your reasons for citation

On pages 119–121 we discussed some of the reasons for citation. As you progress through your academic career, you will come across many citations where the reason for the citation is unclear. Consider, for example, the following sentence from Mary's essay about climate change:

Unless we make substantial changes to the ways in which we live, global temperatures will increase at such a rate that within the lifetime of people alive today, vast tracts of the currently inhabited world will either become desert, or be overwhelmed by rising sea levels (Scott, 2007; Haste, 2008; Melling, 2007).

This is unhelpful as a way of communicating anything at all about the cited sources, since it conveys no information about them, other than that they have some connection to the ongoing debate about human-induced climate change. We are left, as readers, guessing at what the authors cited believe, argue or have done. From what is said we have no idea what kind of people they are, or how reliable their views are. Since Mary fails to say anything about what these authors have written, or said, or done, we cannot, for example, guess at whether they are scientists who have carried out research on climate change; ethicists who have offered arguments about the need for humankind to change our ways, if we are to have a long-term future on earth, or journalists who are interested in selling newspapers. Nor can we tell whether they agree with one another, or represent a range of opinions.

Interestingly, since the author does not give a clear indication about the views held by, or the work undertaken by Scott, Haste or Melling, it is also not at all clear that Mary has actually read them. This is common in much academic writing; many citations give no evidence at all for whether their authors have actually read the sources in question.

Consider, for example, the following:

Many philosophers believe that everyone has the right to decide whether she lives or whether she dies and that therefore we have the right to suicide (Fairbairn, 1995).

This citation should do nothing at all to persuade us that its author has any knowledge or understanding about what Fairbairn has written, or about what he believes and why he believes it. Vague and unhelpful, it could lead someone who reads it to develop the idea that Fairbairn is one of the philosophers referred to, who believes that everyone has the right to kill herself. The problem is that the person citing Fairbairn does not tell us why she is referring to him. As readers we are left to guess at his views. For all we know, rather than believing that everyone has the right to kill herself, Fairbairn might have written a review of philosophical discussions of the question of whether everyone has the right to suicide, and concluded that they don't. Or his position might even be more complicated than that. The point is that from this reference, we can't tell.

Sometimes students include full citations to sources that they have not mentioned in their texts, almost if they are trying to persuade their readers (and especially those who will be marking their work) that they have read more than they really have, in an effort to persuade them to award a higher mark than they might otherwise.

Don't include 'empty' references in your reference list, that is, full references to sources that you haven't cited within the body of your essay. Doing so is unlikely to help you to achieve extra marks, and it is easy to understand why if you think about it. After all why, for example, should the fact that you

> include a reference to Truss's book *Eats, Shoots & Leaves* (2003) or to Parody's *Eats, Shites & Leaves: Crap English and How to Use It* (2004) persuade one of your lecturers that you have actually read them, if you don't mention them in your essay?

Don't allow the desire to convince your lecturers that you have read a lot to dominate your academic writing. It is much better to show that you have thought a lot about a few sources, than to run riot with references, decorating your assignments with them, for no reason other than that you think this will convince those who will mark your work about what a busy bee you have been.

> Don't use citation just to show off how much you have read, or claim to have read.
>
> Don't use citation merely in an attempt to make your work look more scholarly or important. Better to make it scholarly by trying, whenever possible, to really engage with the ideas in sources that you cite, showing that you under-stand them and have something to say about them.

Some students, fearful of the dreadful consequences of being found guilty of plagiarism, include full references to any source that may have influenced them in some way, in their reference list or bibliography. Such students act as they do because they entertain the misguided belief that by doing so, they can somehow protect themselves against the possibility of being accused of intellectual theft, if in their rush to get an assignment completed they have inadvertently included ideas from a source or sources, without acknowledgement.

> Including full references at the end of an essay does not avoid plagiarism, because it does not in itself acknowledge the influence a source has had on what you have written. The only way to do that is by maintaining careful notes about the ideas you gather from, for example, your reading, and then ensuring that if you use ideas that belong to someone else, you acknowledge in your text that you have done so.

On pages 160–164 we discuss plagiarism in more detail, telling you what it is, why it is important and offering more detailed advice about how to avoid it.

Quotation as a form of citation: the basics

The style of citation that most people first come across involves the use of direct quotation, and it is probably at least partly as a result of this that quotation is often overused by undergraduate students, and even by some students at Masters level. Some students even develop the misguided idea that whenever they refer to an author's work, they must directly quote something that she says. This, of course, is nonsense.

> Quotation is handled in every respect, just like citation in which the author's words are not quoted directly, with one additional requirement, which is that in addition to citing the author and the year in which the work was published in your text, with a full reference at the end, you should give the page number(s) on which the words quoted appear, in brackets at the end of the quote.

Directly quoting an author's words can be useful, because, for example, it can help to persuade readers that you are familiar with what she has said. However, it is more likely to do this if, in addition, the quotations you use illustrate your point of view or, better still, if they help you to argue for a point of view. For example, Becky, a student writing an essay in which she was critical of the way in which reconciliation initiatives after human rights abuse are often assumed unthinkingly to be 'a good thing', paved the way for her argument by quoting Dwyer (2002), who writes:

> The notable lack of any clear account of what reconciliation is, and what it requires, justifiably alerts the cynics among us. Reconciliation is being urged upon people who have been bitter and murderous enemies, upon victims and perpetrators of human rights abuses, upon groups and individuals whose very self-conceptions have been structured in terms of historical and often state-sanctioned relations of dominance and submission. (p. 92)

This helped Becky to establish the idea that although reconciliation initiatives are important social and political phenomena, the lack of consensus about the meaning of the concept at their core inevitably calls their validity into question.

To quote or not to quote?

As a general rule, you should not quote another person's words directly unless you have good reason for doing so, for example:

- Because she has managed to say what you want to say more clearly, more elegantly and more economically than you could say it.

- Because it is important, for the purposes of your argument, that you give the exact words she has used. This might be the case, for example, if you wish to criticize what she has written.

- Because the words you are citing are from a literary source such as a novel, poem, play or film script. This is a distinctive use of quotation, and it is clearly different from occasions when you are citing a person in developing an argument.

If you quote directly from another person, you should ensure that you are accurate in your quotation, by taking it directly from the cited source. Whenever you quote, you should be as brief as possible (in most instances quoting more than 50 words is likely to be longer than necessary). In addition, you must make clear why you are doing so.

How much quotation is acceptable in an essay?

Sometimes students ask how much quotation is acceptable in an essay. The answer is that how much quotation is acceptable will depend on the nature of the course, and of the particular essay. As a general guide, in most disciplines, you should probably aim to keep the amount of quoted material in an essay below 5 per cent of the total word limit, and begin to worry if the amount you quote creeps above about 10 per cent. However, in subjects such as English Literature, which involve the detailed study of texts, more quotation is likely to be allowed, and even expected, than in many others.

How should I introduce quotations?

Quotations should always be introduced. The reason for their presence in your essay should be obvious and you should announce their arrival; otherwise, your reader is left to wonder how they relate to what has gone on before and/or to what follows. When they suddenly appear in the middle of a piece of text like decorations on a Christmas tree, without any explanation as to why they are there, quotations are not useful. You should never emulate this kind of thing, for example:

Some authors of textbooks and other guides about study skills believe strongly that quotations should never appear in an essay without being introduced. 'When they suddenly appear in the middle of a piece of text like decorations on a Christmas tree without any explanation as to why they are there, they are not useful' (Fairbairn and Winch, 2011, p. x). In other words, quotations should never be inserted, unannounced, into text.

There is no general rule about how to introduce quotations. However, short quotations are usually indicated by the use of speech marks ('Like this'), while larger ones are often set off from the text as indented paragraphs. Consider, first, the following examples, where quotation is incorporated into the main text.

i. In a conference paper about narrative in medical practice, Kalitzkus, Büssing and Matthiessen (2007) wrote:

> They are trained in anamnestic history taking having the goal of eliciting the relevant medical facts from the patients without too much story, too much 'useless' information around. 'One of the most difficult tasks in health care,' family physician John Launer (2006) states, 'may be to manage each consultation so that it continually meets both *narrative* and *normative* requirements' (p. 338).

ii. In an essay about the problems of living ethically, Bernard, a student pursuing a course in development education, wrote:

> Probably the biggest problem faced by most people who want to shop responsibly, but who realistically have to do most of their shopping in supermarkets, is in deciding which supermarket chain they should use. According to *The Rough Guide to Ethical Living* (2006) '… it's not easy to rank the supermarkets in terms of their overall ethical standards' (p. 220).

iii. In an essay about the evil that people do to one another, Erica, a student of peace studies, wrote:

> When we think of genocide we usually think of the killing off of a whole racial group by killing them, in the way the Nazis tried to eliminate the Jews. However, it is possible to conceive of genocide by means that fall short of killing. Gaita (1998) imagines '… a people forcibly sterilized in order that they be eliminated as a people' and asks, 'Would that count as genocide?' (p. xxviii).

By contrast, compare the two examples below, which illustrate the way in which longer quotations are typically set off from the main body of text in a separate paragraph, or block indent, without the use of speech marks. The first comes from the same paper by Kalitzkus et al, as our first example of quotation using speech marks above. The second comes from a paper by Fairbairn, Webb, Alidu and Medina Bustos (2008):

iv. Narratives, especially patient narratives, incorporate the question of causality and thus foster the understanding of the patient's illness perception. In the words of Greenhalgh and Hurwitz (1998):

> Narrative provides meaning, context, perspective for the patient's predicament. It defines how, why, and what way he or she is ill. It offers, in short, a possibility of understanding which cannot be arrived at by any other means (p. 6).

v. Ignatieff (1996) distinguishes between truths told for the purpose of reconciliation, and truth told for its own sake. He notes that:

> One should distinguish between factual truth and moral truth, between narratives that tell what happened and narratives that attempt to explain why things happened and who is responsible (p. 113).

There is no clear rule about how long a quoted passage has to be to be dealt with in this way, although we would suggest that if you are quoting more than two or three lines you should consider indenting it. Exceptions to this would be occasions where it serves your meaning best to incorporate a longer passage in another person's words, in a sentence of your own.

What if I want to use a quote from an author I haven't read?

Students quite often ask this question. It is quite likely that from time to time you will find that the authors of books and articles you read include in their text, quotations from other authors that would be helpful to you in some piece of writing. As with simple citation that does not involve quoting an author's words directly, it is important to realize that unless you have read the original, you are not in a position to cite it, and in this case to quote it directly. This is especially important with quotation, because you should never attribute words to someone unless you are sure that what you say is accurate. And so, if at all possible (sometimes it isn't) you should locate the original source before using the quotation. If you manage to do so, it will allow you to confirm that the quotation you have found has been used in a careful way; it is, after all, possible to 'bend' the apparent meaning of what someone says, by adding or subtracting words, or by quoting it out of context.

However, even if you are unable to get access to the original, because, say, it is unavailable in your university library, you can still make use of quotations that have been used by third parties, provided that you point out that you have taken it from the source you have read and give a reference to that source, rather than citing and then giving a full reference to the original source from which it came.

If you use a quotation you find quoted by someone else – in a book or article, say – don't cite its author directly, but acknowledge the author in whose work you found it, by citing her in the normal way.

Consider, for example, this passage from Beverley's essay about the relationship between spirituality and religion:

> Discussing the nature of religious experience Holloway (2001) cites Hick's assertion that, '... the forms taken by religious experience are provided by the conceptual equipment of the experiencer'. (p27)

Beverley had read the book *Doubts and Loves* by Richard Holloway (2001), the former Bishop of Edinburgh, but had been unable to access the book by John Hick to which Holloway referred. Note that the page of Holloway's book on which the quote from Hick appears is given, but not the page in Hick's book from which it is taken.

Some final advice about citation and referencing

i   Don't throw in citations just to show off how much you have read. (Or worse, to show off how much you claim to have read.) And don't use citation to make your work look more scholarly and important. Only cite:

- When it is necessary to show that you have evidence for what you are saying.

- If you want to acknowledge that ideas you are using have come from other people.

- When discussing the ideas or arguments in a source can help you to develop your own position.

ii   Since whenever you use other people's ideas you should make it clear that you are doing so, it may at times become necessary to cite the same author and the same source more than once in the course of an essay. However, you need not give the reference repeatedly where you continue to talk about the same author, provided that it remains obvious who you are talking about.

iii Where you refer to more than one source published in the same year by the same author(s), you should distinguish them using lower-case letters. For example:

> Fairbairn and Mead (1993a and 1993b) discuss the use of imaginative storytelling in facilitating nurses' thinking about the ethical decisions they face every day.

iv   In general, you should not give the name of sources, such as books and articles in your text; doing so uses up valuable words and may make your text cluttered and more difficult to follow. One exception to this might be where you are citing a classic work, such as Charles Darwin's *The Origin of*

Species; Wittgenstein's *Philosophical Investigations*, or Marshall Mcluhan's *The Medium is the Massage*. Or you might do so, for example, in a literature essay, in referring to a work of art such as a novel, play or poem, rather than to an academic text.

v   In general, you should use only family names in citation – unless, for example, you are referring, in your essay, to two people with the same family name, when you might use their first names to distinguish them. However, you may come across situations in which personal names are in use. One such situation is when the author being referred to is very famous. For example, Carl Rogers, Germaine Greer, Barack Obama or Bertrand Russell. Another is in the case of literary sources, where an author might, for example, refer to William Shakespeare, Jane Austen or Sylvia Plath.

vi   In general, when you are citing sources within your text, you do not have to give page references, unless you are quoting directly from another person (see the discussion of direct quotation on pages 155–159). However, you may choose to do so if, for example, you are referring to different parts of a large document, or the text to which you are referring is long and/or complex, so that the idea to which you are referring may be difficult to locate.

vii Try to develop the discipline necessary to maintain an up-to-date record of sources you have read and to which you may wish to refer, whether now or at some time in the future; such a record should include full bibliographical details, as well as brief notes about each source. In addition, at times you may decide to copy or scan some pages. Maintaining records of sources in this systematic way will allow you not only to return to them to re-read and check information you have gathered, but to cite them accurately; it will also, incidentally, help you to guard against the dangers of unwitting plagiarism, because it will help you to remain conscious of what you have read and to keep tabs on where ideas you are developing might have their origins.

Plagiarism

Throughout your course you will be told repeatedly that you must avoid plagiarism, which some students mistakenly believe involves copying another person's words. As a result, they spend a great deal of time trying to paraphrase[8], or render into their own words, things that they have read in, for example,

---

[8] To paraphrase a piece of text is to put it into your own words. You will find skill in paraphrasing useful when you want to give an account of an author's ideas or views, before going on to critique them or to compare them with others.

books and articles. Now paraphrase, like précis[9], is something you should practise, because it involves reading with great attention to detail and to meaning,
and making the attempt to render an idea into your own words is one way of
coming to grips with what it means. However, developing, as some students do,
the habit of paraphrasing authors without acknowledging that you are doing
so, is no way to protect yourself against charges of plagiarism, because plagiarism has more to do with a person's ideas than it does with the words in which
she expresses them. And so, unless you explicitly acknowledge that an idea you
use came from the person whose idea it is, paraphrasing it in an essay, is plagiarism just as much as if you had stolen her words, because it involves using as if
you own them, ideas that belong to her.

> Plagiarism involves using another person's ideas as if they are your own,
> whether you do it in writing or in speech.

It is important to be clear that whenever you use another person's ideas,
without drawing attention to the fact that they are her ideas, you will be
guilty of plagiarizing, whether you set out to use them as if they were yours or
not. In other words, plagiarism is plagiarism, whether or not you are aware
that you are engaging in it.

Some universities and some tutors may distinguish between witting (deliberate) and unwitting (non-deliberate) plagiarism, and regard the former as
more serious than the latter. It is easy to see why. Deliberate plagiarism involves
the attempt to deceive others into believing that something that belongs to
someone else – an idea or an argument, say – belongs to you, with the idea in
mind, that if you succeed you will gain more credit than you would have
gained otherwise. Non-deliberate plagiarism, on the other hand, usually results
from poorly developed study skills and disciplines, leading to carelessness in
maintaining notes about what you have read. So, for example, if when you are
reading you are either in the habit of copying out extracts that seem especially
important, or of paraphrasing ideas that interest you, and fail to label them
clearly to remind you about whose words and ideas they are and where they
came from, you might unwittingly copy an author's ideas into an essay.

It would be unwise to expect that unwitting plagiarism will be dealt with
more leniently than deliberate plagiarism, and even if your university distinguishes between the two, because it recognizes that while one represents
the attempt to cheat, the other results from sloppy study habits, it could be
difficult to prove that your plagiarism was of the latter kind.

---

[9] A précis is a summary of a text, which nonetheless contains all of its main points.
Whereas in paraphrase the attempt is made to render text into your own words, précis
usually involves using the author's words, except where another formulation would
allow significant shortening.

As we point out in the context of our discussion of citation and referencing earlier in this book, many students develop the habit of including in a list of full references at the end of essays, references to any source from which they think they may unwittingly have used ideas, in the vain hope that this will protect them from charges of plagiarism. It won't, and the reason is plain: including the bibliographical details of a source in a reference list is not the same as pointing out that ideas that you have used in your essay come from that source, or that your position on a topic or even a particular argument, has been influenced by that source.

> If you use ideas in your essay that have come from, say, an article you have read, and have not acknowledged this, you will be guilty of plagiarism.

Always refer to authors you have read or people with whom you have spoken that you recognize to have had an influence on your work, drawing attention, when you do so, to the ways in which they have influenced what you are writing. Of course, it will be difficult to be aware of everything that has influenced you. However, you should, at the least, avoid using other people's words and thoughts as if they are your own.

At times you will find (as most of us do) that a bright idea you have hit upon has already been advanced by someone else, perhaps even by an important thinker many years earlier and perhaps, in the case of disciplines like philosophy and theology, many hundreds of years earlier. If this happens, you should draw attention to the fact that an idea you have had, has already been explored by others and perhaps to ways in which what you are thinking is different to their ideas.

Why it is important to avoid plagiarism

As we have already said, you will be told repeatedly during your course that you should avoid plagiarism like the plague. The reasons that your institution and your teachers will tell you this so often and so loudly will be varied, but chief among these is the purely pragmatic reason that if you plagiarize you will be open to penalties of the most severe kind, including expulsion from your course and from your institution. Of course, for this to happen, you will have to be found out.

In the past, spotting plagiarism relied on the detective skills of tutors, which depended both on their knowledge of the literature in their field of study, and on their knowledge of their students – of their level of understanding of complex topics, and of their language and style of writing. It does not take Sherlock Holmes to spot the difference between a passage written by someone who can barely write a grammatical sentence, and a passage that uses so many long words and so much jargon, that even the most 'head in the clouds' intellectual would run for cover. And so a student who, rather than working at understanding a passage just copied it into his essay, because he believed it would impress his teacher, could quite easily be caught out, as could one who understood something an author had written, but thought he might be able to claim an idea or an argument as his own if he recast it in his own words. And even a student who was more subtle in his use of pirated text, blending shorter sections with his own words, or who borrowed material from friends, or from students from earlier years who had written on the same topic, could easily be caught out by a tutor who was properly awake when she read his essay. However, the human elements in the detection system meant that deliberate plagiarism was a good deal easier than it is nowadays, because whatever students think, most university teachers are overburdened with work, and getting through their marking as quickly as possible will often be more important than painstakingly checking to see whether students have cheated by stealing ideas and even words from others.

Nowadays, the chances that if you plagiarize you will be caught out (and perhaps kicked out) are much higher, because it is extremely likely that an electronic version of your work will be subjected to checking using computer software that will map it against text stored in a gigantic database.

There are, of course, other reasons for avoiding plagiarism, whether deliberate or non-deliberate.

Deliberate plagiarism is theft and theft is generally frowned upon.

Unwitting plagiarism results from poor work habits, and will be frowned upon for that reason.

Success that arises partly as the result of plagiarism is less sweet than success that comes as the result of hard work.

Avoiding plagiarism

As we have said, plagiarism is of two kinds – witting (deliberate) and unwitting (non-deliberate). Like the theft of more tangible things, like money, cars and mobile phones, deliberate plagiarism is easy to avoid, because committing it involves the intention to cheat by deceiving others into believing that ideas and/or words belong to you when really they belong to someone else. Avoiding non-deliberate plagiarism is harder, because it is difficult to avoid absorbing ideas from others with whom we speak, and it is just as difficult to avoid absorbing ideas from the things we read, whether they are newspapers, magazines, books or journal articles. That is why non-deliberate plagiarism is so difficult to avoid.

It is easy to see why, in some instances, people are unaware of where the ideas in their mind have come from, and find it difficult to pinpoint all of the sources that have influenced them to develop a particular idea. But plagiarism is frowned upon and however difficult, it is your responsibility to avoid it. To do so, you should make sure that you maintain a record of all the reading you undertake for your course, and that in any notes you take about your reading, you make it very clear which ideas and which words have come from authors you have read, and which words represent your comments on, or notes about what they have written.

When you finish the first draft ask yourself the following:

Have I addressed the question asked or task set?

Does my essay make sense at the level of the sentence and the paragraph? (Have I checked each sentence?)

Does each sentence relate clearly to both the one that preceded it and to the one that follows it?

Is each paragraph really a paragraph? Have I inserted any paragraph breaks in the middle of lines of thought? Does each paragraph relate clearly, both to the one that preceded it and to the one that follows it?

Have I made any grammatical errors? (Checking that each sentence actually makes sense and says what you think it does will help you to pinpoint any such errors.)

Have I avoided ambiguity, longwindedness, pomposity, gobbledygook, cliché, mixed metaphors? (Problems with these 'stylistic traps' are addressed in 2.5.

Have I acknowledged all sources that have influenced or contributed to what I have written?

For each item in my reference list, is there a citation within the text and for each citation in the text is there a full reference?

THEN ASK YOURSELF THE SAME QUESTIONS IN RELATION TO EACH SUCCEEDING DRAFT

2.5

Getting your writing right: thinking about style

The word 'style' has many uses. For example, we may say of a person that she has a 'sense of style' because she dresses well, and wine critics often use the word 'style' as a kind of shorthand in describing some characteristics of a wine. We talk of 'life styles', 'hair styles' and 'musical styles'.

In 2.5 we want to talk about some practical aspects of writing, which we are gathering together under the heading of 'style', because they are all concerned with the ways that you will attempt to communicate something of importance in the essays you write as a student. In referring to 'style' in writing, then, we are talking about the character of your writing, and the way in which it can help or hinder the communication of your ideas.

> Get into the habit of asking yourself 'Why am I writing this?' and 'Who am I writing it for?' whenever you are writing. Doing so will help to determine the style in which you write.

Writing successfully involves having not only a clearly thought-out purpose, but also a clear and accurate picture of the audience for whom you are writing. The way in which you structure your writing, including the way in which you punctuate it, the order in which you present your ideas and the relationships you make between them, is just as important a part of your style of writing as are the words and phrases you use.

Developing a clear and effective style of writing

Write as simply as you can. Try to avoid jargon, pompous sounding words and longwindedness.

> Be direct. Get to the point quickly and clearly. Don't waste valuable space making excuses for what you have missed out or been unable to do.

Although it can be helpful to introduce your subject matter by giving an overview of what you intend to cover, it is often best just to get straight to the point of your essay. Don't beat about the bush, as students often do, with introductory sentences of this kind:

> To begin to answer this question, it is first necessary to consider in detail exactly what is meant by ...

> Before attempting to answer this question, we must first define...

Essays that begin with a discussion of the meanings of the words in which the question is written often give the impression that the student is avoiding answering the question. For example, writing an essay about the question 'Should children with disabilities be taught in mainstream classes alongside their non-disabled peers?' Marie began:

> Whether disabled children should be taught in the mainstream depends on a number of things, including what disabilities we are talking about, how severe they are, and also whether being 'taught' in a mainstream class means having their lessons with the mainstream children, or in a separate group, or even individually. Before going on to address the question I am therefore going to offer definitions of a number of terms, including 'disability' and 'mainstream class', and also consider what might be meant by asking whether disabled children should be taught in the mainstream.

Marie's essay then went on to spend more than half of the words allocated discussing the meaning of the question.

If a consideration of the meanings of words is important in answering a question, it is best to make use of such discussion in structuring the essay, rather than, as Marie did, to use it as an overture before the main event – as a way of putting off the awful moment when you get round to trying to say what you think about the question.

Commitment in writing

One of the themes of this book is the need to be able to communicate effectively with a readership. A second theme, no less important, is the need, in academic writing, to develop your own committed points of view in your essays, and to offer evidence and arguments in their favour. In 2.1, discussing some of the forms that essays can take, we argued that even if you are writing about a topic that seems to require nothing more than description of an event, a state of affairs or the views of another person, you will be doing more than pure description, because you will need to select what material to present out of a range of alternatives.

Whenever you write as a student you should commit yourself to a particular point of view, and seek to persuade your readership of that point of view. This may seem obvious to you, but it will by no means be obvious to everyone who reads this book, including some tutors as well as many students. Indeed, in our experience some teachers actually discourage commitment on the part of students, requiring instead that they should present a balanced and neutral (even bland) account of various positions. We find this rather shocking, because it is founded in the misguided belief that a genuine scholar will hold himself aloof from a debate, seeking only to describe the various positions on offer and the arguments for and against them.

> A writer who tries to persuade his readers about what he believes in, is more interesting than one who is merely competent at describing other people's arguments and points of view.

But there is even more to the matter than interesting your readers, important though that is. Commitment injects tension into writing. It forces you as an author to engage more fully with the positions you are adopting, opposing or describing. By stating these positions fairly, you can then put them to work in developing and defending your own position, for example, by contrasting its strength with the weakness of one you are opposing. This tends to impose a structure on your writing that engages the reader and carries him along.

> Try to create tension in your writing by committing yourself to a particular stance. By doing this you will become more involved with your own work.

Showing that you understand other people's positions, and then either defending them or carefully dismantling them by exposing their errors, will help you to develop a vigorous style, through which you can express your commitments.

> If you demonstrate commitment to a point of view that you have reason to support, you are likely to get better marks, even if the tutor who marks your work disagrees with you.

With practice, you will develop a characteristic 'voice' of your own, in which you set out and defend your views.

Sometimes students say that they cannot come up with a definite answer to a difficult question, or a committed view in relation to a complex topic, because they find it hard to choose between competing options. Paradoxical though it may sound, it is perfectly acceptable to argue that you find it impossible to give a definite answer, provided that your problems are well founded and arise, for example, because there is some ambiguity in the question. Of course, arguing like this would involve demonstrating commitment – to the idea that there is no definite answer.

> If a question you are addressing seems to contain some ambiguity, make use of this fact in constructing your answer.

Consider, for example, a student whose essay on the topic 'Is a child who always obeys her teachers necessarily more responsible than one who does not?' began:

> Whether a child who always obeys her teachers is more responsible than one who does not depends on a number of factors including, for example, what is meant by 'responsible'.

Following this Alex went on to build his answer around a consideration of what the question might mean. This was more direct, subtle and interesting than it would have been had he begun with a simple discussion of definitions, in the kind of way that Marie did, in her response to the question about disabled pupils and mainstream classes, that we discussed above. In other words, rather than discussing the ways we use words before attempting to answer the question, Alex used this discussion to structure his answer, in a way that you might find useful, depending on your subject.

Creeping up on your topic

Rather than approaching your topic head-on, it is often possible to seduce your readers into being interested in it by creeping up on it unexpectedly. For example, many years ago one of our students began an essay on 'Authority and the Teacher' with the sentence:

Some people seem to possess an ability to get other people to obey them without using force, and without giving reasons (Wynne, 1985).

Paul then went on to discuss the various different kinds of authority a teacher might possess. Another good way of introducing a topic, whether at the beginning of a piece of writing or midway through it, is to tell a story, or offer an example that illustrates some of the points you wish to make. For example, the philosopher Hart (1966) introduces the idea that there are different varieties of responsibility by relating a story about a sea captain's success or failure in relation to a number of responsibilities, when his ship is hit by a storm. He writes:

> As captain of the ship, X was responsible for the safety of his passengers and crew. But on his last voyage he got drunk every night and was responsible for the loss of the ship with all aboard. It was rumoured that he was insane, but the doctors considered that he was responsible for his actions. Throughout the voyage he behaved quite irresponsibly, and various incidents in his career showed that he was not a responsible person. He always maintained that the exceptional winter storms were responsible for the loss of the ship, but in the legal proceedings brought against him he was found criminally responsible for his negligent conduct, and in separate civil proceedings he was held legally responsible for the loss of life and property. He is still alive and he is morally responsible for the deaths of many women and children. (Hart, 1966, p211)

Although as Hart himself recognizes, this story is rather unsubtle, it nonetheless illustrates several distinct varieties of responsibility, which he then discusses. Hart was working within philosophy, a discipline in which the use of story is common. However, it also works effectively in many other disciplines. For example, Huguette, an undergraduate on a BA in Peace Studies and International Relations, began her undergraduate dissertation with a story from her childhood:

> In 1994, at the age of eight, my friend and neighbour, Lily, came to my house, wanting to play with me, but I didn't want to because I was reading a new book that my dad had just bought for me. When she grabbed my book, I pushed her and got it back. Later that day, she came back again and cut my book into pieces. After that day I was so hurt and angry that I vowed I would never forgive her, and never be friends with her again. Sadly, a few months later we went our different ways as a result of the genocide in our country – Rwanda, and so I never had the chance to talk to her again, or try to sort things out.

This story, told in the first person, was a startling way for Huguette to engage her audience in thinking about forgiveness, which her dissertation goes on to discuss in the context of the genocide of the 1990s, in her home country of Rwanda, which began very soon after the incident described. The personal nature of the story, mirrored throughout her dissertation, was balanced by more theoretical discussion, conducted mainly in the third person.

Should you adopt first or third person?

You are almost bound, at some point in your studies, to come across questions about whether academic writing should use the first or the third person. If you are told to write in the third person, and you are like many of the students with whom we work, it is quite likely that you will think that this is a problem. However, as we argue below, there is no reason why it should be, because whether you are aware of it or not, as an English speaker, you know how to use not only the first and third person, but also the second person. All three feature in the following short dialogue:

John: The cat's just sicked all over the carpet.

Mary: You'd better clean it up then.

John: I'm not cleaning it up. You clean it up. It's disgusting.

John's first contribution to this tale of woe is third person, while Mary's is in the second person. John's second contribution uses all three: first, second and third.

The ***first person*** is best characterized as making it clear that the author is speaking from his own perspective, sharing his views and arguments; giving his opinions and describing his actions and experiences. He does this mainly by using the personal pronoun 'I' (unless the 'author' is more than one person, when they will use 'we').

- I just love gin and tonic.
- I went to bed with my favourite book.
- We had a wonderful holiday at our friend's house in Treompan.

It is because the first person is often associated with communication of a personal kind, such as is illustrated by these examples, that many people believe that it is unsuitable for academic writing. Their preference is for the third person.

The ***second person*** is characterized by the use of the pronoun 'you'.

- You'd better clean it up then.

- You clean it up.

- If I clean it up, you're sleeping on the couch tonight.

We use the second person in this book when we ask you questions, or invite you to think about things or carry out tasks. You understand what we're talking about, don't you?

The *third person* seems to be about things outside the speaker or writer, and allows writers to appear more authoritative and less subjective. That is why it preferred for academic writing by many people.

- The cat's just sicked all over the carpet.

- It's disgusting.

- Contrary to what many people claim, the first person is common in scientific writing.

The third person is often preferred in academic work, because of the apparent sense of objectivity that it conveys. Although this is not the place to enter into a discussion of objectivity, it is worth noting that this is a strange basis upon which to ground the view that the third person is superior to the first person for academic writing. After all, objectivity depends not on the way we write, but on the ways that we think and the ways that we act. In spite of this, however, like many students, you may be given the impression that the third person is somehow superior to other, more personal forms of address, for academic purposes, and it is quite likely that you will be told that you have to write your assignments and essays in the third person. There are good reasons for this in some subjects.

For example, it would sound odd if a chemistry student wrote, 'I loved the bit in the experiment where we mixed the two solutions together and everything started to happen as the mixture bubbled up, especially when the colour suddenly changed.' However, it is important to note that the reason this sentence sounds odd has more to do with the fact that what the student has written is rather casual and imprecise, and reads more like a presentation on children's television, than it has to do with his use of the first person.

Even more formal and precise uses of the first person are most often considered unacceptable in physical science and so, for example, to find the following in the student's lab book would probably still be considered unusual:

When the two solutions were mixed, I noted the following colour changes …

And whereas it would make perfect sense to write 'I compared the chemical composition of a series of samples', in scientific writing it would be more usual to write, 'The chemical composition of a series of samples was compared.'

Despite the strong views of many academic researchers and teachers about the third person's superiority as a medium for conveying serious ideas and arguments in an objective and dispassionate way, to some extent whether you write in the first or third person as a student is a matter of personal preference. However, as we have already said, it may be dictated by the requirements of your course or by the personal preferences of those who teach you. If it is, you should try, if you can, to do what you are asked to do, provided you don't, as a result, end up writing pompous gibberish. Unfortunately, this is what often results when students are told that they must write in the third person, especially when they are told that they must not write in the first person and/or that the use of the personal pronoun 'I' is prohibited.

Pseudo third person: substituting 'The author' or 'The writer' for 'I'

Sound motivations lie behind the advice to students that they should avoid 'I' in their writing. It is about the attempt to stop them writing as if they are speaking to their best friend or their grandmother, who they might justifiably expect to have at least some interest in the story of their life, and in what they are thinking. However, proscribing the use of the first person as a way of trying to prevent students from writing little more than personal biography, even when they are writing about theoretical matters, is like using a sledge-hammer to crack a nut. The results can be just as messy, because for some reason when they are told that they must write in the third person and avoid the use of 'I', many students end up writings things like this:

> The author carried out a review of relevant literature … [I carried out a review of relevant literature …]

> The writer of this essay would argue that … [I would argue that …]

Such expressions convey an air of pretentiousness and are essentially poor translations from the first person versions shown in brackets.

The use of first person constructions translated into what is really pseudo-third person writing is very common among students who are trying to come to terms with the requirement that they should not use 'I' in their essays. Tutors often put this down to the idea that students must have difficulty in using the third person, which makes no sense, since most students, like most other adult English speakers, use the third person every day.

- The bus was late.
- The Kaiser Chiefs are playing in Manchester this weekend.
- The cat's just sicked all over the carpet. It's disgusting.
- Women have the right to do what they want with their bodies.

- Most students have huge debts by the time they get their degrees.

- Akbar's do great veggie pizzas.

Rather than being told to avoid the third person, you should really be being told to avoid allowing your essays to become too personal and too focused on you as an individual. Although as we have argued on pages 00–00, it is good to demonstrate commitment to a point of view in your essays, no academic or intellectual purpose is served by telling people what you believe unless, at the same time, you inform them, clearly and methodically, about the reasons you believe it.

> It is the grounds for your belief in which you can expect people to have an interest, rather the fact that it is *your* belief.

If you are told that you must not use 'I' in your essays, you may have to find ways of translating sentences that you would naturally have written in the first person, as in the examples that follow.

First person	Third person
I observed the behaviour of the twins in the family home.	The behaviour of the twins was observed in the family home.
I think the first person is superior to the third person as a way of engaging the audience.	The first person is superior to the third person as a way of engaging the audience.
We found, on average, fifteen species of insect per square metre of the field.	On average, fifteen species of insect were found per square metre of the field.
I think this argument is mistaken.	This argument is mistaken.
I counted all references to women in the three novels.	All references to women in the three novels were counted.
We split the class into three equal groups.	The class was split into three equal groups.

Task 27: Writing in the third person

Use the examples in the box above as models to help you translate the following from the first into the third person.

   We have given examples of deception on the part of MPs.

> On the tombs I observed markings similar to those found in Orkney.
>
> I counted the number of shops that had closed in the last year.
>
> We will advance two main claims.
>
> I think Broadbent's theory of memory is superseded by later work.
>
> We found that earlier films by these directors all contained biographical elements.
>
> I have presented evidence for greater fluctuations of rainfall during the past ten years.
>
> We divided the volunteers into four groups, according to their level of general fitness.
>
> [Our response appears on page 252]

Although we have been quite critical of the use of expressions such as 'The writer believes ...', we recognize that, used sparingly, they can at times be helpful, for example, where you are writing in the third person and wish to draw on your personal experience without sounding as if you are claiming that your personal experience somehow qualifies you as an authority on the matter at hand. For example:

> How different is the experience at primary school of girls from boys? In the present writer's professional experience, there is no obvious difference between boys and girls in achievement except perhaps in favour of the latter. (Winch, 1985, p. 97)

> This might sound like a crazy idea, but it makes a certain amount of sense, at least to those who write in this kind of way, including one of the present authors, who finds himself disabled if he tries to plan too much, too early. (Fairbairn and Winch, 2011)

The first of these two extracts is taken from what, in the main, is a piece of third person writing. In talking about the author's experience, 'The present writer' is consciously used to avoid jarring of style. The second appears earlier in this book.

Writing academically in the first person

The first person is commonly used in some disciplines including literature, theology and philosophy. It is also increasingly used in science, which makes sense. Canter and Fairbairn (2005) point out:

> ... use of the first person can walk hand in hand with a rigorous and scholarly approach to thinking about most things. After all, you can own

up to having a point of view by using the personal pronoun 'I', while contextualising your position by relating it to those held by others, and testing your views against theirs. (p. 62)

It is possible to write well in the first person and yet avoid lapsing into what amounts to no more than a telling of part of the story of one's life to date. For example, in a paper about 'Status, identity and respect', Bird (2004) carefully sets out the relationship between some ideas in political theory:

> It seems to me that political theorists have taken the concept of respect far too much for granted and have failed to recognize some of its important limitations. My main goal here is therefore to identify some of these limitations and to begin to explore their implications for contemporary political theory. I will advance two main claims. The first, which is my primary concern in this essay, is that once we understand the way in which the concept of respect characteristically functions, the second reinterpretation mentioned above becomes problematic. I suggest that we can make sense of the idea of respect for 'identity' or 'difference' only by threatening the sort of egalitarianism to which the first reinterpretation aspires. So here, my aim is to expose a conflict between the first and second reinterpretations, and a more general tension between egalitarianism and identity-based conceptions of respect. (pp. 207–208)

In this passage the first person has been used in quite a formal way. However, it can also be used successfully in discussing important matters, in a less formal way, as in the next passage, from a paper entitled 'Psychologists are human too', in which Mair (1970) uses the first person in addressing the tendency of psychologists to detach themselves from their subjects.

> When I hear people accuse psychologists of being isolated from the real world, small minded, hidebound by doctrine and method, incapable of learning from experience, I have to laugh. After all, I know, personally, half a dozen (well at least three) psychologists who, after only a few years of dedicated experimentation in their discipline, and despite very expensive and lengthy training to the contrary, have been forced to change some of their fundamental professional beliefs and accept that the subjects they have been herding through their laboratories are human after all. (p. 157)

In this short passage Mair manages, in a personal and witty style, both to engage his readership, and to give them a good idea of what is to come. His intention is to criticize psychologists' habit of attempting to remain aloof and distant from their subjects, almost as if they can pursue research in a totally objective and impersonal way, and so it seems right that he should write in a personal style.

Writing well in the third person

Just as first person writing need not be too personal in the sense that it involves simply giving an account of part of one's life to date, one's personal experiences and so on, so third person writing need not be impersonal, distant and uninvolved. Consider, for example, the following extracts. The first comes from a popular science book, *The Science of Jurassic Park and the Lost World – or – How to Build a Dinosaur*. The second is a piece of travel writing from an article by A.S. Byatt in the *Independent Magazine*:

> The velociraptors of *Jurassic Park* and *The Lost World* are an odd case. They're greedy, selfish, and aggressive – aggressive toward each other and even toward their own infants. On the other hand, they're also skillful pack hunters and appear to put their rivalries aside while chasing their prey: one raptor will maneuver a weak, straying triceratops away from its herd while another waits in hiding to pounce on the prey. But how did orphan raptors acquire the co-operative skills needed for hunting while remaining completely devoid of the similarly cooperative skills needed for living and surviving in a pack? (DeSalle and Lindley, 1997, p. 149)

In this passage the authors use a relaxed third person style to draw us into their imagined narrative about the hunting skills of velociraptors. Byatt, though focused on a less exciting topic, is similarly engaging. Although writing in the third person, Byatt's style is such that we have a sense that we are looking over her shoulder as she walks round this grand old city.

> Nimes is a civilised town. It lies in the sun, its ancient Roman monuments, its beautiful formal garden, the Jardin de la Fontaine, built in the 18th century by a military engineer, its narrow cobbled streets and wide boulevards, its elegant shops and solidly civilised old houses, all part of one harmonious whole. Its name derives from a spring, guarded by a divinity named Nemausus. Augustus Caesar gave this land to the veterans of his victorious Egyptian campaign against Antony and Cleopatra. They must have lived there in a sunny abundance ... (Byatt, 1990, p. 41)

Picking and mixing

Although, as we have illustrated, it is possible to write successfully in both the first and the third person, in practice many authors mix the two, and have been doing so for a long time, as illustrated by a passage from Florence Nightingale's *Notes for Nurses*, which was originally published in the nineteenth century.

> The effect of music upon the sick has been scarcely at all noticed. In fact, its expensiveness, as it is now, makes any general application of it quite out of the question. I will only remark here, that wind instruments, including the human voice, and stringed instruments, capable of continuous sound, have a generally beneficent effect – while the piano-forte, with such instruments as have *no* continuity of sound, has just the reverse. (p. 44)

At the beginning of his famous book *A Theory of Justice* (1971), the philosopher John Rawls moves freely between first and third person.

> These propositions seem to express our intuitive conviction of the primacy of justice. No doubt they are expressed too strongly. In any event I wish to inquire whether these contentions or others similar to them are sound, and if so how they can be accounted for. To this end it is necessary to work out a theory of justice in the light of which these assertions can be interpreted and assessed. I shall begin by considering the role of the principles of justice. (p. 4)

In the next example, Spencer (1989), writing about the ways that anthropologists use language, begins in the third person, but moves into the first person mid-way through his second sentence.

> This article is about recent anthropological questioning of anthropologists' own use of language – the way in which anthropologists use language in representing other cultures, that is the writing of ethnography. It was originally provoked by a recent collection of essays on anthropology as literature entitled *Writing culture* (Clifford & Marcus 1986), but I swiftly found that this was merely the tip of a highly self-conscious and reflexive iceberg, mostly to be found in American anthropology, but with voices intruding from Europe. (p. 145)

We have given examples of authors in a number of disciplines utilizing the first person in discussing their work, including psychology, philosophy, political theory, nursing and anthropology. In each of these disciplines there will be academics who argue that the third person is absolutely essential, and others who have a much more relaxed approach, believing that all that matters is that authors should write clearly and carefully in well argued prose, in ways that engage, inform and challenge their readers. No matter what you are studying, you will probably be able to find authors who write using first, second and third person. This will be true even in the physical sciences, in which, contrary to what many students are told, the first person is becoming increasingly common as part of the way in which people write. For example, in an article in the *New Journal of Physics,* Schachenmayer, Pupillo and Daley (2010) write:

> In this section we introduce the system of bosons moving in 1D in an optical lattice. We first introduce the Hamiltonian describing the system in section 2.1, before discussing the current and general expectations for its stability during time evolution in section 2.2. In order to make stronger connections to quantities that can be measured in an experiment, we introduce the quasi-condensate fraction in section 2.3 ... (p. 3)

Sometimes academic authors use a mixture of first, second and third person writing, as in the next paragraph, from an article – again about language – in a prestigious international nursing journal.

> What is the difference between a gammon steak and a slice of pig's buttock? Are they the same thing? Yes, but I'd rather have gammon with my peas and potatoes than a slice of pig's buttock. If I insist on seeing your gammon as a slice of pig's buttock then, surely, I am not just being 'more scientific' than you, I am making a point. You are not being 'irrational' or 'emotional' if you tell me to shut up. I am perhaps trying to disgust you to put you off, to incline you to vegetarianism. (Hunt, 1999, pp. 52–53)

In this paragraph, the author wants us to think carefully about the language we use. In doing so he moves from the third person into the first, and also uses second person to address his audience directly. We do the same thing throughout this book, sometimes talking in the first person as we do in this sentence, but sometimes in the third person, as we did in the previous one. On the other hand, when we address our readers directly, to invite reflection, ask a question or give an instruction, we use the second person. Have a quick look through what we have written on this page, or even through this sentence, and see if you can locate a use of the second person.

Structure

In developing a style that communicates clearly and simply, you will have to attend carefully not only to the language you use, but also to the ways in which you structure your work. Some of the worst faults we find in student essays occur when it is impossible to tell where they are going, or even to identify their main points. Your job as a writer is to help your reader to find her way round what you have written, so that she can follow your ideas, and assess your arguments and conclusions.

> In structuring your work try as far as possible to ensure that as she reads, your reader has the feeling that she knows where she is going, can remember where she has been, and can see how the section that she is currently reading relates to both.

Unless you do this, your reader can easily lose sight of even the most central ideas you are trying to present.

Signposting

When you are writing, the signposts you use help to make clear what you will be focusing on in major sections of your work. By 'signposts' we mean verbal or structural indications about the direction your argument or discussion is taking, analogous to the signposts we follow as drivers. Attending to signposts as you write can help you to identify major sections for your essay, thus ensuring, for example, that you cover all parts of a question. They can also help in guarding against the possibility of including material that is irrelevant to your main thrust.

Probably the most important signpost used in academic writing is the subheading, which can tell your reader where she is going, by indicating the next point on her journey through your thoughts. So, for example, in discussing a play and its relationship to a playwright's other work, you might use subheadings like these: 'The plot', 'The main characters', 'The relationship of the play to X's other work'. Or, writing an account of an experiment in science, you might employ subheadings such as: 'Hypotheses', 'Method', 'Results' and 'Conclusions'.

The other main species of signpost used in academic writing involves the use of what we might call 'trailers' and 'reminders', which as an author you will use to relate what you are now talking about to what you said earlier, and to indicate the direction your discussion or argument will take as you go further. For example, you may write 'I will argue that ...'; 'Earlier I discussed ...' or 'I have suggested that ...'. Reminding your readers where they have been, and how that relates to what is yet to come, is useful in helping them to grasp your point of view, particularly when your argument is complex. However, as we have already pointed out, it is important to ensure that your trailers and reminders genuinely inform readers about the structure of your text. Often authors claim to have done things that they haven't, or promise things that don't actually come to fruition.

Both trailers and reminders should be short and serve a useful purpose; they should not be simple repetitions of what is said elsewhere.

Every so often, while you are writing, check the trailers and reminders you are using by asking yourself:

- Have I fulfilled promises? For example, if I have written, 'I will argue that ...', have I really offered an argument, that is, given reasons and justifications for my views?

- If I have said that I will enter into more detail about a point later in my essay, have I actually done so?

- Have I addressed all the issues that I claimed I would address and given all the arguments that I claim to have given?

- Have I done everything I say I did, and addressed everything I claim to have addressed?

- If I have employed phrases like, 'It follows from this that ...' or 'This leads me into a discussion of ...' and so on, does whatever I claim follows from an earlier point or argument, really follow from it?

Make every word count

Earlier, in 2.2, we suggested that you should try to develop the habit of writing for five minutes a day without worrying about whether what you are writing is said as nicely as it could be; is correctly spelled and helpfully punctuated; adheres to the common expectations of grammar, or will impress your teachers. Most people are surprised to find not only how much they can write in five minutes when they avoid worrying about these things, but how often the text they write is well formed. Writing for five minutes a day is thus a good way of developing the ability to get ideas out of your head and into text that can be worked on, even when you don't feel inspired and are unsure about what you want to write. This is one of the main abilities you must develop if you are to become a successful writer. Another is the ability to shape text carefully, ensuring that so far as possible, every word counts, and that there is no clutter of extra ideas that do not contribute sufficiently to your main thrust to justify inclusion.

We want, now, to give you some help in developing the skills, discipline and courage necessary if you are to be able to choose rationally, which ideas in the draft essays you write should make it through to the next draft, and which should either be consigned to the recycle bin or stored for use on another occasion. We will do this by introducing you to two literary forms, in which severe constraints on length mean that every word has to earn its keep:

- The mini saga
- The 200-word 'reflection'

Small but perfectly formed: the 50-word 'mini saga'

Mini sagas are a literary form that came to prominence in the 1980s, when the UK newspaper the *Daily Telegraph* staged a mini saga competition. Good mini sagas are perfectly formed miniature stories. Of course, the name 'mini saga' is a joke, because the 'sagas' with which we are most familiar are the long stories, often covering many generations, that are important in the traditional folklore of Scandinavian countries. Successful mini sagas often deal with big issues.

The Postcard[10]

Friendless, he despatched a letter to the twelfth century. Illuminated scrolls arrived by return post. Jottings to Tutankhamen secured hieroglyphics on papyrus; Hannibal sent a campaign report. But when he addressed the future, hoping for cassettes crammed with wonders, a postcard drifted back with scorched edges. It glowed all night.

Mini sagas are a very specialized form of writing. Like novels and short stories they tell a tale, but what makes them interesting is that they are so compact and condensed. Whereas a short story might be many thousands of words in length, the mini saga has to be exactly 50 words long – not a word longer and not a word less. This is what gives mini sagas their special character, because the limitation of 50 words means that every word has to earn its keep. They are rather like some forms of Japanese poetry; for example, haiku should contain 17 syllables arranged in 3 lines of 5, 7 and 5 syllables respectively[11].

I kill an ant
and realize my three children
have been watching.

Kato, Shuson

[10] We are grateful to the authors of this mini saga and the two others that follow a page later: 'The Death Touch!' and 'Who Dares Wins', though we don't know who wrote them, since the person who shared them had failed either to note down where she collected them, or who their authors were. Of course, if we become aware of their authors before this book goes into another edition we shall, of course, acknowledge them properly next time round.

[11] These examples and many more can be found on the website *Haiku for People*: http://www.toyomasu.com/haiku/#murakami

Clouds appear
and bring to men a chance to rest
from looking at the moon.
          Basho, Matsuo (1644–1694)

First autumn morning:
the mirror I stare into
shows my father's face.
          Murakami, Kijo (1865–1938).

Like Haiku poets, mini saga authors are compelled to think creatively about how best to say what they want to say, and about how best to achieve the effects they desire. When you only have 50 words in which to say what you want to say, there is no room for ostentation or irrelevance.

The Death Touch!

When a daughter went away to college, she reluctantly left her plants and her goldfish in her mother's care. Once the daughter telephoned and her mother confessed that the plants and the goldfish had died, there was a prolonged silence. Finally, in a small voice, the daughter asked, 'How's Dad?'

Who Dares Wins

He was scared. It was his first drop. The transport shuddered violently on its journey through the night. They were over the dropping-zone. Soon it would be knives into unsuspecting bodies. Killing silently. 'Ready?' said the Sergeant. 'Go.' He said a prayer and jumped into the streets of Troy.

Task 28: Try writing mini sagas

Try writing some mini sagas. They must have exactly 50 words, but in addition they can have a title of up to 15 words. Although they should be narrative in form, make sure your mini sagas address 'big' issues.

Then try writing some 'mini essays' with the same rules as mini sagas – 50 words; title of up to 15 words.

The 200-word 'reflection'

For several years Leeds Metropolitan University promoted the use of a new literary form, the 200-word 'reflection', by publishing on its website, series of such reflections on a range of topics, including research and ethics. These 'reflections' were constrained in two ways: by the requirement that they should be exactly 200 words long; and by the requirement that they should contain only two paragraphs. You may find ludicrous the idea that it is possible to write about important matters in just two paragraphs containing only 200 words. If you do, you will be in good company, because this is a common reaction when people first come across the reflection as a literary genre. However, most people who try writing in this form eventually view it as helpful, because it forces them to think carefully about each and every word. The three examples that follow are all 'ethical reflections' from the Leeds Met web pages.

Saving Life or Saving Death – Who should call it?

Technology has widened the space between dying and death. We are living longer and with higher expectations; as a consequence dying is sometimes prolonged. Consider a patient who was brought into the Emergency Room in cardiac arrest. She had been defibrillated and adrenaline had been administered. The clinician said 'This patient's brain is dead' but continued resuscitation. After a further hour of CPR, he said 'This patient's heart is dead, her brain is dead, does everyone agree?'

The cerebral cortex is redundant after being starved of oxygen for four to six minutes. This woman's brain had not received oxygen for forty minutes prior to resuscitation. In cases like hers, advances in knowledge and technology increase options, but bring with them complexity and dilemmas. Emergency services had correctly followed protocol and using advanced technology had been able to return this woman's heart rhythm to one compatible with life. However, even if she had survived the resuscitative effort, she would have remained in a persistent vegetative state. Her personality and capacity to be who she was, had been lost. Would you want resuscitation in such circumstances? At all costs? Who should decide? How can they ensure that their decisions are ethical ones?

Cara Bailey [When she wrote this in 2008, Cara was a PhD Student at the University of Nottingham]

The Value of Natural Assets

The Indian Government has recently approved the environmental clearances necessary to allow Vedanta, a UK FTSE–100 company, to proceed with a controversial bauxite mining project in Niyamgiri, Orissa. The proposed site, an area of extraordinary natural beauty, supports a diversity of wildlife within its extensive forests. It is also home to the Dongria Kondh, one of India's remotest tribes, who worship the Niyamgiri Mountain as their 'living God'. Their unique tribal identity will be destroyed when the mining begins. Anthropologist Felix Padel calls it cultural genocide: 'a slow death of everything which makes their lives meaningful'. Though several companies have withdrawn their investments from Vedanta over concerns about its environmental and human rights record, they seem intent on proceeding with the project.

Pavan Sukhdev, Head of Deutsche Bank's Global Markets business in India, believes that much of the economic world considers Nature to be an externality. The global economy, he claims, is losing natural capacity at a rate of between two and five trillion dollars every year from the disappearance of forests – a financial loss even greater than that experienced by the current banking crisis. Ironically, Deutsche Bank still has investments in Vedanta, as does the UK's Universities Superannuation Scheme.

Mark Helyar [Writer, theatre director and musician]

Suicide, Ethics and Minding Our Tongues

The words we employ affect the ways we think and the ways we act. That is why, in discussing the morally challenging phenomenon of suicide, it is important to mind our tongues.

For example, since murder is killing from bad intentions, describing suicide as 'self murder' begs the question of whether it is morally wrong. And since most acts that are committed are illegal – consider, for example, robbery, arson and fraud, the common practice of referring to suicide as an act 'committed' clearly begs the question of whether it is wrong. This problem could be overcome by substituting the neutral expression 'he killed himself' for 'he committed suicide'. However, doing so would produce another problem. After all, a person could kill himself without being a suicide. For example, he might drink paraquat, believing it to be gin, in which case his act would not be suicide, even if he died. Another, arguably better, strategy would be to use the verb 'to suicide' to indicate no more than that a protagonist acted so as to achieve his death, because he wished to be dead, thus leaving open the question of how his act should be judged, both legally and ethically.

Gavin Fairbairn

Task 29: Write some 200-word 'reflections'

Now try your hand at writing '200-word reflections'. The topic can be of your choice, but it should be related to your academic work. Remember that this text should be serious and self-contained. It is neither a snippet of a larger piece, nor an introduction to a larger piece. In approaching your first draft for this exercise, you might find it helpful to aim at three things:

- *Engaging* your audience, that is, interesting them in the topic.

- *Informing* your audience, that is, telling them something they don't know already (or that you believe they don't know).

- *Challenging* your audience, that is, finding ways of persuading them to think, or to question their assumptions about a topic.

MAKE EVERYWORD COUNT!

Writing very short texts, such as mini sagas and 200-word reflections, might seem to be a strange way to practise writing, when the essays and other assignments you have to write as a student will be much longer. However, we hope you will spend at least some time on Tasks 28 and 29, because doing so will enhance your ability to write well – clearly and concisely, at any length. One of the most important skills every writer has to learn is cutting work down to size by removing material that is not essential. Practising on very short texts, in which every word has to earn its keep or it gets removed, is a good way of developing this skill for use when you are writing on a bigger scale.

Improving your work by cutting it down to size

Almost every text, however nicely written and however carefully edited, will improve if it is made shorter, and so if you want to improve your written work, try 'cutting it down to size'.

i   Every so often, when you are writing as a student, print out a draft of your text and read it carefully with the intention of doing nothing other than removing some words from it.

ii Decide on a number of words you will remove from each page, then get brutal.

iii Pretend, if you have to, that the text was written by someone else. The number of words you decide to excise from each page doesn't really matter, but it should be more than 10 and we find that 17 words is often a good place to start.

Task 30: Practise cutting some texts down to size

i   Find a text – any text will do, but something that purports to be informative
     will be best – an article from an academic journal, say; or a chapter from
     a book. Read it carefully with a view to improving it by cutting it down to
     size, following the procedure outlined in the box above. This is best done
     on a printed copy, so if necessary, photocopy the text, because it's best if
     you 'mark it up' like a copyeditor.

ii   If you are working on an assignment at the moment, print out a draft and
     try cutting it down to size. If you aren't writing anything right now, get out
     an old essay or two and practise on them.

Clarity

During the 1988 US presidential election campaign, in which he successfully
stood for Vice President alongside George H.W. Bush, Dan Quayle gave a speech,
part of which was cited in an article that appeared in the UK newspaper, the
Guardian:

> I suppose three important things certainly come to mind that we want to
> say thank you. The first would be our family. Your family, my family –
> which is composed of an immediate family of a wife and three children,
> a larger family with grandparents and aunts and uncles. We all have our
> family whatever that may be ... time and again I'm often reminded, espe-
> cially in this presidential campaign, of the importance of a family, and
> what a family means to this country. And so when you say thanks I
> suppose the first thing that would come to mind would be to thank the
> Lord for the family.
>
> (From the article 'Family man Dan goes rambling for Thanksgiving',
> *Guardian*, 8 November 1988, p. 24)

As a student, the demands upon you in, for example, seminars or tutorials, are
hardly likely to be as stringent as those that will be made upon a presidential
candidate, although your tutors would probably hope that you and your peers
might achieve a little more direction and clarity in their essays than Quayle
managed in this snippet from Dan Quayle's speech. Your teachers' expecta-
tion will be very different in relation to your writing, because when you write
you have more time to think. However, students and even professional
academics at times write things that are in some ways very similar to our
extract from Quayle's speech. For example, discussing the treatment of

human embryos, Nigel S. de Cameron (1989) wrote the following remarkable sentence:

> May we not argue that the way in which such conflicts should be met in our society involves (a) a cautious and conservative approach to fundamental change; (b) a recognition that certain courses of action are ruled out, since they are profoundly offensive to many people (majority? substantial minority? – so much depends on how the question is framed); (c) an aware-ness that there are arguments unconnected with Christian religious and ethical convictions which tend to support them, or (put it another way) to show that they are reasonable (in this case we are working with a concept of human rights and human dignity as co-extensive with Homo sapiens)?

Task 31: What does de Cameron want to communicate?

Try writing down what you think de Cameron intends to communicate. Although it is clear he means something, the convoluted nature of this sentence with its three-point list, asides and questions, makes it difficult, by the end, to remember what the beginning of the sentence was about.

[Our response appears on page 253]

Some writers give the impression that they have something to say which is of profound importance even when they do not, even when they are unclear about what it is that they want to say. They may do this by using important sounding words and phrases, by using references to literature, and by the liberal use of metaphor. For example, the passage that follows has the appearance of academic rigour and scholarly content and yet we can make very little of it. Note the use of words drawn from Latin and Greek and the (allegedly pertinent) reference to the derivation of the term 'Academy' from Akademus. Note also the use of the odd term 'an essential resonance of transcendence', which probably means something, although we can't imagine what.

> Education is to do with educing, with releasing, with liberating. It would seem to do with the free and animated play of mind over experienced phenomena. Educating Rita is not training her; it is essentially releasing her into the life of thought and, therefore, existential possibility. It is no accident that the word 'school' derives from the Greek word 'schole' meaning both leisure (freedom from necessity) and discussion; freedom we might say, for discourse. It is pertinent that the word 'academy' derives from Akademus, the man who owned the garden/grove in which Plato and his students discussed philosophy. The metaphor of the garden – a protected place where utile pressure is off, where the mind can struggle to

think its own thoughts – gives an essential resonance to this cluster of key words; education, school, academy. Certainly education bears within it the distinct resonance of transcendence.

(Peter Abbs, 'Training spells the death of education', *Guardian*, 5 January 1987)

Task 32: What is Abbs trying to say?

In Part 3 we argue in favour of adopting a generous approach when reading what others have written, and this is what we have tried to do in reading what Abbs has written. Even so, however, we can still make very little of it.

Try to work out what you think Abbs is trying to communicate in this passage, and write it down in your own words. Aim to capture the general flavour of what he is saying rather than trying to translate each word and phrase. Make your version shorter.

[Our response appears on page 253]

In an essay about the ways that small children begin to understand the world for his undergraduate course in teacher education, Daniel, a student on a teacher education course, wrote:

We are aesthetic beings long before we are rational beings, since, from a new-born babe, a person begins to mediate his or her world through the basic senses of sight, sound, smell, touch, and taste, thus bringing together through pain, pleasure or a sense of well-being, intimations of the nature of our world, and with it, a commitment to basic understanding; the development of which demands a particular kind of imaginative attention to things made, performed or learned; and in doing so, become critically reflective in his or her responses to them.

Task 33: What was Daniel getting at?

Daniel's sentence is so long that although it gives the impression of coherence and sounds quite intelligent, it is difficult to hold on to its sense right through to the end. It has several strands and the use of semi-colons towards the end suggests that the writer is aware that there are too many separate ideas for one sentence. Try rewriting it in, say, three or four sentences to see whether this can help to make its meaning clearer.

[Our response appears on page 253]

Make sure that the language you choose helps you to communicate meaning, rather than concealing it.

Coherence

Whenever you are writing as a student you must ensure that what you write is coherent, in other words, that it hangs together, not only at the level of individual statements and paragraphs, but as a whole text. It may be helpful to consider an example.

Suppose that an undergraduate history student is writing an essay about the causes of the Second World War, during which she wants to claim that in some sense the Soviet Union caused the war. Her argument for this contention might involve the claim that, as a result of the Soviet Union's interference in German politics in the 1920s and 1930s, divisions on the German Left allowed Hitler to come to power.

Now suppose that in the course of her essay our undergraduate historian asserts that Germany caused the outbreak of hostilities with the Soviet Union by invading Soviet territory in 1941. At first sight this seems to lay her open to a charge of inconsistency, because it looks as if she is claiming both that the Soviet Union was responsible for the war, and that Germany was responsible for it.

With luck, however, our historian may have anticipated such difficulties, because she has tried to imagine what a critical reader might say about her essay. And so in developing her argument she could avoid the accusation of inconsistency by distinguishing between various senses of 'cause'. She might point out, for example, that whereas the Soviet Union caused the war in the sense that its actions in interfering in German politics in the 1920s and 1930s were decisive in enabling Hitler's rise to power in Germany to take place, this is not inconsistent with the further claim that Germany's invasion of the Soviet Union caused the outbreak of hostilities between these two countries. Whether or not her argument is convincing, or even plausible, she has at least attempted to achieve clarity and to maintain consistency in what she has written.

Remember that the people who read your work (including your tutors) will not be able to ask questions about what you intended by what you have written. Bear in mind the fact that, as a writer, you have a variety of sources of information available: your memory, files, notes, reference books and so on, but that your reader probably doesn't. And so, since your reader cannot ask for clarification, you need to ensure not only that what you write is clear, but that there are no gaps in your text that prevent others from understanding it.

Attending to the needs of a readership

Whenever you are writing as a student, it is important that you should think about your readers and about their needs, if you are to help them to understand what you want to communicate. Make sure that there are no gaps in your essay that prevent them having a clear idea of what you are saying.

> As you write, try to do so with the idea in mind that your readers may not be as knowledgeable about your topic as you are, and that they may not have access to the same sources as you.
>
> Remember, also, that even though your tutors are likely to know much more than you, they may not have read the same things, or thought about things in the same way as you.

As a writer you can only safely assume that your readers have one source of information, namely what you have written. When you are writing essays, you therefore need to ensure that you include all the important information in your text, even much that you think that a reasonably well-informed reader might well know.

> In developing your essays, take the time, every so often, to read what you have written as if you were a novice in relation to the subject matter, to identify places where a reader might fail to understand because vital information is not presented. Then ensure that this information is included in an understandable form in your essay.

There is an important difference between providing adequate background to enable your readers to follow your line of thought or argument and insulting or patronizing them. You will not insult their intelligence by ensuring that they have access to important items of information. You may well do so by employing careless arguments or by withholding vital information or references from them. To continue with our example of the Second World War, our history undergraduate may well wish to refer both to the Comintern (the Third Communist International, the organization that effectively controlled the Communist parties of the inter-war period and was itself effectively controlled by the Soviet Union) and the Weimar Republic (the name given to the German state of the pre-Hitler period). If she does, she will need to briefly introduce these terms, before using them to develop her argument.

> Read and re-read what you have written with the needs of your readers in mind, and if those demands seem not to be fully satisfied, take the time to rewrite what you have written. Doing so will improve your essay.

Choosing words carefully

Words are the tools with which you make meaning and the better suited to the job the tools you use, the more likely you are to succeed in conveying your ideas. Try to choose short, everyday words whenever you can, not because there is anything wrong with the longer words of the English language, but because they are often misused and even abused by writers whose desire to impress people with their cleverness is stronger than their wish to communicate clearly. Impressing your teachers is, of course, a commendable aim. Unfortunately, many misguided students form the view that using difficult words and a convoluted style of writing will help them to do so. It won't. Difficult and important sounding words do not necessarily do their job well, however good they sound.

The thing that is most likely to impress your teachers is clarity. Show them that you understand your material by writing about it in a simple and clear way, using words that are appropriate, in ways that show you understand them. If, at the same time, you can show that you have developed your own point of view and can write about it in an accessible way, you are likely to do well.

> Never use words with which you are unfamiliar, in the hope that your reader will be impressed. It is likely that you will simply demonstrate your ignorance.

Synonyms

Synonyms are words that mean the same thing, or very nearly the same thing, as one another. The English language is particularly rich in such words because of having emerged from a hotchpotch of other languages. The happy result is that there will often be a choice of words, which may be used with equal correctness. However, having a rich language available on which to draw can lead to problems, because of the temptation to substitute a word that is similar in meaning to the one you would have used naturally, in the attempt to make your work more interesting, or perhaps more important and impressive sounding. The problem is that although they may mean very nearly the same as one another, synonyms are not necessarily interchangeable. For example, although 'start' and 'begin' can mean something very similar to one another, you would not write 'The Judge began the race by firing a gun', you would write that he 'started' it. And although 'home' and 'residence' are synonyms, you wouldn't write 'An Englishman's residence is his castle' rather than 'An Englishman's home is his castle', because 'residence' does not carry the same cosy feeling as 'home'.

> Always ensure that whenever you consider using a synonym for a word you might have used, that it makes sense to use it in the context in question, particularly when you are using a word with which you are unfamiliar.

Your job as a writer is to convey meaning and so you should aim to use words with which you are comfortable, whose meanings you understand. Don't risk using words that are new to you, or the meaning of which you are unsure of; if you do, you risk looking foolish. Not only should you avoid words that are unfamiliar to you, you should also, if possible, avoid words that you do not expect your readers to understand. Do not assume too readily that your teachers will be familiar with specialized vocabulary you want to use, unless you are sure that it is part of the general vocabulary of their discipline. This point applies both to jargon and to common words that have been hijacked from everyday language and made to fulfil a particular function; it applies also to 'newspeak' words, that is, words that have been invented relatively recently to fulfil a particular function. Whenever you are going to use new words or old words with new meanings, you should first consider whether their use will help you to be clearer, and explain their use when you first introduce them.

> Avoid confusing your reader by the use of words that she may not understand.

Whenever you feel tempted to abandon a familiar word for a more impressive sounding one, ask yourself whether you need the particular meaning the less common word conveys. If you are going to use a word with which you are unfamiliar, make sure, before doing so, that you are going to use it accurately.

Avoid jargon and technical language whenever possible

'Jargon' is the specialized vocabulary of a specific field of work or study, for example, sociology, the law, computers or economics. Within such fields its use can often be justified because it can help meanings to be communicated more accurately and more briefly. However, problems frequently arise when jargon is used in addressing people outside the relevant specialist area. That is why, outside the linguistic community from which it stems, it is best avoided.

> Avoid using jargon just because you think it sounds good, or because you want to look knowledgeable. Use everyday terms rather than jargon, where possible.

Jargon is acceptable only when you are writing for an audience whom you have every reason to believe will be familiar with it, or if you are willing and able to explain it to your readers. After all, you wouldn't write in French for an audience who didn't speak French, so why write in some jargon such as 'Computerese' for readers who don't understand it?

Avoid jargon and difficult words unless their use can make your meaning clearer.

Phrases that include unnecessary words

There is a family of phrases that include words that are redundant. Consider, for example:

- The use of the expression 'quite unique' to refer to some individual, thing, place or event, where the addition of 'quite' is redundant, since uniqueness does not come in degrees. Something can't be a bit unique, very unique or absolutely unique; it's just unique.

- The claim that an object was found in 'close proximity' to something else, in which the use of the word 'close' is redundant, since 'proximity' already suggests closeness.

- Occasions when you feel tempted to say that you are basing your opinion on 'prior experience', almost as if you could, if you wished, base your opinion on future experience.

- The claim that a situation is 'absolutely impossible' or 'really impossible'.

Or consider these examples, in which, in each case, the version in brackets is preferable:

a total of 35,891 visitors (35,891 visitors)

an added bonus (bonus)

completely eradicated (eradicated)

end result (result)

free gift (gift)

personal opinion (opinion)

prior experience (experience)

repeat again (repeat)

completely exhausted (exhausted)

summarize briefly (summarize)

triangular in shape (triangular)

very widespread (widespread)

adequate enough (adequate)

surrounded on all sides (surrounded)

Task 34: Look out for redundant words

Have a look through some of your old essays and in a few magazines and newspapers for examples of phrases that include redundant words. **Try to avoid using such phrases**.

Don't confuse your readers with abbreviations

Like all intelligent people, your readers, including your tutors, will be familiar with many abbreviations, including shortened forms of words, such as Prof (Professor) and contracted forms, such as Mr (Mister) along with acronyms such as UNESCO or NATO, and initialisms like AA (Automobile Association) and MA (Master of Arts). However, it is important to realize that since they have not engaged in the same research and reading that you have, they might not be familiar with some abbreviations that to you seem commonplace, and therefore you should always introduce abbreviations carefully. You can do this either by using the full name followed by the abbreviation in brackets when you first use it, or by using the abbreviation and following it with the full name in brackets.

The United Nations International Children's Emergency Fund (UNICEF) is active in many parts of the world.

The School of Applied Global Ethics (SAGE) was created in 2004.

SPUC (The Society for the Protection of Unborn Children) is completely opposed to abortion.

Over the years the WHO (World Health Organization) has regularly taken issue with Nestlé over their marketing of formula baby milk in developing countries.

Having introduced the abbreviation alongside the full name of what it stands for, it is then usually okay to use it on its own, although in a long document, such as an MA dissertation or a PhD thesis, it is often helpful to remind readers of the meaning of abbreviations that have not appeared for several pages.

When many abbreviations are used in such a document, it is also a good idea to include a comprehensive list or table of abbreviations, to which readers can refer if necessary.

There is nowadays such a proliferation of acronyms and initialisms that it is worth thinking carefully before introducing them into your written work. In general, you should only do so if either:

- the body or organization to which it refers is always or very often referred to by the abbreviated form;

- by using the abbreviated form you can make your text shorter and or more elegant.

Stylistic traps

So far we have discussed some aspects of style to which you should attend when you are writing as a student. In doing so we have hinted at dangers that lie in wait for unsuspecting students, particularly those who are anxious to impress their teachers. We want to end by briefly visiting some stylistic traps into which all writers are in danger of falling.

'Empty' words and phrases

There are lots of phrases in the English language that mean nothing, but have a certain attractiveness, perhaps because they are heard so often that they become like old friends. We're talking about phrases like these:

- all things considered
- at the end of the day
- for all intents and purposes
- I mean to say
- in a real sense
- it has to be said that
- on the whole
- very real
- when push comes to shove

You will often find phrases of this kind in journalistic writing, and in the responses of politicians and others in media interviews. For example, when he was being interviewed, Tony Blair, Prime Minister of the UK from 1997 to 2008, had a tendency to use the phrase 'I mean to say ...' repeatedly, almost as if he knew that he wasn't saying what he really wanted to say, or what he should have been saying.

You should avoid the temptation to use empty phrases like these in your academic work, because they add nothing and use up words that you could use to say something of value. Closely related to the problems caused by the use of empty phrases is the use of phrases like the following, which serve to do nothing other than fill up space, because they could be replaced by much simpler and shorter alternative [shown in brackets]:

- at the present time [now]
- in the event that [if]
- has a tendency to [tends to]
- in many instances [often]
- during the time that I was engaged in a study of ... [While I was studying...]

Avoid using several words where one will do. Be especially aware of the dangers that come at the beginning of an essay, or even at the beginning of a sentence, when there is a temptation to talk yourself into what you want to say:

In beginning to address this aspect of my topic, I would first like to...

To make clear the extent of the involvement of the Pied Piper in the exit from the village of Hamelin, not only of the rats, but of the children, it is first necessary to give an overview ...

Such sentences can usually be cut down to size, or even omitted completely, without making any significant difference to the text, because most often they serve no other purpose than delaying the point at which the writer says what she actually wants to say. As a result, they can usually be omitted without changing the point that is being made.

Phrases of this kind are often heard in discussion, and at times they appear in clusters so large that they end up piling on top of one another so densely that they almost disguise the fact that anything meaningful is being said at all – as, for example, in the following answers by politicians, during television interviews:

With reference to the claim that I misled the House about the extent of my involvement in this affair, I should just like to say that at no time have I set out intentionally to deceive anyone.

At this moment in time, given the constraints under which we are operating and the very difficult situation in which we find ourselves, I want just to say that the measures we have put in place are essential if we are to improve things in the long term.

In the first of these two examples, everything up to '... at no time have I ...' is irrelevant, and serves no purpose other than buying the speaker time to think. In the second the same is true, up to '... the measures ...'. In a way, filling space like this is understandable in a live interview. But it's unforgivable in writing, because when we write we should think ahead and only write what actually communicates. Indeed, it seems to us to be disrespectful of a reader to expect her to wade through a lot of unrelated or only vaguely related verbiage before she gets to the point you're trying to make; in addition, if there's too much verbal junk around, it's possible to miss the point totally.

Phrases like 'It follows from this that ...' and 'This leads me into a discussion of ...' can perform a useful function. However, they often give the appearance of planning and structure, of cohesiveness and logicality where none exist. So make sure that if you have used such phrases, you have actually done or are going to do what they claim you have done, or are going to do.

Frozen language

At times language becomes frozen, so that rather than being used creatively to express ideas, stylized forms of words are used, which show that the speaker or writer has not really thought about what she is wishing to communicate but has simply grabbed at whatever ready-made phrases she has to hand. The best known example of frozen language is the cliché – a common word, phrase or sentence that trips easily off the tongue, but which has lost its original effectiveness through overuse.

Cliché is as far as possible to be avoided in speech. More particularly, however, it is to be avoided when you write. Whereas when a person speaks her direct contact with her listeners allows them the opportunity to clarify whatever thought or emotion underpinned an individual's use of a cliché, in writing this is not possible. So, for example, you should avoid using expressions such as 'at the sharp end' to refer to activities in which people engage practically with problems; 'in the cold light of day' to refer to occasions when problems or possibilities are considered calmly; and 'At this moment in time' to indicate that a problem is being addressed now, as opposed to some other time, since it is obvious that the individual is writing, or speaking, now and not at some other time.

Many clichés were once rather powerful metaphors, conveying meaning in strikingly new ways, until overuse made them pale and insipid, even something to be laughed at. Most of us use clichés at times, and some people use them a great deal. Some speak or write in ways that suggest that they have not thought too clearly about what they are communicating, because they involve juxtaposing metaphors with contrasting images in 'mixed metaphors'. For example, in an unfortunate attempt to establish how hard he had worked as a teacher, an ex-colleague of ours who was a master of cliché, once came out with the following:

Unlike some colleagues I came into teacher education straight from the coal-face with my pockets still full of chalk dust.

Listen carefully to yourself, both when you are speaking and when you are writing, and avoid excessive use of clichéd expressions and frozen metaphors, otherwise you risk looking as silly as the colleague we referred to in the last example.

Task 35: Collecting clichés

Make a list of clichés that you hear on radio or TV, or in the pub; or that you read in books or the papers.

Own up to clichés that you find yourself using (then try to avoid using them). For example, when was the last time you used these expressions: 'it goes without saying'; 'in any shape or form'; 'last but not least', or 'to all intents and purposes'?

[Some other clichés appear on page 254]

Ambiguity

If someone wrote 'Every boy loves some girl', it would be unclear whether she meant that for every boy there is a girl that he loves, or that there is a particular girl who is loved by every boy. The expression 'All the nice girls love a sailor' also leaves it unclear what is intended. One possibility is that there is a particular sailor that all nice girls love, even though it is highly unlikely that any sailor is known to all nice girls. A little less strange perhaps is the claim that since all nice girls love sailors, every nice girl must love every sailor she sets eyes on.

Ambiguity often leads to amusement. Consider, for example:

- The child who had lost a glove at school and who came home delighted a few days later and told her dad, 'I found my glove walking up the corridor'.

- The sign in a restaurant that proclaimed, 'Patrons who think our waiters are rude should see the manager'.

- The article in a local newspaper that began, 'Brian kept his pigeons down the garden with his brother Sid'.

- The advertisement offering a dog for sale that read, 'Dog for sale. Will eat anything. Loves children'.

> Avoid ambiguity, that is, writing things that have more than one meaning.

Spotting ambiguities in your own writing is difficult, and so you should try to get someone else to check your work for such problems.

> Be alert to the possibility that what you have written is open to different interpretations. Don't assume that because you know what you mean your audience will also know what you mean.

The use of non-standard forms of English can lead to ambiguity, which is perhaps the main reason you should avoid them in your academic writing, the other being that the use of standard English means more people will be able to understand and interact with what you write[12]. For example, in Yorkshire, the word 'while' is often used to mean what 'until' means in standard English. So 'I'm waiting while school finishes' means 'I'm waiting until school finishes'. In certain contexts, this use of 'while' could have interesting consequences. Imagine, for example, a situation where someone from Yorkshire, driving through a strange area, came across a level crossing with a sign saying, 'Wait here while trains pass'.

What can you do to improve your writing?

In Part 2 we have tried to persuade you that it is worthwhile learning to write well as a student and we have looked at some ways in which you might approach writing that will increase your chances of doing so. Let us end by recapping briefly on some of the more important points we have made.

---

[12] What you do in speech or in other kinds of writing is up to you, although it is worth noting that the use of dialect or even just a regional accent can convey certain advantages in some contexts, while in others the use of standard English, spoken in a more neutral accent, will convey such advantages.

REMEMBER:

Write as simply as possible, avoiding long and complex sentences and using simple words where possible.

Avoid jargon, unless using it can help to make your meaning clearer.

Stick to the topic and don't allow yourself to be side-tracked into issues that are only marginally relevant.

Write grammatically, and make sure that what you write makes sense.

Make sure that your punctuation helps readers to understand what you are saying.

Take care over the structure of your written work. Make sure your ideas are presented in the best (most logical, most helpful) order.

Use subheadings or other signposts to help guide readers around your ideas, and to help them to understand how your ideas relate to one another.

Work at making your text flow easily, so that one sentence follows another without your reader having to wonder why.

Make sure your paragraphs really are paragraphs – that is, that they are containers for separate points in a topic or argument.

Check your spelling.

As it develops, check your essay again and again to make sure it makes sense and says what you think it does.

Avoid longwindedness, pomposity, gobbledygook and cliché.

Seek and heed the advice of others, but be your own worst (and best) critic.

Follow conventions relating to the citation of sources.

Checking your work

In our discussion of the writing process in 2.1, we looked at the importance of copyediting and proofreading and we have touched on these also during our discussion of some of the more technical aspects of writing: punctuation, spelling and grammar as well as the conventions of citation and referencing. As a result, you might think that by now we should feel happy that we have said often enough, how important it is to check your work at every stage. You would be wrong, because writing well depends so much on the discipline of checking your work, that we feel the need to draw your attention to it again and again.

Re-read and check your work frequently

In preparing essays and other assignments, re-read what you have written regularly, to check whether you are adequately addressing your topic, and whether your use of language is as good as you can make it. As you read, ask yourself questions such as these:

- Is what I have written easy to follow?
- Does it communicate what I intended?
- Have I answered the question or carried out the task I was set?
- Have I said enough to persuade readers of my point of view?
- Are my arguments well structured?
- Have I made good use of every source I've cited? Is it clear why I have cited them?
- Do my examples and illustrations do their job well?
- Is any of what I have written irrelevant?
- Do I repeat myself unnecessarily?
- How can I improve what I have written to make it even easier and even more interesting to read?

In addition, you should check whether you have made any mistakes relating to spelling, punctuation or grammar. Ask yourself:

- Have I made any spelling mistakes?
- Have I made any grammatical mistakes?
- Have I made any mistakes in punctuation?

Finally, you must check to ensure that you have not committed the offence of plagiarism, by checking that whenever you have used ideas or words that come from another person, you acknowledge their source, both by giving a citation within your essay and by giving a full reference to that source, using the conventions for citation and referencing that we outline on pages 117–151.

Part 3

Developing arguments in your writing

In Part 3 we aim to help you develop skills in persuading people through your writing. We will show you how to develop arguments aimed at persuading your readers by presenting them with reasons and evidence in support of your views. However, we also want to give you help in analysing and evaluating arguments that you come across, so that you become adept at detecting whether there is good reason to accept the conclusions in favour of which others argue. This will involve learning to distinguish between good and bad reasons, and between rational and non-rational means of persuasion.

> Learn to distinguish persuasion that takes place through the use of tricks or appeals to the emotions, from persuasion that is supported by sound evidence.
>
> We recommend that you use the latter and become good at detecting and exposing the former.

Section 3.1 is concerned in a general way with the distinction between rational persuasion, where people are persuaded to believe in something by rational argument, and non-rational persuasion where, for example, they might be persuaded by appeals to their emotion. Section 3.2 introduces and gives you practice in recognizing different forms of argument. Section 3.3 discusses the evaluation of arguments.

3.1

Influencing the beliefs of others

In this section, we will use ideas about informal reasoning deriving from the work of Stephen Toulmin (2003) that employ a few simple and easy to understand ideas to help you to take apart arguments and to construct and evaluate your own.

When we set out, develop or defend a position in our writing, we are hoping to persuade our readers to believe that what we are saying is true or at least plausible. In doing so, we make a claim or claims, which we try to defend by providing grounds for believing it.

Some terminology

Claim: What we want readers or listeners to believe.
Grounds: Statements that support our claim.
Argument: A *claim* supported by *grounds*.

It is important to distinguish between means of persuasion that respect the rationality of those we are seeking to persuade and others that do not. It is possible to give all the stylistic indications of setting out a case in a rigorous fashion, without actually doing so. For example, you might write:

'It follows from what I have just said that ...', when in fact nothing follows.

'I have argued that ...', when in fact no argument has been offered.

'I refute the suggestion that ...', when the suggestion is merely contradicted, not argued against.

'It has been shown that ...', when nothing of the kind has been done.

The use of phrases like 'It follows that ...', 'I have shown that ...' and 'I have argued that ...' will often be justified. However, the mere use of such expressions does not mean that what has been written is coherent or rigorous. In other words, saying that you have argued something or shown it, or claiming that a conclusion follows from something you have said, does not mean that you have done what you claim to have done. Often such phrases are used as mere decoration, rather than to indicate when argument is taking place.

> A well-developed style is a good thing and can help to make a passage more persuasive, but it can also cover up the lack of substance beneath the stylistic glitter.
>
> Try to avoid giving the appearance of rational argument, unless you really are offering arguments.

Rational and non-rational forms of persuasion

If I try to persuade you to believe something without attempting to give you any evidence or good reasons why you should do so, then I have employed a non-rational form of persuasion. Suppose, for example, that you very much want to become Vice-President of Ruritania, although you are endowed with only mediocre political abilities. Given your ambition, there may be independent rational reasons for running, at least from your point of view. For example, it may be that in Ruritania (and in some other countries) even a donkey would succeed in running for vice-president if he were to run for office with a popular presidential candidate. However, if I persuaded you to run for office by telling you how brilliant you are, and you accepted my flattery, then you would have been persuaded via appeals to your vanity. My *claim* that you should become Vice-President of Ruritania was based on the *ground* that you are a brilliant politician, and if you accepted you would have done so, because your vanity allowed you to be persuaded by that *ground*, and not because you had considered the evidence as to whether or not you actually are a brilliant politician.

On the other hand, I may persuade you to believe something through what appears to be a rational argument even though it is not. (It is possible that I may not realize this myself.) For example, I may say that the Welsh Nationalists are going to win the general election because a recent poll in Gwynedd has shown them to be in the lead, even though this is hardly good grounds for predicting the result at a national level – can you see why? Perhaps my enthusiasm for the cause of Welsh nationalism has led me to put this argument forward without pausing to consider the relative strength of Welsh nationalism in Gwynedd compared with the rest of Britain. Again, if I have red spots on my face, you may assure me that I have chicken pox, on the grounds that anyone who has chicken pox has red spots on their face. But though I may well have chicken pox, this argument would not show it; having red spots is *evidence* for my having chicken pox, but on its own it is not very strong evidence. On the other hand, having red spots is rather stronger evidence for my having some illness from a range of alternatives including chicken pox.

Sometimes showing someone evidence can persuade him in a rational way. For example, if a certain kind of scar is the only sign that a person has suffered a particular kind of snake-bite, and he has such a scar, it would be rational for him to be persuaded that he has been bitten by such a snake. On the other hand, we might attempt to provoke an emotional response as part of an attempt at non-rational persuasion. This might be the case both where John uses a photograph of a fetus aborted during the twenty-eighth week of pregnancy in the attempt to persuade Rachel that abortion is abhorrent, and where Rachel uses the fact that where abortion is illegal women can die at the hands of back street abortionists, in the attempt to persuade John that abortion is acceptable.

When you are writing you will rarely get a chance to show evidence directly. Instead, you will have to use statements about evidence as grounds. It is therefore important that you do your best to put the reader in a position to *verify* the truth of those statements by providing the means of accessing the evidence (see Part 2, where we discuss citation). This shows once again the importance of citing sources of information, even when those sources may in themselves contain only indirect evidence.

It is not always possible to distinguish clearly between good and bad evidence, or to distinguish between bad and good arguments (this is discussed in Section 3.2). The important point is that you should make the attempt to provide good evidence or good arguments in favour of any position you wish to defend or advocate. At times, of course, despite the honest attempt to argue or give evidence in favour of your position, you will fail, although you could not be accused of using non-rational means. For example, in the chicken pox case above, you would have presented an argument in the attempt to persuade me that I should see the doctor because of my chicken pox, even though the argument you employed is a bad one. The ground simply does not support the claim.

Illicit ways of persuading others

There are many ways of persuading people to act in the ways that we want them to act, some of which, notably torture, are obviously unacceptable in a civilized society. The expression 'We have ways of making you talk' hints at the use of physical coercion to get a person to do something against her will, which is easier than getting her to change her beliefs. For example, although by pointing a gun at a bank clerk I might be able to persuade her to open the safe, it would be much harder to persuade her to believe that it is right that I should help myself to the contents.

We will now examine a range of different ways in which beliefs may be influenced without respecting the rationality of the reader.

Indoctrination

The term 'indoctrination' refers to a family of practices that are used to induce beliefs in others. We are particularly interested in written means of persuasion that fall within this family.

Indoctrination is difficult to describe in a thoroughly convincing way. A person who is indoctrinated is taught so that her freedom to think independently about the material being taught is radically curtailed. This may arise either through the censorship of material prejudicial to the case the indoctrinator wishes to present, or by the selection only of material favourable to his own case. It is easy to see indoctrination taking place in an institutional setting such as a military staff college or labour camp, where influences that might undermine the indoctrination process can be rigorously excluded. It is important to realize that it is still possible to indoctrinate (although perhaps in a less thorough fashion) in a free and open setting through the one-sided presentation of a case and through the exclusion of prejudicial material. Indoctrinators are also very keen on non-rational forms of persuasion, as we shall see.

Practices that could be considered indoctrinatory also find their way into areas in which we might be less inclined to expect them. Consider, for example, this extract from a course booklet published in a university. Could it be indoctrinatory?

> The rise of liberal democracies: the course will show how free societies developed market-oriented parliamentary systems.

This looks innocuous, since nearly all parliamentary democracies are, in fact, also market-oriented in their economic organization. But this is not the same as saying that a liberal democracy *is* a market-oriented system, let alone that only a market-oriented society can be a free society. The authors of this booklet fail to acknowledge that their course is based on an ideological stance, describing it rather as if it rests uncontentiously on a fact about the way things are in society, and may thus be open to the charge of indoctrination. You should always take care that you are not seduced into accepting views because their proponents manage to put them forward as if they are true, without, for example, considering the reasons against (or even those in favour).

Failing to distinguish between fact and opinion

Presenting material in an indoctrinatory way is a pitfall of which teachers and writers, especially those strongly committed to particular positions, need to beware. In particular, they need to be very careful to distinguish between fact and opinion. Facts should be presented as facts, opinions as opinions. Although knowledge of particular facts can sometimes be taken for granted if a writer can safely assume that her readers share a degree of background knowledge, her own opinions should certainly not be taken for granted, but should be made plain and distinguished carefully from the factual content of what she is writing. For example, although when we were writing this in 2010, it could safely be assumed that nearly everyone in Britain over the age of 25 would know that Tony Blair was once the Prime Minister, it *could not* be assumed that everyone believed that he was incompetent in this role. Generally speaking, it should be possible to distinguish between fact and opinion by asking yourself whether or not there is evidence to substantiate a factual claim. If there is not, then the information or point of view put forward should be indicated as the view of the author, rather than something for which there is clear evidence. For example, I may state:

All the westbound number 11 buses were late at Lillie Road yesterday.

If I am able to give evidence of this by showing a log of actual times of arrival, compared with the advertised times, then even if I don't present the evidence in my text, I can put this statement forward as fact. I may wish to *cite* my evidence by giving a reference so that sceptical readers can check for them- selves. Indeed, I would be well advised to do so. In the Introduction we pointed out that in speech there is usually the opportunity to ask for clarification; this possibility does not exist when we are communicating in writing. This means that if I do not have evidence for the assertion that the number 11 bus is always late, I should not put it forward as fact, but only as my opinion, hunch or guess.

Persuading by non-rational means

We want now to discuss some dubious techniques that people often use in attempting to convince others of the rightness of their opinions. These are all techniques that we would caution against using. Convincing others by using them does not show how right you are, it simply shows how cleverly you can box with words. It is likely that after reading about these you will realize that you have been using the same or similar techniques in your writing to date. This does not necessarily mean that you have been using them deliberately because it is quite possible to be unaware of doing so. We suggest that you pay close attention to your writing and try as far as possible to avoid these techniques. We have adopted the expression 'persuader' to refer to words and phrases that illicitly persuade someone to accept a point of view, 'crafty conflation' to refer to a particular way of confusing the meanings of words, and the notion of the 'You won't believe this' challenge, from Oswald Hanfling's excellent work on the uses and abuses of argument (Hanfling, 1978).

Here are some of the main techniques to look out for:

- The use of emotive language

- The use of 'persuader' words and phrases

- The crafty conflation

- Begging the question

- The 'You won't believe this' challenge

- Rash generalization

- Assertions posing as arguments

Emotive language

Sometimes writers use emotive language to try to persuade a reader into accepting a point of view that otherwise she might reject. Emotive language may refer to the same individuals, events, things or properties of things as more neutral language. However, it differs by exciting a reaction of approval or animosity in the listener or reader through the associations that it evokes. The use of expressions such as 'rabble' for 'crowd' or 'riot' for 'demonstration' would be examples of the use of this technique, as would the use of 'workshy layabout' for 'unemployed person'. Sometimes whether language is experienced as emotive depends on the point of view of the individual using it, or reading it. Thus, for someone who is in favour of choice in the matter of abortion, the use of the word 'baby', rather than 'foetus', would be viewed as emotive, whereas for anti-abortionists, the opposite would be true. The use of emotive language is, for example, common in discussing civil disobedience, when it tends to be used to discredit those who, in good faith, may be attempting to change things by direct action, because they believe that the influence they can exert by the use of their vote is not powerful enough. Consider, for example, the way in which people who demonstrate against new roads being constructed in areas of natural beauty are often attacked by the media and politicians. Or, consider the way in which the term 'extremist' is often used by politicians in power to refer to individuals who disagree strongly with policy and official government views.

Task 36: Look out for emotive language

Look out for uses of emotive language: in the newspapers, in the electronic media, in the pub. Particularly rich sources of examples are likely to arise whenever people are campaigning for something in which they believe very strongly. Whenever you find yourself moved to support a cause or point of view by arguments that are at least partly couched in such language, we suggest that you think carefully before committing yourself. Ask yourself, 'Am I being persuaded by rational argument or by an appeal to my emotions?' And we suggest that you avoid persuasion by such means in your essays.

The use of persuaders

By persuader words and phrases, we mean words and phrases that are put into an assertion illicitly to persuade the reader to accept what is said by other than rational means. A writer may or may not be conscious that she is using 'persuaders'. Persuaders suggest that the point being made is obvious, that it needs no argument. They are used to persuade listeners and readers to accept as undeniable statements that are perhaps quite doubtful. For example:

> Surely all teachers must realize that their job is one of the most important in the country.

> We have to remember that Russia is just waiting for an opportunity to expand into Western Europe and so we have to install an anti-missile capability.

> Only a fool could fail to see that George W. Bush was the best President the USA ever had.

> It is clear to anyone with any sense that the UK has never had such a lying and shifty Prime Minister as Tony Blair.

> It has to be admitted that whatever the risks that nuclear weapons bring, without them we would not have had peace for over sixty years.

> We can't go on using up the earth's resources at this rate and expect mankind to survive as a civilized species beyond the twenty-second century; this is obvious.

What persuaders are used in these examples? Here are the ones we can find: 'This is obvious'; 'It is clear that'; 'We have to remember'; 'It has to be admitted that'; 'Only a fool could fail to see'; 'Surely'.

Task 37: Persuader words and phrases

Write a list of persuader words and phrases with some examples of their use. Having done so, look out for them in the books and articles you read and try to avoid using them when you write.

[Our response appears on page 254]

When someone consciously uses words or phrases as 'persuaders' she is trying to trick others into accepting unsupported assertions. By asserting that 'plainly' or 'obviously' or 'clearly' or 'undeniably' something is the case, she is trying to make the listener or reader agree. If it is *plainly* or *obviously* or *clearly* or *undeniably* so, then the listener or reader would have to be rather foolish not to see it; and who wants to admit to himself that he is foolish?

It is important to note that not all uses of words or phrases that might in certain contexts be seen as 'persuaders' are necessarily devious; in other words, the context in which a word or phrase is used is important in determining whether or not it is being used as a persuader. For example, we could say 'All students at King's College are expected to attend lectures. This is undeniable.' Are we using a persuader here?

Many phrases that can be used as 'persuaders' are acceptable if they are supported by argument or evidence. The statement 'Members of the caring professions face moral decisions every day. This is undeniably true', for example, could be used in connection with firm evidence that members of professions such as social work and nursing do face moral decisions daily. In this case, the phrase 'this is undeniably true' would not be serving as a persuader but rather as a mark of emphasis.

Let us make one last point about a very common species of persuader, in which appeals are made to science. It is worthwhile looking out for statements such as: 'Modern science has shown ...' or 'According to physics ...'. Such appeals are often accompanied by references to famous scientific personalities. The idea is that science, which is supposed to be objective (and hence fair, honest and reliable), is the best arbiter of any claim to human knowledge. But apart from the fact that this isn't true, as anyone who has studied science at a reasonable level will know (did you spot the persuader in that comment?), unless appeals to science are backed up by a detailed account of the way in which the conclusion was reached, they are no more reliable than any other kind of appeal. Referring to science as a source of truth in a general and unsupported way is an example of an appeal to authority, and in this case it is not a justified one. You should note, however, that some appeals to authority are unavoidable and justified; we look at such cases in 3.2.

Crafty conflation

Crafty conflation involves running together or conflating a number of ideas, which, in spite of their similarities and connections are actually distinct, and often mean very different things.

For instance, in writing an essay a student may wish to assert that something (call it A) is the case, but have some doubt about whether he can simply assert it. If he can't really find a way of arguing for it he may craftily conflate A with B, because he knows that it would be safe to assert B, by writing 'A, in other words B', thus implying that A and B are the same thing.

> When someone uses crafty conflation, she slides from one word or phrase to another, as if the two phrases were one and the same. Crafty conflation can take a number of forms including:
>
> - A, in other words B.
> - A, that is to say, B.
> - A or B.
>
> Or even simply
>
> - A, B.

Here are some examples of crafty conflation:

Our aim is to secure equal opportunities for ethnic minorities, in other words, an anti-racist policy.

The best President this country has ever had, that is to say, George W. Bush.

Ladies and gentlemen, I give you the greatest rock and roll band in the world: the Rolling Stones.

Totalitarian Communist regimes collapsed like ninepins all over Eastern Europe; socialism could no longer claim any validity as a form of political organization.

Task 38: Can you spot the crafty conflation?

Here is an example from the famous eighteenth-century economist, Adam Smith. Can you spot an example of crafty conflation here?

It is not from the benevolence of the butcher, the brewer, or the baker that we expect our dinner, but from their regard to their own self-interest.

We address ourselves, not to their humanity, but to their self-love, and never talk to them of our own necessities but of their advantages.
Adam Smith ([1776] 1981, pp. 226–227)

[Our response appears on page 255]

Task 39: Write some examples of crafty conflation

Try writing some examples of crafty conflation; and try to spot occasions when people you are speaking to, or authors you read, use this method of illicit persuasion.

Begging the question

By 'begging the question' we mean one of two things. Strictly speaking, to 'beg the question' is to offer an argument in which the claim to be argued for is already stated. The phrase is also used more generally to apply to cases where something questionable is taken for granted. Crafty conflations are one way of begging the question, because they take it for granted that assertions mean much the same, even though this is questionable.

One indication that someone might be begging the question comes when he uses words and phrases like 'remember', 'point out', 'see' and 'remind'. If we remind someone of something, point it out to her, or ask her whether she remembers it, we take it for granted that what we remind her about, point out to her, or enquire whether she remembers, really is as we say it is. For example,

Someone might say, 'You'll remember that water is lighter than air'. There is a presupposition here not only that water is lighter than air but also that you know that it is (of course both of these presuppositions are actually false). You can't legitimately be asked whether you remember that something is the case unless it actually is the case.

Another person might say, 'I pointed out to him that there were more road deaths in 2008 than there had been in 2005'. She might be justified in pointing this out because, as a matter of fact, there were more road deaths in 2008 than there had been in 2005. However, it would be possible for her to talk of 'pointing it out' even though this was untrue. To use the form of words that she has used presupposes that there really were more deaths in 2008 than in 2005.

Here is an example that teachers often use: 'Why did you talk just now, Smith?' This presupposes that Smith actually did talk just now. This is like the classic, 'Are you still beating your wife?'

If someone asks you whether or not you saw a man with a bag marked 'swag' running from the bank, this presupposes that there really was a man with a bag marked 'swag' running from the bank for you to see. Something similar is true with the word 'know'. For example, a friend could ask 'Did you know that the President was attending the same psychiatric clinic as the Prime Minister?', which presupposes that both people are receiving psychiatric care. And a committed vegetarian might ask, as you are eating your T-bone steak, 'You are aware, aren't you, that people who eat meat are five times more likely to die of heart disease than vegetarians?'

It is important, when you are writing, to avoid begging the question. It is equally important, when you are reading or listening to others speaking, to notice when they are begging the question.

Task 40: Look out for question begging

Try to spot examples of question begging that you come across in your reading on radio and television, and in the conversations you have. Speeches by politicians (when they make sense) are a particularly rich source of examples of question begging.

The 'You won't believe this' challenge

The 'You won't believe this' challenge relies upon the tendency of people to believe an incredible story more readily than one that is merely unlikely (Hanfling, 1978). The challenge may be put in several ways: 'You are never going to believe this ...'; 'Of course most people find it hard to accept that ...'; 'I know that your intuitive reaction will be to reject what I have to say ...', and so on.

When someone uses such phrases she is often asking you either to accept her assertions or to admit to being a narrow-minded person who cannot face facts, or who cannot rise above intuition to see the truth of what she is saying. Such a person, it is implied, so lacks imagination that he is not prepared to believe new ideas just because they are, well, unbelievable.

Of course the fact that someone uses a form of words that approximates to the 'You won't believe this' challenge does not necessarily mean that we should reject what she says. Many facts now taken for granted have seemed unbelievable to people in the past. Just be alert when this form of words is used.

Task 41: You won't believe this

Try out the 'You won't believe this' challenge on a few of your friends. How outrageous a point of view or alleged fact can you get them to accept? Try to avoid the challenge in your written work.

Rash generalization and universal statements

Sometimes writers use bold statements that are quite unwarranted, such as 'Everyone knows that ...', 'It is commonly believed that ...', or 'Many people would argue that ...'. The use of generalizations of this kind can be rather rash and when used by a student may result in marks in the margin of an essay such as these: 'Actually, I don't know this; in fact, I don't even believe it!'; 'I don't know anyone who believes this', or 'Who would argue it?'

Rash generalizations are often unsupported by facts, although they appear to be factual claims. It is better to make a less bold statement or at least to give some evidence for your generalizations. For example, if you do want to claim that many people would argue something, you should give references to some who do.

Not all generalizations are rash. A generalization can be supported by good evidence or it can be a restatement of what is already claimed by a number of statements about individuals. For example, if I know that it is true of each parliamentary seat in Scotland that the Tories do not hold it, I can assert 'There are no Tory MPs in Scotland' without being rash.

Assertions posing as arguments

Sometimes writers make a series of assertions which they surround with verbal devices that suggest they are supported by arguments. For example, they might write, 'I will argue that ...' or 'I will employ an argument for the belief that ...', or claim to have used arguments when in fact no argument is offered. In Part 2 we warned against claiming to offer an argument when you do not. Remember that there is a difference between arguing for a point of view and asserting it; you should be clear about when you are simply stating an opinion or belief and when you are arguing in its support or offering evidence in its favour. In the next section, when we come to discuss the nature of argument, we will go into more detail about the distinction between argument and assertion. For the moment, we would like to invite you to reflect on the need to find support for views or ideas that you would like to persuade others to believe.

Task 42: What could be used to support these statements?

Imagine that you have been asked to argue in favour of one of the following four claims in a debate.

Claim 1: Euthanasia should be legalized.

Claim 2: Along with problems around the commodification of sex, human trafficking is probably the most significant moral problem in the world today.

Claim 3: The world is a more dangerous place now than it was before 9/11.

Claim 4: There is no ethical reason why newly born infants should not be allowed to die or even killed, if they have serious defects at birth.

To help you decide which claim to choose, we have provided below some possible supporting statements that might help you. Decide which of the four claims you would want to defend, by deciding how helpful each of these statements is and why.

Claim 1: Euthanasia should be legalized

Additional statements

i. No-one has the right to tell another person that they must live even when life is intolerable for them.

ii. If a dog or a horse was suffering terribly, we would not think badly of someone who put it out of its misery.

iii. Everyone should have the right to decide the course of their own life and to decide the time of their own death.

iv. More than half of all doctors who responded to an anonymous questionnaire admitted to having knowingly acted in ways that 'hastened a patient's death' on more than one occasion during their professional life.

v. Euthanasia, which literally means 'a good death', has nothing whatsoever to do with the so-called 'euthanasia programme' by which the Nazis set out to eliminate those that they referred to as *Lebsensunwerten* or 'unworthy of life'.

Claim 2: Along with problems around the commodification of sex, human trafficking is probably the most significant moral problem in the world today

Additional statements

i. Each year, an estimated 600,000 to 800,000 men, women and children are trafficked across international borders (some international and non-governmental organizations place the number far higher), and the trade is growing.

ii. The UN describes trafficking as a form of 'slavery'. It knows of victims from 127 countries and of their exploitation in 137.

iii. In the UK, the gangs behind the trade in human beings buy and sell women for between £2000 and £8000. Some have been forced to work 16 hours and have sex with 30 men a day.

iv. No country is immune from human trafficking. Victims are forced into prostitution or to work in quarries and sweatshops, on farms, as domestics, as child soldiers, and in many forms of involuntary servitude.

v. An estimated 17,500 foreign nationals are trafficked annually in the United States alone. The number of US citizens trafficked within the country is even higher, with an estimated 200,000+ American children at high risk for trafficking into the sex industry each year.

Claim 3: The world is a more dangerous place now than it was before 9/11

Additional statements

i. More people died in the 9/11 attacks than died in any other terrorist attack in the US.

ii. The attacks of 9/11 had a huge impact on the America psyche, probably because citizens of the US are not used to their enemies attacking them 'in their own back yard'.

iii. The explosion of the plane as it hit the second World Trade Center Tower, shocked those who watched it to the core.

iv. Research carried out by the social scientists in the Department of Peace Studies at the University of Beeston shows that 70 per cent of all adults in the UK are more conscious of the potential dangers of international travel than they were before 9/11 and 7/7.

v. Since 9/11 there have been more security alarms in international airports than there were in the whole of aviation history before that time.

Claim 4: There is no ethical reason why newly born infants should not be allowed to die or even killed, if they have serious defects at birth

Additional statements

i. Many babies that survive in the rich world would not survive if they had been born to mothers in poorer countries.

ii. Kuhse and Singer (1985) point out that throughout history disabled neonates have been allowed to die in many parts of the world.

iii. Scientists are quite clear in their prediction that if the population of the world continues to increase at the rate it has been increasing in the last hundred years, the human race will not survive beyond the twenty-second century.

iv. Many severely disabled babies that now survive through pregnancy and birth would have miscarried had they been conceived fifty years ago.

v. Since they have not yet developed any of the characteristics by which we define persons, including self consciousness, language and the ability to remember and form hopes and expectations about the future, newly born babies are not yet people, but only potential people.

[Our response appears on page 255]

Task 43: What is being argued for? How? How successfully?

Try rewriting these arguments, so that it is clearer what the person presenting them wants to argue for. Decide whether you think the argument in each case is convincing, and how you could make it stronger.

i.   People who wear leather shoes, or who drink milk and eat dairy produce, can't really justify their vegetarian beliefs on the grounds that eating animals is wrong because it involves cruelty. After all, we get leather by killing animals and the dairy industry involves terrible cruelty to both cows and calves, which get separated from their mothers just because we want to use their milk.

ii. It's almost certain that Smith was the murderer, because nobody else could have got access to the victim and what's more his fingerprints were found all over the murder weapon.

iii. Cannabis should be legalized because it isn't any more harmful than, for example, alcohol or tobacco, both of which are legal. Since laws that ban things are usually intended to protect us from harm, there shouldn't be a law against the use of cannabis, unless there is also a law against alcohol and tobacco.

iv. It always annoys me when I hear people being praised for being brainy, even when it is true. Working hard and studying, maybe, but not just being brainy. I don't think it's right to praise people for their intelligence. After all, we'd think it was wrong if we heard someone being praised for being six foot tall or having brown eyes, because eye colour and height are natural characteristics, rather than something over which we have any control.

v.   Breast feeding is best, even in developing countries where HIV/AIDS is a major problem, because it helps to protect babies from many early childhood diseases, from which they are more likely to die in the short term.

[Our response appears on page 257]

3.2

Arguments of a different kind

We are all familiar with arguments in the sense of people airing their differences of opinion. They are most likely to do so through face-to-face disagreement. Arguments in this sense can range from a civilized exchange of views through heated discussion to bad-tempered shouting that stops just short of fighting. Typically, an argument in this common sense of the word involves the conflict of opposing points of view.

There is another sense of argument in which an individual will attempt to persuade others of their own point of view by making a claim and giving grounds for that claim. When a ground is given for a claim, we have the basis for an argument in its favour. We will restrict our use of the term 'argument' to refer to the giving of grounds for claims. When we wish to refer to arguments in the more common sense of the word, we will use the expression 'disagreement'.

In this section, we will begin by discussing the difference between argument and assertion. Then we will say a little about the nature of argument in general and about some common types of argument. Finally, we will discuss arguments from authority.

Arguments and claims or assertions

There is a distinction between arguing for a point of view and merely asserting it. Imagine that you believe that something is true and further that you want to persuade someone else to believe that it is true. Say, for example, that you believe Bruce Springsteen is a brilliant guitarist and that you wish to persuade someone of this. How might you go about it?

Claiming that Springsteen is a brilliant guitarist would involve merely stating something of this kind:

Bruce Springsteen is a brilliant guitarist!

This may persuade some people to believe that Springsteen is a brilliant guitarist but note that in making it you have not offered any grounds why they should. If, in addition to making the claim, you were to offer grounds, then you would be offering an argument. For example, you might say:

Bruce Springsteen is a brilliant guitarist because he plays very fast and my friend who plays in a band says so and he's a great guitarist.

This is an argument in favour of the claim that Springsteen is a brilliant guitarist. Note, however, that by its being an argument does not mean that it is any good. (What do you think would make it a good argument?) Note also that the fact that it is not a good argument, does not, in itself, mean that the statement is untrue; it simply means that it does not offer very strong support for it.

Later we will discuss the question of what makes the difference between good and bad arguments. For the moment, it is important to distinguish clearly between argument and assertion. In arguing a case we offer grounds, which are often called 'reasons' for the point we are making. In claiming or asserting something, on the other hand, we offer no grounds or reasons, we simply say that such and such is the case.

It is usually not enough simply to claim something to be the case. Of course, in arguing for a point of view, we will invite others to accept some claims that we make and on the basis of these we will build up our argument. So we're not saying that you should never make claims, only that claiming on its own is rarely good enough. In general, offering arguments is superior to simply making claims.

If you claim something I might say, 'Well, very interesting, but why should I believe that?' Unless what you claim is so reasonable that anyone who knows what you are talking about would accept it (and of course many claims are of this kind), if you don't go on to give me grounds, I may very well reject it. Arguments have a structure that allows us to see how the claim is backed up by grounds. The claim is sometimes called the *conclusion* and the grounds on which it is based are known as *premises*. In offering an argument, you are giving me reasons for believing something, provided that the premises are true.

| Initial grounds for a claim | Often called 'premises' |
| Claim | Often called 'conclusion', especially when it comes after 'Therefore', 'So', 'It follows that ...' |

There is a very well known argument which goes:

Socrates is a man

Therefore: Socrates is mortal

In this argument, the first line is the ground and the part of the second line that comes after 'Therefore', and follows from the ground, is the claim.

Although it is possible to set out arguments so that the relationship between claims and grounds is made clear, when arguments develop in the course of a disagreement, this relationship is often much less obvious. There are a number of reasons for this that are worth looking at before we consider the setting out of arguments on the printed page.

In a disagreement, the claim a person is attempting to defend is usually set forth first and, as it is challenged, grounds are given to back it up. At the same time, the other party or parties are trying to defend their own point of view, which is usually opposed to that of the first party. So very often there are at least two arguments developing within a disagreement. Disagreements usually develop on an unplanned basis, and so the arguments they express develop haphazardly. This dynamic and changing quality of arguments within spoken disagreements is not always so clear on the printed page, but it is useful for you to think of arguments as the to-ing and fro-ing of a disagreement so that you can keep in mind what objections there might be to a claim and how you might deal with them.

Finally, an argument developed in the course of a disagreement very often contains gaps that may be picked up on during the course of the disagreement. Consider, for example, the following argument:

G.F. is a Scottish philosopher

Therefore: G.F. is handsome

Considering this argument, someone may say, 'Just because G.F. is a Scottish philosopher doesn't mean that he is handsome'. On the face of it, this appears to be a fair point, so how might the person making the claim that G.F. is handsome respond? Well, he might add to what he has already said, the statement that 'Scottish philosophers are handsome', thus offering a way of getting from the ground that G.F. is a Scottish philosopher to the claim that G.F. is handsome. We must assume that in his initial argument he didn't state this link, because he hoped that the person he was arguing with would take it for granted, because he assumed that everyone is aware that Scottish philosophers are handsome. Adding this link to the original argument produces the following:

G.F. is a Scottish philosopher

Scottish philosophers are handsome

Therefore: G.F. is handsome

Adding in this link, which was unstated in the original argument, makes it much more convincing. A link of this kind that gets you from ground to claim is sometimes called a 'warrant'.

Ground	Statements that support our claim
Warrant	The link that gets the argument from ground to claim
Claim	What we want readers or listeners to believe

If the warrant is that Scottish philosophers are handsome, that statement, once it is made, is likely to be challenged. Possible responses include: 'How do you know?', 'All the ones I know are ugly' and 'I met a very plain one yesterday'. If this happened, the person making the claim that G.F. is handsome could clarify the warrant by saying, 'All Scottish philosophers are handsome'. The trouble is that he is unlikely to be able to produce evidence for this and therefore no-one will believe him. The only evidence that would help would be that all Scottish philosophers had been observed and that they had all been found to be handsome. That would be a tough call. Even the warrant 'Nearly all Scottish philosophers are handsome' is likely to be greeted with disbelief. However, if we were to suspend disbelief and admit that there was evidence for the warrant 'Nearly all Scottish philosophers are handsome', then the argument might be acceptable, because the ground would appear to support the claim.

Let's return to the argument about Socrates that we considered above:

Socrates is a man

Therefore: Socrates is mortal

In this case, although the warrant 'All men are mortal' is not stated, it does not matter, because everyone understands and is aware that all men are mortal. So there is no need to state it. Of course, if someone were to challenge that warrant, we could point out that a very large number of men had been observed, over a very extensive period and that all had eventually been found to die and that there was compelling biological evidence that this would continue to be the case. We tend to think that the 'all' in 'All men are mortal' really does refer to every single human being who has lived, is living and will ever live, because the evidence seems to point overwhelmingly in that direction.

Deductive arguments

Sometimes, as we have seen in the case of the argument about Socrates' mortality, it is possible for the warrant in an argument to be implicit or unstated, because it is so obvious that it does not need to be said. However, it will more often be necessary to spell your arguments out more fully, stating the warrant explicitly so that it becomes another ground for your claim. Sometimes, when you do so, the argument becomes almost impossible not to accept, because the warrant, when stated, is obviously acceptable. You can then say that because the argument is a good one (the grounds support the claim) and the grounds are true, then the claim is *proved*.

Sometimes people say, 'Suppose, for the sake of the argument ...', and then ask you to consider whether you would accept the claim if you accepted that the grounds were true.

Consider the argument:

David White is a Manchester policeman (ground)

Therefore: David White is a racist (claim)

Most people would say that the ground that David White is a Manchester policeman does not support the claim that David White is a racist, because the warrant, that all Manchester policemen are racists, would not be believed. However, someone who believed that it is true that David White is a racist, because he is a Manchester policeman, could elaborate the argument further:

All Manchester policemen are racists (ground 1)

David White is a Manchester policeman (ground 2)

Therefore: David White is a racist (claim)

If grounds 1 and 2 are true, then the claim that David White is a racist *must* be true. You can't agree that the grounds are true and deny the conclusion.

Such arguments, where *if* you accept the truth of the grounds then you *must* accept the truth of the claim, are known as deductive arguments. When you can't deny the claim if the grounds are true, you have a *valid* deductive argument.

It is customary for logicians to include the warrant 'All As are Bs' as one of the premises or grounds, thus making the argument more explicit than it normally would be, by turning the warrant into a ground. So the pattern of the form then is:

All As are Bs (ground 1)

X is an A (ground 2)

Therefore: X is a B (claim)

Not all deductive arguments are valid. Some are invalid. In an *invalid* argument the claim does not follow from the grounds, even if the grounds are true. Invalid arguments can lead from true grounds to false claims. Suppose that it is true that if you have chicken pox you are covered in red spots, and further suppose that Martin is covered in red spots. Someone may be tempted to argue:

If you have chicken pox you are covered in red spots (ground)

Martin is covered in red spots (ground)

Therefore: Martin has chicken pox (claim)

This argument is invalid. Even if the grounds are true the conclusion may be false because the form of the argument is invalid; valid and invalid forms of argument are discussed below. Martin may have red spots but be suffering from measles. Even the fact that Martin had chicken pox would not mean that this argument was valid, because the claim does not follow from the grounds. You can show this by giving an example of an argument like it where the grounds are true but the claim is false, for example, by supposing that Martin has the measles or heat rash.

Examples

Here are two more examples of invalid arguments. Think a little about why they are invalid, before looking at the discussion that follows.

All whales are mammals (ground 1)

Some mammals are seagoing (ground 2)

Therefore: All whales are seagoing (claim)

All shopkeepers eat sweets (ground 1)

Some sweets are harmful to the teeth (ground 2)

Therefore: All shopkeepers eat sweets that are harmful to the teeth (claim)

The first of these arguments leads from two true grounds to a true claim (all whales are seagoing!). In spite of this, the claim does not follow from the grounds, because it refers only to 'some mammals'. This is obvious if we re-cast it as:

Some mammals are seagoing (ground)

Therefore: All whales are seagoing (claim)

The second of these arguments goes from one false ground (not all shop-keepers eat sweets!) and one true ground (some sweets are harmful to the teeth) to a false claim that does not follow from the grounds. Consider, however, the argument:

Some sweets are harmful to the teeth (ground)

Therefore: All shopkeepers eat sweets that are harmful to the teeth (claim)

for which the warrant is:

All shopkeepers eat sweets

The inadequacy of this argument is obvious, as not only is the warrant invalid (it is not true that all shopkeepers eat sweets), but it is irrelevant, since the warrant says nothing about sweets that are harmful to the teeth.

Another, more formal way of assessing these arguments is to reinstate the warrant as a premise or ground and to do the following. In the first argument, try substituting 'voles' for 'whales'. You will then have an argu-ment of the same form that leads from true grounds to a false claim. You will also be able to see much more clearly that the claim does not follow from the grounds.

To see that the second argument is invalid, try substituting 'orchestral players play' for 'shopkeepers eat', 'musical instruments' for 'sweets', and 'trumpets' for 'harmful to the teeth'. You will then have an argument that is the same in form as the shopkeepers' example, but which leads from true grounds to false claims.

Remember that the validity of an argument has nothing to do with whether its grounds are true. Both valid and invalid arguments can lead from true grounds to true claims, from false grounds to true claims, and from false grounds to false claims. However, valid arguments, unlike invalid arguments, never lead from true grounds to false claims. Logicians would say that a valid argument with true premises is said to prove its conclusion. In other words, a valid argument *proves* the claims its author makes by stating true grounds for those claims.

Deductive arguments are said to be valid or invalid in virtue of their form, rather than the truth or falsity of their grounds. Whether or not a particular argument is valid or invalid depends on whether or not its form is valid or invalid. The idea of the form of an argument will become clearer with some more examples.

So far we have been discussing relatively short and simple arguments. Sometimes, however, arguments are more complex. At times an argument is made up of several smaller arguments, the claims of which then serve as grounds in the next step in the larger argument; these are known as 'intermediate steps' in the larger argument. Very often they are not stated in the course of a disagreement or a discussion because it is assumed, rightly or wrongly, that the other person grasps the moves implicitly. In a disagreement it is possible for a listener to interrupt and ask for amplification of a particular argument and thus have intermediate steps spelled out. Intermediate steps are often left out of written arguments also. The difference in a written argument is, of course, that there is no direct opportunity to ask for amplification.

Intermediate steps

To show how intermediate steps may be spelled out as the discussion proceeds, consider the development of an argument as it might grow in the course of a conversation. We may argue:

John is a Falkland Islander (ground)

Therefore: John does not need a visa to visit Britain (claim)

Here we have connected a ground to a claim and produced the basis of an argument. This may be enough for someone well acquainted with the status of the Falkland Islands. However, someone who is not may ask for clarification. She may not be able to see how this claim is supported by this simple ground. We need to supply the *warrant* for getting from the ground to the claim. It could be:

All Falkland Islanders are British citizens (warrant)

For most people this would be enough to allow them to see how the claim follows from the ground. However, it may still not be enough for our listener, so we may add by way of further elucidation:

No British citizen needs a visa to visit Britain (ground)

This would be a further ground for the original claim. Is the argument satisfactory now with the additional ground and the warrant spelled out? Most people would say 'yes', but it would still be possible to point out that the argument is not complete, not through lack of grounds and a warrant, but because, given these three, the conclusion still does not follow from them. We need a warrant for the step that takes us from the ground that

John is a British citizen

to the claim that

John does not need a visa to visit Britain

This warrant is:

No British citizen needs a visa to visit Britain.

The complete argument now looks like this:

John is a Falkland Islander (ground)

All Falkland Islanders are British citizens (warrant)

Therefore: John is a British citizen (claim)

No British citizen needs a visa to visit Britain (warrant)

Therefore: John does not need a visa to visit Britain (claim)

As we said before, you do not usually need to spell out the warrant for an argument. In this example, if you are arguing in the context of a course on British citizenship, it may be enough to move from the ground

John is a British citizen

to the claim that

John does not need a visa to visit Britain

because everyone involved with the course takes it for granted that you do not need a visa to visit Britain if you are a British citizen.
  Is the complete argument above a deductive argument? *Answer*: Only if

All Falkland Islanders are British citizens

is taken to mean that *by definition* everyone who is a Falkland Islander is a British citizen, *and*

No British citizen needs a visa to visit Britain

is also true by definition. There is no reason why there may not be exceptions, for example, because someone from Argentina swam ashore and became a Falkland Islander. The point is that 'all' may stand for literally everyone or everything for a formal logician, but in everyday usage it can be taken to mean 'nearly all'. Therefore, we should be wary of classifying this as a deductive argument unless there are good grounds for doing so, like making Falkland Islanders British by definition.

Backing statements

There is one further point about warrants worth making. In the example above, in a course on British citizenship, where both lecturers and students share background knowledge about the rights of British citizens, the warrant won't be questioned. But someone who does not share such background knowledge may enquire, 'Why don't British citizens need visas to enter Britain?' In doing so, they are questioning whether or not the warrant really works in this argument. In such cases, one is being challenged to justify the warrant:

No British citizen needs a visa to visit Britain

A reason for accepting this warrant is required, such as:

By Act of Parliament no British Citizen needs a visa to visit Britain

Resting on evidence of the relevant law passed by Parliament, this would be a *backing statement* used to justify the use of the warrant to get to the claim that John does not need a visa to visit Britain from the ground that he is a British citizen.

So a pattern that you might find in a discussion is that someone makes a claim and is asked for the ground for the claim. They supply it and then the warrant is asked for. This should settle the matter, but the other person in the argument might question the warrant and ask why the maker of the claim feels justified in its use. At this point, it would be appropriate to bring in the backing statement. This pattern often occurs in spoken arguments but it is useful to bear in mind when you are constructing your own arguments. You can imagine someone 'in your head' who is debating with you:

'What is the ground for your claim?' he asks

Then

'What is the warrant for getting from ground to claim?'

And then:

'How can you justify using that warrant?'

Going through these steps as you are constructing an argument is a very useful way of checking that you are, in fact, putting together good arguments.

Ground	Statements that support our claim
Warrant	The link that gets the argument from ground to claim
Claim	What we want readers or listeners to believe
Backing statement	The statement of evidence for accepting the warrant

---

Task 44: Is Darren a beast? (With apologies to all Darrens, wherever they are)

Consider the following argument:

Darren is a man
Therefore: Darren is a beast

(a) Write down what you take to be the claim of the argument.

(b) Write down what you take to be the ground for the claim.

(c) Write down what you think the warrant is.

(d) Does the argument prove the conclusion?

(e) Can you think of a backing statement for the warrant?

[Our response appears on page 258]

Task 45: George, the Scottish millionaire

Consider the following argument:

George has lots of money (ground)
Therefore: George is a Scottish millionaire (claim)

(a) What warrant is this argument relying on?

(b) Does the warrant actually work in getting from the ground to the claim?

(c) If it doesn't, why is this?

[Our response appears on page 259]

You should not get hung up worrying about whether an argument that you encounter is deductive or not. Most of the deductive arguments that you are likely to come across will be in logic books and if you don't read logic books you won't come across too many of them. However, they do turn up in real life, as we shall see in 3.3, so you need to be aware of them.

Logic encourages us to look for similarities in arguments, and logic textbooks deal largely with argument structures rather than with particular arguments. Seeing similarities in arguments can be very useful when we are assessing whether or not they are good arguments. Logic books don't talk about warrants, they invariably put the warrant into the argument as a ground or premise. There's nothing wrong with doing this if you want to make a formal study of deductive arguments. In logic books, as we have noted, the warrant is the form under which the argument is offered, rather than any particular statement. So,

All As are B

Darren is an A

Therefore: Darren is a B

would be the warrant for the Darren argument if it is set out as a deductive argument with the warrant turned into one of the grounds. However, in everyday conversation and in most academic texts, that is not the practice followed and you should not try and judge your arguments and those that you read as if they were always deductive arguments. The key issues are:

- Does the warrant allow you to get from the grounds to the claim?

- Are the grounds true?

Seeing similarities among arguments

Recognizing that arguments have the same form requires practice. There are a number of very common forms that it is possible to learn to recognize; doing so would help you to understand better what is involved in setting out arguments. Those who wish to go deeper into examples of valid and invalid forms in deductive arguments should look at Salmon (1984, Chapter 2).

Look again at the argument about Darren:

All men are beasts (warrant)

Darren is a man (ground)

Therefore: Darren is a beast (claim)

Is the following argument of the same form?

All Northamptonians are friendly (warrant)

Rosina is a Northamptonian (ground)

Therefore: Rosina is friendly (claim)

If we spell out the warrant for this argument we can see that it shares the *same form* as that about Darren. We can see that they have this common form by removing what is particular to them and leaving what is common. Thus, in the warrant of the Darren argument we will remove 'men' and 'beasts'; in the ground we will remove 'Darren' and 'man'; and in the claim we will remove 'Darren' and 'beast'. Replacing these words with the letters A, B and C we get:

All As are B

C is an A

Therefore: C is a B

Task 46

(a) Try substituting A, B and C for what is particular in the Rosina example to satisfy yourself that it has the same form as the Darren example.

(b) If you accept the warrant and the ground is true, does the ground support the claim?

(c) What would make the Rosina argument a deductive one? Try working out whether the ground could be true and the claim false if the warranted is accepted.

[Our response appears on page 259]

The following are some of the argument forms that you are likely to come across in the course of your reading. You will probably find yourself using these as well.

Examples

not B (ground); If A then B (warrant); therefore not A (claim)

Example: You haven't got a high temperature (ground)

　　　　　If you have flu, you have a high temperature (warrant)

　　　　　Therefore: You haven't got flu (claim)

Do the grounds support the claim? Try using the method of finding a true ground and warrant and a false conclusion, as in the exercise above about Scotsmen and millionaires.

A (ground); If A then B (warrant); therefore B (claim)

Example: If you are a millionaire you have lots of money

You are a millionaire

Therefore: You have lots of money

If A then B (ground); if B then C (warrant); therefore if A then C (claim)

Example: If you have flu you have a high temperature

If you have a high temperature you feel unwell

Therefore: If you have flu you feel unwell

In this example, you could say that 'if you have flu you feel unwell' is the claim; 'if you have flu you have a high temperature' is the ground for the claim and 'if you have a high temperature you feel unwell' is the warrant that takes you from claim to ground.

All As are B; some Cs are not B; therefore some Cs are not As

Example: Some mountains are not climbable (ground)

Therefore: Some mountains are not hills (claim)

What seems to be the warrant for this argument? Does it actually support the move from ground to claim? *Answer*: The warrant seems to be

All hills are climbable

However, although an acceptable warrant, it does not seem to be particularly relevant to getting from the ground to the claim.

Inductive arguments

Even more important than deductive arguments are *inductive* arguments. Rather than having the properties of validity and invalidity, like deductive arguments, inductive arguments are either *sound* or *unsound*. Given that the grounds presented are true, sound arguments give you good reasons for believing the claims they make, while unsound arguments do not. Consider the following example:

Roberta is a traveller

Nearly all travellers will reach their destination safely

Therefore, probably: Roberta will reach her destination safely

The fact that this is an inductive argument is signalled by the use of 'probably' after 'therefore', showing that the claim that Roberta will reach her destination should not be taken to be certain. The warrant presented – about nearly all travellers reaching their destination safely – gives us good reason for accepting the conclusion.

However, in inductive arguments even though the grounds support a claim to some extent, and we are justified in *believing* that claim if the ground presented is true and we accept the warrant, the claim may actually be false. With induction, in other words, even though the argument is sound, the grounds true and the warrant perfectly acceptable, the claim may be false, meaning that what the conclusion states is simply not the case.

As we have seen, sometimes the claim of an inductive argument is prefaced with 'probably'. This indicates that we are advancing the claim with a certain degree of caution. The term 'probably' is not part of the argument, but is an explicit indication that the argument being used is an inductive rather than a deductive one. The use of 'probably' shows that the person who is presenting the argument is signalling to the listener or reader that he intends the argument to be taken as an inductive one, rather than leaving its interpretation to intuition or experience.

In inductive arguments the grounds advanced may support the claim made to different degrees. For example, if the warrant for the above argument was changed to

Most travellers reach their destination safely

we would be inclined to say that the claim is now supported a little less strongly. This is because 'most' means any quantity greater than half of the total, whereas 'nearly all' suggests a much larger proportion. The *content* (what it actually states rather than its form) of an inductive argument is, therefore, important. The content of the grounds and the warrant affects the soundness of the argument.

Sometimes the warrant in an inductive argument is spelled out as one of the grounds, especially when it has a precise numerical value. For example, if the ground:

99.9 per cent of travellers reach their destination safely

was substituted for the first ground in the Roberta argument, it would make the argument more sound than substituting

80 per cent of travellers reach their destination safely

Those readers who have studied or are studying the social sciences will already have realized that many arguments in subjects like sociology and politics are inductive. In induction, the number and content of the grounds influence the degree of soundness or unsoundness we are prepared to allow it. For example, most people would not be prepared to accept the following as a sound inductive argument:

0.01 per cent of the electorate were asked how they would vote if there were a general election held tomorrow

90 per cent of those asked said they would vote Conservative

Therefore: The Conservatives would win an election if it were held tomorrow.

In formal inductive reasoning, the warrant is very often spelled out as a further ground and the warrant for the whole argument becomes the form under which the argument is offered. However, whether the warrant is accepted or the form of the argument is accepted as a good one, will depend on the subject matter. This is not the case with deductive arguments.

Task 47: Why unsound rather than sound?

Can you work out why most social scientists would reject as unsound the above argument for the conclusion that the Conservatives would win a general election if it was held tomorrow?

[Our response appears on page 260]

Arguments from authority

None of us is an expert in every subject. Even in those subjects where we can lay claim to some knowledge, we are not infallible. However, because of this very situation we are obliged, if we wish to gain reliable information about subjects about which we know little or nothing, to consult *experts* or *authorities*. If someone states that such and such is the case, for example, if they were to assert that 'It will rain in Perth tomorrow', we would not normally accept that it will rain merely on that person's say so unless she is a recognized authority on the area in question, in this case, the weather. The reason for this lies in the distinction between *argument* and *assertion*, which was discussed at the beginning of Part 3. To use symbolism similar to that used earlier when showing the form of certain particular deductive arguments: if Peter says that p (where p is any statement), we do not accept p without evidence or further argument. We will suggest below that Peter's being an authority on the subject area in question would count as such evidence.

Using 'A' to stand for any person and 'p' to stand for any statement, we would not accept the following as a good argument:

A asserts p (ground)

Therefore: p is true (claim)   (argument A1)

Nevertheless, we do need to be able to make judgements as to whether or not a person's statements can be relied upon. Another way of putting this point is that we need to know whether or not a particular person is a reliable authority on what we need to know. How would we go about judging whether or not this is the case?

No-one is infallible; we all make mistakes of fact at one time or another. Therefore, this version of the argument from authority will be unsound in all cases. Some people would argue that as it stands it is not really an argument at all, since all it does is back up the claim that p is true with the further statement that A has claimed it, which is the ground. However, adding a warrant is helpful. The warrant could be

Nearly everything A says is true

Adding this warrant produces

A asserts p (ground)

Nearly everything A says is true (warrant)

Therefore: p is very likely to be true   (argument A2)

Note that we are here dealing with an *inductive* argument. Note also that if the warrant were

Everything A asserts is true

and was taken to mean literally everything A ever said, is now saying and will ever say, and was then 'promoted' to being a ground, the argument would become a *deductive* one:

Everything that A asserts is true (ground 1)

A asserts p (ground 2)

Therefore: p is true (claim)   (argument A3)

Task 48: Why does this argument become a deductive one?

Can you work out why the above argument would become deductive? Check to see if it has the same warrant as any of the other arguments above. Note also that it is an argument that, although valid, is unlikely to prove anything. Why is this?

[Our response appears on page 260]

Our inductive argument about A (argument A2), although sound, is not of any more practical use than the deductive argument just given (argument A3). It is simply not true of any of us that nearly everything that we say is true. Even if we are not telling lies all the time, we are almost certainly making some mistakes, particularly when we pronounce on matters about which we know very little. The most we can say with confidence about anyone is that there is some restricted area of knowledge about which she is a reliable authority. We might now have:

p is a statement made by A about subject S (ground)

Therefore: p is true (claim)

And the warrant would be:

Nearly everything A says about subject S is true   (argument A4)

This is an argument from authority and it is sound because it gives good grounds for believing that p is true, given that the warrant is acceptable and the ground is true.

There are ways in which the argument from authority can be misused. The most obvious way is for A to be an accepted authority on S but for her to pronounce in an authoritative way on a subject that is not S. To be sound, the argument from authority has got to be used in a way that is sensitive to the boundaries of competence of the authority in question. The following is, therefore, an unsound form of the argument from authority:

p is a statement made by A (p is about subject T) (ground)

Therefore: p is true (claim)

Where the warrant is:

Nearly everything A says about subject S is true   (argument A5)

It is very tempting for an authority to pronounce or to be persuaded to pronounce outside his area of competence. In addition to the respect that they enjoy as experts in their chosen field, authorities very often carry an aura of *mystique* about them that may incline people to believe what they say even when there are no rational grounds for doing so. When authorities capitalize on this by pronouncing on issues about which they are not legitimately considered as authorities, they are clearly attempting non-rational persuasion in the sense in which this was introduced in 3.1. The authority relies on the admiration, respect or devotion she evokes in respect of her expertise in a particular field, in order to win assent for statements not backed up with good reasons or evidence in another field. The philosopher Bertrand Russell, a leading figure in the field of mathematical logic and epistemology, who also wrote widely on marriage, war and education, could be considered a writer whose authority in one field gave him a prestige in other fields that was not really matched by his expertise in those other fields. You may recognize this technique as it is commonly applied by advertisers, who often pay some famous personality to endorse the product that they wish to sell.

A second way in which arguments from authority can be problematic is when there is a genuine dispute between authorities within a particular field of competence. It may be the case that most or nearly all of what George says about the visual apparatus of a particular species of spider found in Rainforest is true. However, Gloria may also be an authority on the visual apparatus of the same species, and assert one thing while George asserts the opposite. How are people to decide between the two? In many cases, it may be impossible to come to a rational decision. However, it would be a mistake to believe one authority rather than another simply because of her or his greater prestige, popularity, fluency, plausibility or charisma. This would be a mistake similar to the one illustrated in the unsound argument from authority above, where it was assumed that A's being an authority on subject S gave her the right to pronounce on subject T.

Being *An Authority* and being *In Authority*

We have discussed some of the problems with arguments from authority. You should also be aware of the distinction between being *an authority* and being *in authority*. Someone may be an authority on medicine, for example, because of her acknowledged expertise in the field. She may also be a senior figure in a medical institution, such as a hospital. Although many people who are authorities in their subjects are also *in* authority in their profession or institution, their being *in* authority does not make them *an* authority. It may even be possible for a person who is in authority to abuse her position of being in authority unjustly to bolster her prestige as an authority. An example might be an indolent university professor who achieves fame by requiring that all publications by her postgraduate students contain her name as first author.

Authorities in dispute with one another will have to deploy arguments in support of their own positions and in criticism of those with whom they disagree. In doing so, they will allow the possibility of evaluation of their own arguments by others. Most often it will be difficult for someone without *any* specialist knowledge of the subject area to make a judgement as to the cogency of these arguments. But someone with a reasonable background knowledge of an area will be able to evaluate arguments. She will be able to note unstated warrants and form these, together with stated grounds, into more fully articulated arguments. She will also be able to form judgements as to the likely truth or falsity of grounds in arguments used, as well as to question the validity of the warrants used by asking, for example, what the justification for a warrant is. A degree of expertise, however achieved, gives one a right to form judgements about disagreements between authorities. Where an authority uses an argument that is explicitly articulated and clearly invalid or unsound, the thoughtful non-expert should be in a position to make a judgement about the quality of the argument without knowing very much about the subject matter. The point to remember is that while we should maintain a proper respect for individual expertise and the complexity of particular subject matters, we do not have to surrender our rational faculties in situations where it is still possible to form judgements on the evidence and arguments available.

For example, the humorous writer Bill Bryson has written a book called *A Short History of Nearly Everything* (2004) in which he gives a brief account of the most important scientific discoveries. Why should anyone believe a word of what he says, because, as he would be the first to admit, he is not a scientist of any description. The answer is that we do have good grounds for believing Bryson. First, he makes no claim to scientific expertise. Second, he has consulted authoritative sources for the claims made in the book. Third, he has had specialists check what he has written for accuracy. Bryson thus passes the test for being a legitimate author of a popular science textbook even though he is not an expert on what he writes about.

Dealing with arguments and disagreements in what you read

You need to be sure that you understand the arguments and evidence deployed in favour of different points of view in what you read. A good way of helping is to make notes on relevant passages in which you try to set out the arguments put forward in as explicit a manner as possible. This may mean inserting what you take to be unstated warrants and grounds to obtain the best possible construction of what you think authors are trying to say. This is a theme to which we will return in 3.3.

3.3

Analysing and evaluating arguments

A contrast is often made between two sorts of criminal justice system – the *adversarial* and the *inquisitorial*. In the adversarial approach, typified by judicial practice in the United Kingdom and the United States, trials are seen as a contest between the defence and the prosecution, in which the prosecution aims to overcome the presumption that the defendant is innocent, while the defence aims to maintain that presumption. On the other hand, in the inquisitorial approach, typified by the French system of justice, the object of a trial is to determine what actually occurred, that is, whether or not a crime actually took place at the time and place alleged and, if so, whether the defendant was the perpetrator.

In a similar way, it is possible to evaluate the arguments you read in either an adversarial or an inquisitorial way. Adopting an adversarial approach would involve the attempt to pinpoint places where a writer has argued badly, while a more inquisitorial approach would involve the attempt to discover what the author actually meant by what she wrote, even if her meaning is unclear or her argument poor. Adopting a generously inquisitorial approach in evaluating the arguments of others is much more useful as a way of coming to understand what an author is arguing than adopting an adversarial approach, where the object is to show where he is mistaken.

Let's try out being generous in our attempt to understand what someone is arguing by looking closely at an argument that, rather than being presented in written form, was developed in conversation.

Charles M.

Take a look at the following passage, cited by Labov (1969) in which Charles M. talks about his views of witchcraft and other supernatural things. Cooper (1984) argues that although Charles M. seems muddled, it is possible to view him as presenting a coherent argument, if the appropriate concealed ground is made clear.

> Well, I even heard my parents say that there is such a thing as something in dreams some things like that, and sometimes dreams do come true. I have personally never had a dream come true. I've never dreamt that somebody was dying and they actually died, or that I was going to have ten dollars the next day and somehow I got ten dollars in my pocket. I don't particularly believe in that, I don't think it's true. I do feel, though that there is such a thing as – ah – witchcraft, or some sort of science of witchcraft; I don't think that it's just a matter of believing hard enough that there is such a thing as witchcraft. I do believe that there is such a thing that a person can put himself in a state of mind, or that – er – something could be given them to intoxicate them in a certain – to – to a certain – to a certain frame of mind – that that could actually be considered witchcraft. (Labov, 1969, pp. 197–198)

Questions

Before reading our discussion of the passage, which appears below, take some time to think about and try to answer the following questions about it:

i. What is the claim in favour of which Charles is arguing?

ii. What are the grounds or warrants, stated or unstated, on which his argument rests?

iii. Set out the argument in a clear and unambiguous way.

Discussion

At first sight what Charles is saying looks incoherent. There is a lot of hesitation, there is repetition, and there appear to be great gaps in his argument. Since we cannot interrogate Charles, it is not possible for us to say whether or not he was aware of or would have been able to supply the missing grounds or warrant that would make his argument more convincing. However, filling in some of the possible unstated grounds and warrants, Charles could be seen as offering a valid argument as outlined below:

(i) The claim is: 'I don't believe that dreams come true'

(ii) There are two grounds, one of which is unstated:

In all matters of the supernatural, personal experience is the only criterion for belief (warrant)

Dreams that come true are an example of supernatural matters (unstated ground)

I have never had personal experience of a dream coming true (stated ground)

(iii) Taking these together, we can construct the following valid argument:

Dreams that come true are an example of supernatural matters (unstated ground)

The only criterion for believing that dreams come true is by having personal experience of dreams coming true (claim)

In all matters of the supernatural, personal experience is the only criterion for belief (unstated warrant to get from ground (a) to claim (b)[1])

I have never had personal experience of a dream coming true (ground)

Therefore I don't believe that dreams come true (claim)[2]

Given the information we have about what Charles thinks and the impossibility of gaining any further information about his thinking, this seems to be a sympathetic interpretation of his position that is quite consistent with what we know him to have asserted.

The following is a longer example:

Conversation between C. R. and Larry

In the following conversation, based on an example taken from Labov (1969), two people, C. R. and Larry, are having a conversation about what might happen to people after they die.

> *C. R.:* Have you ever thought about what happens to people when they die? I know you were told about it in Sunday School and so on, but I want to know about your own thoughts.
> *Larry:* Well, I do have my own views on that.
> *C. R.:* What are they then? I'm dying to know.
> *Larry:* What I think is, when you die, your body just decomposes.

---

[1] This counts as a warrant as it is a relatively general and uncontroversial principle that most people would be inclined to agree with and that would not normally need to be stated.

[2] Warrant (c), 'In all matters of the supernatural, personal experience is the only criterion for belief (unstated warrant to get from ground (a) to claim (b))', again unstated, can once again be used as a warrant to license the move from (d) to (e).

C. R.: So tell me something new. I thought you'd been giving this some thought. I want to know what you think happens to your soul.

Larry: Your soul leaves you when you die.

C. R.: Where do you think it goes then?

Larry: Well, I'm not really sure about that ...

C. R.: Come on. I thought you'd been thinking this over.

Larry: OK. A lot of people still think that if you're good your soul goes to heaven and if you're bad your soul goes to hell. I think that's a load of rubbish, quite frankly. In the long run, we're all going to hell.

C. R.: I'm beginning to be sorry I asked you now! Whatever makes you think like that?

Larry: Look, nobody really knows if God exists. You know. I've travelled a bit in my time and I've seen more gods than you've had hot dinners. They can't all exist and I don't think that any of them do. So when folk say if you're good, your soul will go to heaven, that's absolute rubbish because there isn't a heaven for it to go to. Good or bad, your soul is going to hell anyway.

The next two tasks are designed to help you to come to an understanding of Larry's position. Spend some time on the questions each raises, before reading our response at the back of the book.

Task 49: What is Larry doing in this conversation?

i.   How many arguments is Larry developing?

ii. What claims does he make?

iii. What are the grounds of Larry's argument or arguments?

iv. Does Larry make any ambiguous statements?

[Our response appears on page 260]

Task 50: What is Larry arguing?

i.   Set out the arguments that you think that Larry is developing, arranging them as sets of grounds, and claims, in that order. If you think that the warrants are not made explicit, state what you think they are.

ii. Are the arguments developed by Larry any good?

[Our response appears on page 261]

Larry's arguments look very different once they are laid out explicitly in the way we have done in our response on page 261, which contrasts markedly with the fragmentary and implicit form that they took in the conversation between Larry and C. R. presented above. This illustrates how important it is to try to be as clear as you can about arguments before trying to set them out. Of course, it is much harder to do this in the context of a conversation, such as that between Larry and C. R. than when we are constructing a written argument. Larry could hardly be blamed for failing to state his argument clearly and without ambiguity, because the conversation in which he was doing so was not one over which he had full control. Rather, he was engaged in a competitive battle of wits. As a writer, on the other hand, you do not face such constraints, although you do face others.

> Work hard at stating arguments clearly and without ambiguity.

No author can hope to include all of the possible grounds and warrants for her claims. Neither can she hope to provide arguments for the truth of all her grounds. She must, therefore, take into account the knowledge and assumptions that she can reasonably expect her audience to have, depending on whether it is a general or specialized one; its degree of education, and its willingness to give sympathetic attention to her views. When this has been done, she must ensure that her arguments are unambiguous by, for example, ensuring that she has included all crucial intervening steps.

As an author (and as a student you are an author), you must try to maximize clarity. To do so, it is often helpful to make a clear statement of the claim or claims you want to support, before setting out the grounds for that claim or claims. Let us take one last look at Larry's argument. How might he have gone about presenting it in writing if he had had some lessons in the clear presentation of arguments? He might have proceeded like this:

> *I am going to argue that the view that the souls of good people go to heaven and the souls of bad people go to hell when they die, is false*

(This statement would focus the reader clearly on the aim of what was to follow)

> *Suppose, for the sake of the argument, that if you are good your soul goes to heaven and if you are bad your soul goes to hell*

(Here Larry states the grounds on which he is basing his argument, beginning by supposing that the view which he is arguing against is true)

> *Now, it is false that if you are good then your soul is going to heaven, since there is no heaven, and you cannot go somewhere which does not exist.*

(Here Larry's claim that 'It is false that if you are good then your soul is going to heaven' is supported by a smaller argument with a further ground, signalled by 'since', namely that 'there is no heaven'. The warrant here is 'you cannot go somewhere which does not exist')

So far, Larry has supposed one ground for the sake of argument and argued in favour of another:

- If you are good your soul goes to heaven and if you're bad your soul goes to hell.
- It is false that if you are good then your soul is going to heaven.

However, since these two grounds implicitly contradict one another, he would have to point it out.

Given the truth of my earlier supposition, it follows that if you are good then your soul is going to heaven. However, I have just argued that it is false that if you are good then your soul is going to heaven.

Since it is not possible for both these statements to be true it can, therefore, be concluded that the statement that if you are good then your soul is going to heaven and if you are bad then your soul is going to hell, is false.

At this point Larry would have stated his argument as clearly as possible.

When you are evaluating arguments presented by others, whether in writing or in speech, try always to offer a sympathetic interpretation of what they mean, before raising objections to, or criticisms of, them.

Being your own most rigorous critic

Although we think you should always aim to be generous as a reader, because that gives you the best possible chance of properly understanding and therefore benefiting from what you read, our view is somewhat different when it comes to reading and evaluating your own writing, when we suggest that you should adopt a more adversarial approach.

When evaluating your own writing, it pays to be your own severest critic.

Why this use of different standards when reading your own and other people's work? When you are reading what an author has written, you should be trying to understand what she says, even if you disagree with her, because you need to understand what someone is saying properly before you can criticize it.

> When you are *writing* for an audience, you need to provide as clear a statement of your case as possible, if you want them to understand what you are saying.

Try to recall what we wrote in Part 1 about the peculiar demands of written as opposed to spoken communication. You are writing for a non-present audience, maybe an unknown audience, who cannot interact with or question you.

> As you write, try to think yourself into your reader's shoes.

You need to test your own writing for readability, relevance, fairness and consistency before you submit it to a wider audience. You can do this best, we believe, if you get into the habit of subjecting your own writing to adversarial criticism.

Evaluate your own work

Style
Have you written in clear, accessible and unambiguous prose, eliminating jargon and cliché whenever possible?

Representing others' points of view
If you are reporting or evaluating what someone else has said or written, do you understand what they are saying and show in what you have written that you do?

If what they are saying is ambiguous, have you at least alerted your readers to that possibility?

Have you given a fair and comprehensive account of what they say? Are you sure that you are not distorting what they are trying to say?

Quoting what people say
If you are quoting someone, does the passage you have chosen really reflect the point that you want to make about what the author is saying?

Have you quoted the relevant passage properly, without omitting key words or phrases in ways that alter the author's meaning?

Citation
Have you ensured that your readers have the opportunity to check what you have said about other authors' arguments and contentions, by giving full bibliographical references to all sources?

Argument
Do you argue well? In other words, are your arguments clear, easy to follow and sound?

Are you consistent? Have you avoided contradicting yourself?

Have you managed to avoid the temptation to use irrational means of persuasion, such as those described in Section 3.1?

Evaluating other people's arguments

We end Part 3 by offering you some practice in tracking arguments in short texts. Task 51 invites you to identify and evaluate the arguments in four short texts. In undertaking this task you will probably find it useful to begin work on each passage by identifying and copying out all of the statements (which might be claims, grounds or warrants that the passage contains) before trying to work out what the author is trying to persuade you to believe. In doing so, you will also have to reflect on whether there are suppressed or unstated elements in these arguments. Task 52 gives you more practice in relation to short passages from two very distinguished academics, one a linguist and the other a philosopher.

Task 51: What is being argued for?

Read the passages that follow and in each case decide what the author wants to persuade us about, how she supports her claim and whether there is any material in the passage that is not directly relevant to the argument.

   Sir Paul McCartney wrote some of the best pop and rock songs of all time. Despite the fact that there are people who consider some of his output rather 'twee', he is not only a great rock singer but a fantastically successful songwriter, because he comes from Liverpool and songwriters from Liverpool are always fantastically successful.

As a result of the focus on issues of real importance in their course, most students on courses in the School of Applied Global Ethics (SAGE) at Leeds Metropolitan University, develop a strong sense of right and wrong, along with a commitment to try their best to live in ways that are ethically defensible. Therefore, all SAGE students know the difference between right and wrong and try always to do what's right in all areas of their life, including campaigning about issues they feel strongly about.

Lots of high street stores in the UK source their clothes from manufacturers in developing countries that pay their workers a pittance. You have to be very careful whom you buy your clothes from if you want to be ethical. Some retailers manage to sell clothes really cheaply. Sometimes they're really good value, even if they're a bit 'iffy' ethically speaking. There have been lots of newspaper articles about how such retailers work with suppliers that only pay their workers about 10 pence an hour, which means the workers don't have enough to live on.

Like most of the major acting talents working in film at the moment, Sir Ian McKellen has also worked in the theatre and in television. He is not only a great actor but a great man, whose long career has brought him fame for film roles such as Gandalf in the *Lord of the Rings* movies, as well as for acting many of the major roles in Shakespeare in live theatre. At one point a few years ago he even spent a few weeks as part of the cast of *Coronation Street*. However, he is probably most likely to go down in history because of the work he did, in the 1980s, to raise awareness of the problems of HIV and AIDS.

[Our response appears on page 262]

Task 52: Tracking arguments

Read the two passages that follow and try to work out what their authors are trying to persuade us to believe and how they set out to do it. In each case decide whether the author is successful.

Passage from The English Language (Crystal, 2002)

Teachers often express surprise that a child who has been quick to learn to read should be a poor speller. They assume that reading, once taught, automatically means that spelling will be 'caught'. But there is no correlation between reading ability and spelling ability. Totally different skills are involved. Spelling involves a set of active, productive, conscious processes that are not required for reading. To take just one contrast: it is possible to read very selectively, by spotting just some of the letters or words in a piece of writing, and 'guessing' the rest (as we do when we 'skim' a newspaper story). You can't spell in this way. Spellers have got to get it *all* right, letter by letter. (p. 73)

Passage from Enhancing Evolution: The Ethical Case for Making Better People (Harris, 2008)

Suppose a school were to set out deliberately to improve the mental and physical capacities of its students. Suppose its stated aims were to ensure that the pupils left the school not only more intelligent, healthier and more physically fit than when they arrived, but more intelligent, healthier and more physically fit than they would be at any other school. Suppose they further claimed not only that they could achieve this but that their students would be more intelligent, enjoy better health and longer life, and be more physically and mentally alert than any children in history. Suppose that a group of educationalists, outstanding ones of course, far more brilliant than any we know of to date, had actually worked out a method of achieving this, in the form perhaps of an educational and physical curriculum. What should our reaction be?

Well of course our reaction would be one of amazement; it would certainly be an unprecendented event – a breakthrough in education. But should we be pleased? Should we welcome such a breakthrough? We might of course be sceptical, we might doubt such extravagant claims, but if they could be sustained would we want our children to go to such a school? And if the school our own children attended was not run according to the new educational methods, would we want those to be adopted as soon as possible? (p. 1)

Responses to tasks

Task 1: How is writing different from talking?

Among the more important differences is the fact that when we write we don't usually have the opportunity to offer clarification, if someone who reads it does not understand; or to elaborate what we have written to take account of objections he or she might have to our position. (Can you think of a time when, as a writer, this would not be true?) So talk has the advantage, over writing, that it allows a two-way conversation. On the other hand, writing has the advantage over most talk that it allows you to think through your point of view or argument very carefully, before revealing it.

Task 2: How is talking face-to-face different from talking on the phone?

When we talk face-to-face we can pick up facial expressions and body language that, together with deliberate gestures (e.g. pointing) will often help us to understand what a person is saying. Unless we are talking to someone using a videophone, these elements are absent in telephone talk, which thus usually demands more precision when one is speaking and more concentration when one is listening.

Task 3: Communicating directions to your new address

To some extent it depends how complex the directions are. Giving them in written form takes away the need to remember and offers the possibility of including a spatial representation of the route (a map) as well as written instructions. Giving them face-to-face includes this as an option, but has the added advantage (shared with giving instructions over the phone) of allowing the person to whom you are giving them, the opportunity to ask for clarification or re-iteration if necessary.

Task 4

To say what was going on when your attention lapses as you are reading would take a lot of space, and would be better discussed by a psychologist working in human attention, than us. However, it is easier to guess at why it happens, which probably has something to do with the text (it might, for example, simply be boring or written in rather a difficult style) but is likely, also, to arise at least partly because of your approach to reading. Advice about making the best use of reading, which is offered throughout Part 1, will help you to avoid this experience. Especially important is the suggestion on pages 34–35 that you should always approach reading with definite questions in mind, so that you are actively seeking particular pieces of information, or understandings, as you read.

Task 5: Read the passage that follows and answer the questions

Answers

1 Toby was new years old.

2 Toby had a holl of oun ret.

3 Toby lev Fred each week.

4 Toby gave him holls of welt to pock

5 He was able to pell in the gelt of Toby's fing, because he was mump enough.

6 Fred remp his juges.

Task 6: What are your reasons for reading as a student?

No response

Task 7: Where and when do you read as a student?

No response

Task 8: What kind of academic reader are you?

No response

Task 9: Circuit training for reading

No response

Task 10: Trying out SQ3R

Survey
In surveying the book you will probably have looked at both the index and the contents page and discovered that Part 3 is about 'Developing arguments

in your writing' and that within it there is a section entitled 'Influencing the beliefs of others' and further subsections entitled 'Rational and non-rational forms of persuasion' and 'Persuading by non-rational means', which might contain more detailed material on what you want. The subsection entitled 'Illicit ways of persuading others' might also be relevant, since it is likely that in most cases persuading by non-rational means is going to be illicit. Skimming these areas of the text will have allowed you to establish that closer reading will help you to answer the question you have been set.

Question
Preparing to read the areas of the text you pinpointed for close reading and deciding what you want to get from it, will have involved settling on the specific questions to which you should seek answers, which might have included 'What does non-rational mean?' and 'What kinds of means of persuasion are non-rational?'

Read
In carefully reading the areas of text you have earmarked you will have found several different ways in which non-rational persuasion might be described, including the idea that it does not involve cogent argument and may involve appeals to the emotions. You will have realized that the range of techniques of persuasion that might be described as non-rational is quite large and you will have read about and come to understand the ways in which some of them work.

Recite
Following your detailed reading of some bits of Part 3, you should have a reasonable idea of the nature of non-rational persuasion and be able to summarize what you have learned by reciting or noting down some examples of the techniques that might be employed, including sophistry, indoctrination, begging the question, crafty conflation and the use of 'persuader words'.

Review
In the review stage it might occur to you that to really understand the nature of non-rational persuasion, you will first have to find out a little about its opposite – rational persuasion. In that case you will perhaps enter into a second cycle of SQ3R, during which you will find yourself learning about, for example, inductive and deductive reasoning, and about the conditions for valid and cogent arguments.

Task 11: What distinguishes one form of writing from another?

It would take up too much space to give a detailed account of the differences between these forms. However, we would, for example, expect you to refer to the likelihood that while poems will most often make use of devices such as metaphor and alliteration, rhythm and rhyme, scientific reports are likely to be more literal in their use of language, as well as being a good deal more formal in style, perhaps using visual devices like graphs, tables and charts to share information in helpful ways. You might note that while both a field guide to British birds and an illustrated biography of a famous painter are likely to provide factual information supported by the use of helpful photographs, few novels will be written with the idea in mind of providing such information, and few will contain photographs. We would expect you, perhaps, to argue that an essay written as part of an undergraduate degree is likely to be more carefully written than an estate agent's details about a house for sale, although a brief look over many student essays might call this assertion into doubt, and some estate agents are very careful about what they write. Finally, you might lump blogs, emails to colleagues and messages on social networking sites together, because they are subspecies of communications that are usually intended to be read on-line, while newspapers – both serious and tabloid – are usually intended to be read in printed paper form. (Of course, this is gradually changing as more and more newspapers have an on-line version and some begin to be presented entirely on-line.)

Task 12: Turning essay topics into questions

In what ways are the music of Scotland and Ireland similar? And in what ways are they different? Is the traditional music of Scotland as good as that of Ireland?

What can an examination of party policy and media reports tell us about the mental health of a party political leader of your choice?

How can we produce synthetic living organisms from raw materials found in the average student fridge? (Your answer should include a detailed account both of the process involved and of the necessary equipment.)

Task 13: Description, discussion, evaluation or comparison?

In a way this was a 'trick question', because we cannot imagine a decent answer to any of the seven questions that did not utilize all of these approaches. If you decided that all of these questions demanded description, discussion, evaluation *and* comparison, you probably thought about them quite carefully. If you found it difficult to decide, you probably also thought about them carefully, and perhaps even more carefully. If, however, you managed to persuade yourself that some of these questions demanded only one or two of these approaches, you might not have thought carefully enough and we suggest that you think again, trying to imagine how you would actually go about answering those particular questions. What arguments would you use and how would you convince your reader of them?

Task 14: Excuses for not getting round to writing

No response

Task 15: Writing for five minutes

No response

Task 16: Write for five minutes a day

No response

Task 17: What is Julia planning to do in her next draft?

She has spotted the need to cite Silverman to support her use of case study and the likely date – 2005. Realizing that a reference to 'holistic and meaningful characteristics' might be thought vague has led her to conclude that she needs to explain what she means. She notes that her reference to Moore would be more helpful if she said something about what he or she says. Finally, she notes the need to mention some of the criticisms of case study, and notes that Yin (1994) will probably fit the bill.

Task 18: Mistakes in proofreading and copyediting

i.   Clever items of climbing equipment, climbing towards the summit on their own, leaving their wearer behind.

ii. Perhaps the student had dinner on his mind as he wrote the second sentence. Or perhaps he simply hit the wrong jey on his ketboard and theb didn# proofread well enough.

iii. Although ensuite shower rooms are common, how odd for a hotel to provide each bedroom with its own breakfast room and also a (continental style) female undergarment that can provide snacks and beverages.

Task 19: It's or its?

Correct answers appear in **bold** and incorrect answers in *italics*

The mechanic who examined my car told me that **its** radiator needed to be replaced.

It's important to get punctuation right, otherwise **it's** likely that those who read your essay will get *it's* meaning wrong.

The comma should be used carefully, because *it's* overuse can lead to a lack of clarity.

The Royal Bank, which was rescued by the government after coming near to financial ruin, has awarded all of *it's* senior staff large bonuses.

It's only rice pudding, but I like it.

Its not right that we have to wait so long for the train.

It's a shame that so many people find problems with the use of the apostrophe.

In writing the possessive pronoun *it's*, *its* important never to use an apostrophe.

Task 20: What homophones catch you out?

No response

Task 21: Make a list of problem words

No response

Task 22: Spotting spelling errors

The correct spellings are given first in each case

  i.   poll/pole; principal/principle; taxes/taxis; far/fair; too/two high

  ii.   broach/brooch; in/inn

  iii. descent/decent; begged/bagged; to/too; great/grate care

  iv.   off/of; seesaw/see saw; right/write; write/right; for/four; two/too.

Task 23: Practise proofreading

Mistakes are indicated below by the use of italics

How much time *do* students spend using mobiles? Researchers at the University of Billericay conducted *an* experiment about mobile *use* among students. Nocci and Ohtou (2003) *reported* that on average students *use* cameras on mobiles ten times a week. They also find that mobile use *increases* with the age *of* students, until a final year student *spends* up to two hours day speaking to friends, texting and *accessing* the internet.

Writing *is* difficult. It *involves* more mental and physical effort than speaking, which probably explains why people *are* often reluctant to rewrite what they *have* written.

This year was the 200th anniversary of *the* birth of the Polish composer Chopin. He has been *credited* with the production of many essentially romantic masterpieces. His compositional style *portrays a* miniature approach to piano playing, which many commentators think has done little to further appreciation of the instrument. Nevertheless many people in *his* homeland *regard* him as a national hero.

The use of citation to indicate the relationship of one's work to what others *have written*, is one of *the* characteristics that *distinguishes* academic writing from other species of writing, including fiction and intelligent journalism. It is *expected* of all academic authors, whether they *are* first year undergraduate students, lecturers, or professors.

Task 24: Which use of citation is most helpful?

In example 1, the first paragraph uses citation more helpfully because, for example, it tells us about what Majewski did, and hints at what he found, whereas in the second we are left guessing at this.

In example 2, the second paragraph is more helpful than the first, because it gives information about Smith's research, and about both Thompson's criticism of Smith, and Cullen's criticism of Thompson.

Task 25: What is the purpose of the citation?

The first example introduces us to the fact that Davis has developed a model of global warming, and the second to the fact that a number of different groups are interested in citation analysis.

The third example informs us that although several researchers consider the methodology adopted by Jameson in his research to be flawed, they find his work on empathy among torturers interesting.

The fourth example tells us no more than that Wing carried out research on the history of leek growing competitions in North East England, while the fifth goes into some detail about which of the researchers compared by Thomas used the same techniques, and also informs us that Thomas argues they all made the same errors.

The sixth example informs us that Smith believes apes should have the same rights as us (assuming you are not an ape) and explains the reasons he believes this.

The seventh example reports on the conclusion of research by McCormack, into the eating habits of gerbils, but let's us know that he reached this conclusion on the basis of flawed evidence, while the eighth informs us both that Smail is sceptical of the idea that psychotherapy can be scientifically justified, and that he contends that it is, in some ways, similar to prostitution.

In the penultimate example, we learn that Ignatieff draws attention to two versions of the truth – that told for its own sake, and that told for the purpose of reconciliation.

The final example draws attention to Tschudin's definition of sympathy.

Task 26: Practise writing full references

No response

Task 27: Writing in the third person

Examples of deception on the part of MPs have been given.

Markings similar to those found in Orkney were observed.

The number of shops that had closed in the last year was counted.

Two main claims will be advanced.

Broadbent's theory of memory is superseded by later work. Or, Broadbent's theory of memory is thought to be superseded by later work.

Earlier films by these directors were all found to contain biographical elements. (Earlier films by these directors all contained biographical elements.)

Evidence has been presented for greater fluctuations of rainfall during the past ten years.

Volunteers were divided into four groups, according to their level of general fitness.

Task 28: Try writing mini sagas

No response

Task 29: Write some 200-word 'reflections'

No response

Task 30: Practise cutting some texts down to size

No response

Task 31: What does de Cameron want to communicate?

Try as we might, we cannot quite fathom what this remarkable sentence is getting at. However, so far as we can tell, de Cameron wants the conflicts to which he refers to be addressed cautiously and conservatively, in ways that avoid courses of action that might offend many people. He appears, also, to want to draw attention to the way that certain Christian religious and ethical convictions may be supported by arguments that are rooted elsewhere. Finally, he seems to want to let us know that he is aware of the relationship between humanity and the species Homo sapiens, although we can't quite tell what he means by saying that 'we are working with a concept of human rights and human dignity as co-extensive with Homo sapiens?'

Task 32: What is Abbs trying to say?

To be fair to Abbs this passage does convey meaning; it is just that his meaning is clouded by the language he has chosen to use. He seems to believe that schools and teaching should be about enabling students to think for themselves and that thus, in some sense, about giving them freedom to determine their lives. Had he thought more clearly about what exactly he wanted to say before beginning to write, he could probably have said what he wanted to say using simpler language, avoiding the use of unusual words such as 'utile' (what does 'utile' mean? Look it up), and vague phrases such as 'an essential resonance' and 'the distinct resonance of transcendence'.

Task 33: What was Daniel getting at?

We are aesthetic beings long before we are rational beings. From a new-born babe, a person begins to mediate his or her world through the basic senses of sight, sound, smell, touch and taste and thus brings together through pain, pleasure or a sense of well-being, intimations of the nature of our world. Through these experiences comes a commitment to basic understanding, the development of which demands a particular kind of imaginative attention to things made, performed or learned. In so doing, the person becomes critically reflective in his or her responses to them.

This is still rather pompous and inelegant, but at least it is easier to read.

Task 34: Look out for redundant words

No response

Task 35: Collecting clichés

Here are a few more to add to your collection:

- Let sleeping dogs lie
- It takes two to tango
- The thing is …
- Too much information
- Like chalk and cheese
- Take it with a pinch of salt

- In at the deep end
- Too much of a good thing
- It isn't all it's cracked up to be
- The writing's on the wall
- It isn't rocket science
- Too much of a good thing

Task 36: Look out for emotive language

No response

Task 37: Persuader words and phrases

Some suggestions:

- Surely
- Plainly
- Obviously
- Clearly
- Self-evidently
- Undeniably
- Naturally
- It has to be admitted that
- It is clear/obvious that
- Everyone must agree
- We must remember
- I need hardly remind you
- Everyone knows that
- As you will no doubt agree
- It is true that
- The fact is that
- Everyone has had the experience of
- No-one would deny the fact that
- Only a fool could fail to realize

Task 38: Can you spot the crafty conflation?

Note how Smith moves from 'self-interest' to 'self-love' in the space of two sentences. These are not quite the same idea, as I can include within my 'self-interest' all kinds of things and people that are at the centre of my concerns: friends, family, even country. 'Self-love', on the other hand, suggests that it is myself alone as an individual who concerns me. It may be the case that my self-interest is bound up with myself alone, in which case I would probably be counted as a selfish person, but it need not be. Smith appears to be suggesting that it always is and this is controversial, to say the least.

Task 39: Write some examples of crafty conflation

No response

Task 40: Look out for question begging

No response

Task 41: You won't believe this

No response

Task 42: What could be used to support these statements?

Claim 1: Euthanasia should be legalized

  i.   This could be useful, because the law against euthanasia is about restraining behaviour aimed at helping people to die, and could be construed as telling them that they must live even when life is awful for them.

  ii. Although emotive, this misses the point of the law against legalizing euthanasia, which is arguably mainly focused on the likelihood that ick (probably old) people might be persuaded to ask to be killed, were it legally possible, and dogs and horses could not be persuaded to ask for death.

  iii. This is such an open permission that few would accept it. If you feel inclined to do so, imagine what you'd think of a four-year-old who wanted 'euthanasia' because a friend stole his teddy bear.

  iv. We are not told whether they felt they'd done the right thing. Think about whether they would have given same answer in a non-anonymous questionnaire.

v.   This is true, but does that get us anywhere? It does not, for example, guarantee that if legalized, euthanasia would not then become the preferred option for dealing with the aged and infirm. Does it?

Claim 2: Along with problems around the commodification of sex, human trafficking is probably the most significant moral problem in the world today
All of the evidence cited here seems strongly to support the view that trafficking is an extremely serious and widespread moral issue, although it is difficult to say whether it is more or less important than other issues, including the fact that we live in a world where so many babies die each day for lack of food and basic health care. The numbers cited: of people trafficked every year; of the hours a day a trafficked person might have to work; of the number of people she might be forced to have sex with during a 16 hour 'shift'; the monetary value placed upon a human life, and the numbers of people trafficked in the US every year (perhaps especially the number of children in the US at risk of being trafficked into sex work each year, which we might assume is mirrored in many other countries), all add strength to the view being argued for. The world is full of bad people.

Claim 3: The world is a more dangerous place now than it was before 9/11
To some extent whether these statements help to support the claim depends upon what we mean by the world being 'a more dangerous place'. The number that died, although shocking, doesn't make the world more dangerous, even though it might have made many people feel as if it is. On the other hand, the fact that the 'war on terror' began at least partly because the US isn't used to being attacked 'at home', may well have made the world more dangerous; and since that was the result of 9/11 and the number of people who died, who knows? Provided that the research methods were sound and carried out scrupulously, the research carried out by the University of Beeston supports exactly what it says – the contention that 70 per cent of all adults in the UK are more conscious of the potential dangers of international travel than they were before 9/11 and 7/7; this doesn't support the idea that the world is a more dangerous place now, but merely the fact that some UK residents believe it is. The last statement supports a similar point in the international arena.

Claim 4: There is no ethical reason why newly born infants should not be allowed to die or even killed, if they have serious defects at birth
The fact that many babies that survive in the rich world would not survive if they had been born to mothers in poorer countries has no relevance to this claim. Nor do the facts that throughout history disabled neonates have been allowed to die in many parts of the world, or that many severely disabled babies that now survive through pregnancy and birth would have miscarried had they been conceived fifty years ago, just as the fact that many people die of hunger in the developing world does not mean that it doesn't matter

whether people die of hunger in the UK. Whether you give any credibility to the facts claimed about whether newborn babies have developed features that are alleged to be those by which we 'define' persons, is up to you. However, it is important to note that even if it is true that neonates do not display many attributes that are regarded as indicators of 'personhood', that does not support the idea that it is okay to allow disabled babies to die.

The prediction about increasing population certainly supports the idea that we need, as a species, to think carefully about how we live, including how we share or don't share the world's resources, but it has little to do with the fate of individual disabled neonates.

Task 43: What is being argued for? How? How successfully?

i.   The use of leather in making shoes involves cruelty, because it necessitates the killing of animals.

The production of dairy products is cruel, because it involves distressing cows and their calves by separating them.

Those who wear shoes and consume dairy products are thus implicated in cruelty to animals.

It therefore makes no sense for anyone who wears leather shoes and consumes dairy products, to cite cruelty to animals as a reason for their vegetarian beliefs.

[This seems like a successful argument]

ii. Smith must have held the murder weapon because his fingerprints were found all over it.

There is no possibility that anyone else could have gained access to the victim.

It therefore follows that Smith was the murderer.

[To sustain this line of argument, it would be important to give evidence for the fact that only Smith could have had contact with the deceased; perhaps they were locked in a room together, when the automatic locking system failed, and a large group of trustworthy others kept vigil outside until it opened again]

iii. It is legally permissible to use both alcohol and tobacco.

Cannabis is no more harmful than alcohol or tobacco.

Laws that ban things are usually intended to protect us from harm.

There is no law to protect us from the harm caused by alcohol and tobacco.

Therefore, there should be no law to protect us from the harm caused by cannabis, unless there is a law to protect us from the harm caused by alcohol and tobacco.

[Although it might seem unfair to cannabis users who don't use either alcohol or tobacco, that their pleasure is denied while others' pleasure is permitted, the many cannabis users who also use alcohol and/or tobacco might want to be wary of arguing too loudly, lest their argument is turned round in arguing that 'If cannabis is illegal, because of the harm it can cause, then alcohol and tobacco should also be made illegal, because of the harm that they can cause']

iv. People should not be praised for being tall, or for their eye colour, which do not result from anything they have done, since they have no control over them.

By analogy, people should not be praised for being brainy, because like height and eye colour, they have no control over how intelligent they are.

On the other hand, we think it is okay to praise people for working and studying hard.

[It would be important, in making this argument, to produce evidence that while knowledge and skill may be enhanced by hard work, intelligence can't]

v. Breast feeding babies helps to protect them from early childhood diseases, from which they may die in the short term.

Babies in developing countries are more likely to die, in the short term, from childhood diseases, than they are from AIDS, even if they develop HIV through drinking mother's milk.

Breast feeding is thus the best way of feeding babies, even in countries where HIV/AIDS is a major problem.

[This seems like a convincing argument]

Task 44: Is Darren a beast? (With apologies to all Darrens, wherever they are)

(a) The claim is 'Darren is a beast'.

(b) The ground is 'Darren is a man'.

(c) The warrant is 'All men are beasts'.

(d) It doesn't unless you really do think that men are beasts by definition or that every single man who has ever existed has been shown to be a beast. Either of these could be the backing statement for the warrant.

(e) A backing statement for the warrant might be, 'Every man who has ever existed has been shown to be a beast.'

The full argument would look like this:

Darren is a man (ground)

All men are beasts (warrant)

Every man who has ever existed has been shown to be a beast (backing statement for warrant)

Therefore: Darren is a beast (claim)

Task 45: George, the Scottish millionaire

(a) The warrant is: 'If you are a Scot with lots of money then you are a Scottish millionaire' or 'All Scots with lots of money are millionaires'.

(b) No.

(c) It is unlikely that all, nearly all or even most Scots with lots of money are millionaires.

It is worth noting that if all rich Scots are *by definition* millionaires, then the argument would be a deductive one. But this is implausible. The attempt to use a backing statement that stated that every rich Scot had been examined and found to be a millionaire would quickly result in a realization that this was obviously false.

Task 46

(a) Let 'A' stand for 'Northamptonians', 'B' for 'friendly' and 'C' for 'Rosina'. You should get:

All As are B

C is an A

Therefore: C is a B.

(b) Most of us would say 'yes', just as we would with other arguments that share the same form.

(c) We would turn the warrant:

All Northamptonians are friendly

into a premise. Logicians would call this the major premise, and

Rosina is a Northamptonian

the minor premise. The warrant for the argument would then be of the form:

All As are B

C is an A

Therefore: C is a B

Since 'All' in this kind of argument is assumed to mean 'without exception', it will not be possible to find an unfriendly Northamptonian and so it will not be possible to find an example where the minor premise (what was the ground in the original argument) is true and the conclusion (what was the claim in the original argument) false.

Task 47: Why unsound rather than sound?

The reason is that no indication is given as to whether the sample of voters who were asked is in any sense representative. If, on the other hand, the argument gave details about how the sampling had been carried out, most social scientists might form a different opinion of it. If, for example, the following additional ground was added:

Those asked constituted a random stratified sample of the electorate

those of us who understand that random stratified sampling is a statistical method of achieving the best possible prediction would happily accept the argument as more sound than it was before, even if the rest of the argument remained unchanged (see Smith, 1981, Chapter 6). If, however, the additional ground was:

The names of those asked were drawn from a register of Conservative Party members

most people with any sense would realize that the argument was less sound as a result of adding this ground.

In sampling theory, the way in which the sample is selected and the size of the sample are as important as the proportion of the population that the sample represents in influencing our willingness to accept an argument's soundness. The example further illustrates that the addition of extra grounds to an inductive argument may increase or decrease its soundness. This contrasts induction with deduction, where the addition of grounds will not affect the form of the argument, assuming of course that when we come to evaluate it, the warrant or warrants have been made overt.

Task 48: Why does this argument become a deductive one?

The argument becomes deductive, because the first ground has become a universal statement. Although valid it is unlikely to prove anything because it is unlikely to be the case that everything that A says is true.

Task 49: What is Larry doing in this conversation?

i.   Larry is developing two arguments.

ii. There are two claims. One is that it's absolute rubbish to say that if you're good your soul is going to heaven and if you're bad your soul is going to hell. The second is that, good or bad, your soul is going to hell.

iii. The grounds of the first argument are:

   (a) There is no heaven for your soul to go to.

   (b) It is absolute rubbish that if you are good your soul will go to heaven. (This follows from (a); strictly speaking it is an intermediate step.)

   (c) If you're good your soul goes to heaven and if you're bad your soul goes to hell. (This is an unstated premise that is *supposed* in the course of the argument.)

iv. We don't think so but some people might. They might think that Larry's statement, 'A lot of people still think that if you're good your soul goes to heaven and if you're bad you're soul goes to hell. I think that's a load of rubbish, quite frankly' is ambiguous. They might think that it is ambiguous because they think it is unclear whether Larry intends to say that both the idea that *if you're good your soul is going to heaven*, is rubbish and the idea that *if you're bad your soul is going to hell*, is rubbish, or rather that *if you're good your soul is going to heaven and if you're bad your soul is going to hell*, is rubbish. A sympathetic reader will take him to mean the second interpretation, because otherwise he appears to contradict himself since he also says that we are all going to hell.

Task 50: What is Larry arguing?

There are two arguments:

i.   First argument:

   (a) There is no heaven for your soul to go to (ground)

   (b) It is absolute rubbish that if you are good your soul will go to heaven (intermediate step)

(c) If you're good, your soul goes to heaven and if you're bad your soul goes to hell (second, unstated ground, which is *supposed* for the sake of the argument but not asserted)

(d) If you're good, then your soul goes to heaven (intermediate claim that follows from (c))

(e) If you're good, then your soul goes to heaven and it is rubbish that if you're good your soul goes to heaven (intermediate claim obtained by joining together (b) and (d))

(f) Therefore: It is rubbish that if you're good your soul goes to heaven and if you're bad your soul goes to hell (final claim)

The conclusion to the argument is obtained by denying the ground that was supposed for the sake of the argument (c). This can be done because supposing (c) has led to (e), which cannot be true, since it is self-contradictory.

Second argument:

The second argument has one ground, which is:

In the long run, we're all going to hell.

and the claim:

Therefore: Good or bad, your soul is going to hell

ii.   We think that both arguments are good arguments. However, someone who thought that Larry was being ambiguous in the way described in our discussion of question (iv) in Task 50 might argue that Larry's first argument was a bad one and that Larry was a muddled rather than an astute thinker. If you are interested in reading about why they might conclude this, you may care to look at what William Labov (1969) and David Cooper (1984) have to say about this example.

Task 51: What is being argued for?

Sir Paul McCartney example
This argument is straightforward once we have identified the claims and warrant, and removed some tangential claims that have no direct part in the argument. Removing these claims and re-arranging, we arrive at:

Paul McCartney, the songwriter, comes from Liverpool (ground)

Songwriters from Liverpool are always fantastically successful. (warrant)

Therefore: Paul McCartney is a fantastically successful songwriter (claim)

This is a valid deductive argument with a claim that is undoubtedly true. However, the warrant is untrue, despite the great success of many Liverpudlian songwriters.

Tangential claims

(a) Paul McCartney is a great rock singer.

(b) Some people consider some of Paul McCartney's output rather 'twee'.

SAGE example

There are two arguments here, the first leading to a conclusion that serves as a new ground in the second.

Argument 1

Students in the School of Applied Global Ethics (SAGE) at Leeds Met are taking courses that focus on issues of real importance (ground)

Therefore: Most students on SAGE courses develop:

- A strong sense of right and wrong (claim 1)

- Commitment to trying to live in ways that are ethically defensible (claim 2)

To get from the ground in this argument to claims 1 and 2, there is a need for a warrant, which is unstated. We might state it like this:

Students who undertake courses that focus on issues of real importance, develop as people who have a strong sense of right and wrong, and are committed to trying to live life in ethically defensible ways. (unstated warrant)

Argument 2

As a result of their university course, all SAGE students have a strong sense of right and wrong and a commitment to trying to live their lives in ways that are ethically defensible (ground)

Therefore: All SAGE students try always to do what's right in all areas of their lives, including campaigning about issues they feel strongly about (claim)

To get from the ground to the claim in this argument, we need a warrant, which has not been stated. It is:

People who have a strong sense of right and wrong and who are committed to trying their best to live in ways that are ethically defensible, know the difference between right and wrong and try always to do what's right in all areas of their lives, including campaigning about issues they feel strongly about (warrant)

Whether we should be convinced by either of these arguments will depend on whether there is evidence to support the warrants offered in each case. In other words, in argument 1, whether studying in SAGE really does have the effects on students that are claimed, and in argument 2, whether it really is the case that having a strong sense of right and wrong and a commitment to living in ethically defensible ways, actually changes people's behaviour in the ways claimed.

High street stores example

This argument contains some material that is not directly relevant, which has to be put to one side if we are to understand what is being argued. Removing this material (which appears below) leaves a simple argument. To make sense of it, we also have to insert two missing warrants, one relating to the ethicality of paying workers a pittance if that is insufficient to live on, and one relating to the question of whether buying clothes from stores with ethically dubious business contacts is, in itself, unethical.

> Lots of high street stores in the UK source their clothes from manufacturers in developing countries that pay their workers very poorly, only about 10 pence an hour, which means the workers don't have enough to live on (ground)
>
> Paying people too little to live on is ethically wrong (unstated warrant)
>
> Buying clothes from shops that source them from unethical manufacturers is ethically wrong (unstated warrant)
>
> Therefore: You have to be very careful who you buy your clothes from if you want to be ethical (claim)
>
> *Material that is not directly relevant*
>
> Some shops manage to sell clothes really cheaply.
>
> Sometimes they're really good value, even if they're a bit 'iffy' ethically speaking.

Sir Ian McKellen example

> Sir Ian McKellen is a great actor (ground)
>
> Like most of the major acting talents working in film at the moment, he has also worked on TV and in live theatre (ground)

He is famous for acting many of the major roles in Shakespeare in live theatre, as well as for film roles, such as Gandalf in *Lord of the Rings* (ground)

In the 1980s he worked to raise awareness of the problems of HIV and AIDS (ground)

That is why he is not only a great actor, but also a great man (claim)

To get from the grounds to the claim, we also need a warrant, which is unstated:

People who work for humanitarian causes, such as raising awareness of the problems of HIV and AIDS, are great people (warrant)

Material that is not directly relevant

Ian McKellen's long career has brought him fame for film roles such as Gandalf in the *Lord of the Rings* movies, as well as for acting many of the major roles in Shakespeare in live theatre.

Sir Ian once spent some time on the cast of Coronation Street.

Task 52: Tracking arguments

Passage from The English Language (Crystal, 2002)

We might set out Crystal's argument as follows:

There is no correlation between reading ability and spelling ability, because these activities involve different skills (ground)

It is possible to read by spotting just some of the letters or words in a piece of writing, and 'guessing' the rest (warrant)

By contrast, spelling involves a set of active, productive, conscious processes (warrant)

Unlike readers, spellers have got to get it *all* right, letter by letter (warrant)

Therefore: Teachers should not be surprised when a child who has been quick to learn to read has problems with spelling (claim)

Passage from Enhancing Evolution: The Ethical Case for Making Better People (Harris, 2008)

Stated more straightforwardly, Harris's argument is that:

A school claims that by the time they leave its students are:

• More intelligent, healthier and more physically fit than when they arrived.

- More intelligent, healthier and more physically fit than they would be on leaving any other school.

- More intelligent, enjoy better health and longer life, and be more physically and mentally alert than any children in history.

[This is the ground of the argument]

In spite of scepticism about its claims, this school's educational and physical curriculum achieves its aims without exception (warrant)

Given this, any parent who wants the best for their children would want them to attend this school (claim 1)

If this was impossible, because of the rush on places, they would want other schools to adopt the same methods (claim 2)

Discussion
Rather than arguing straightforwardly Harris invites us to follow his reasoning so that we discover the claim he is making for ourselves. This is clever, because his argument thus becomes our argument. At first sight it seems to be a good argument. However, it would be as well to bear in mind the fact that Harris hasn't told us about any negative changes that might go along with children becoming healthier, more intelligent, etc.; for example, an unstated side-effect of the schools miracle method might be that they become horrible people.

There are also some other problems with Harris's story. Exactly how clever, healthy and fit do the children become at this school? Do they all leave at exactly the same level? And if it's the case that they are more intelligent, healthier and fitter than any other children in history, does this mean that each successive generation of pupils will surpass their forbears? Of course, what Harris wants to do with his story is to get us to think about what matters to us, and this story is a staging post in a bigger argument about genetically modifying children to make them fitter, healthier and brighter than any other children in history.

References

Abbs, P. (1987) 'Training spells the death of education', *Guardian*, 5 January.

Alidu, S., Fairbairn, G. and Webb, D. (2011) 'TRC and Transitional Justice: The Ghanaian Experience', under consideration by the editors of the *International Journal of Transitional Justice*.

Barnes, R. (1995) *Successful Study for Degrees*, 2nd edn, London, Routledge.

Beard, R. (1990) *Developing Reading 3–13*, 2nd edn, London, Methuen.

Bird, C. (2004) 'Status, identity, and respect', *Political Theory*, 32 (2) 207–232.

Bryson, B. (2004) *A Short History of Nearly Everything*, New York, Doubleday.

Byatt, A.S. (1990) 'Nimes', *Independent Magazine*, 3 March, p. 41.

Candlish, G.N. (2010) 'On the smoothness of the multi-BMPV black hole Spacetime', *Classical and Quantum Gravity*, 27, 1–17.

Canter, D. and Fairbairn, G. (2006) *Becoming an Author: Advice for Academics and Other Professionals*, Buckingham, Open University Press.

Clark, D. (2006) *The Rough Guide to Ethical Living*, London, Rough Guides Ltd.

Concise Oxford Dictionary (2006) Eleventh Revised Edition, Oxford, Oxford University Press.

Cooper, D. (1984) 'Labov, Larry and Charles', *Oxford Review of Education*, 10 (2) 177–192.

Crystal, D. (2002) *The English Language*, 2nd edn, London, Penguin Books.

Crystal, D. (2004) *Rediscover Grammar*, 3rd edn, London, Pearson Longman.

de Cameron, N.S. (1989) 'Embryos again', *Ethics and Medicine*, 5 (2) 17.

DeSalle, R. and Lindley, D. (1997) *The Science of Jurassic Park and the Lost World – or – How to Build a Dinosaur*, London, Harper Collins.

Dworkin, R. (1975) *Taking Rights Seriously*, London, Duckworth.

Dykes, B. and Thomas, C. (1989) *Spelling Made Easy*, Sydney, NSW, Hale and Iremonger Pty Ltd.

Etherington, K. (2002) 'Working together: editing a book as narrative research methodology', *Counselling and Psychotherapy Research* (internet) 2:3, 167–176.

Available at: http://dx.doi.org/10.1080/14733140212331384795 (Accessed 12 December 2007).

Fairbairn, F. (2005) Personal communication.

Fairbairn, G. J. (1995) *Contemplating Suicide: The Language and Ethics of Self Harm*, London, Routledge.

Fairbairn, G. (2008) *Citation and Referencing: A Simple Guide for SAGE Students*, Leeds, School of Applied Global Ethics, Leeds Metropolitan University.

Fairbairn, G. and Fairbairn, S. (2001) *Reading at University: A Guide for Students*, Buckingham, Open University Press.

Fairbairn, G. and Fairbairn, S. (2005) *Writing Your Abstract: A Guide for Would-be Conference Presenters*, Tollard Royal, Wiltshire, APS Publishers.

Fairbairn, G. and Winch, C. (1996) *Reading, Writing and Reasoning: A Guide for Students*, 2nd edn, Buckingham, Open University Press.

Fairbairn, G. and Winch, C. (2011) *Reading, Writing and Reasoning: A Guide for Students*, 3rd edn, Buckingham, Open University Press.

Flew, A. (1998) *How to Think Straight*, Amherst, NY, Prometheus Books.

Gaita, R. (1998) *A Common Humanity: Thinking About Love and Truth and Justice*, London and New York, Routledge.

Gee, R. and Watson, C. (1990) *The Usborne Book of Better English*, London, Usborne.

Hanfling, O. (1978) 'The Uses and Abuses of Argument', Arts Foundation Course A101, Milton Keynes, Open University.

Harris, J. (2008) *Enhancing Evolution: The Ethical Case for Making Better People*, Princeton, NJ, Princeton University Press.

Hart, H.L.A. (1966) *Punishment and Responsibility: Essays in the Philosophy of Law*, Oxford, Clarendon Press.

Harwood, N. (2009) 'An interview-based study of the functions of citations in academic writing across two disciplines', *Journal of Pragmatics*, 41, 497–518.

Holloway, R. (2001) *Doubts and Loves*, Edinburgh, Canongate Books.

Hunt, G. (1999) 'Abortion: why bioethics can have no answer – a personal perspective', *Nursing Ethics*, 6 (1) 47–57.

Iga, M. and Tatai, K. (1975) 'Characteristics of suicides and attitudes toward suicide in Japan', in Farberow, N. L. (ed) *Suicide in Different Cultures*, Baltimore, MD, University Park Press.

Kalitzkus, V., Büssing, A. and Matthiessen, P.F. (2007) 'Severe illness episodes and inner development: a biographical-narrative approach', *The Narrative Practitioner*, an international conference at the North East Wales Institute of Higher Education in June 2007.

Kearney, R. (2002) *On Stories: Thinking in Action*, London, Routledge.

Kennicutt, R. C., Jr. et al (2003) 'SINGS: The SIRTF Nearby Galaxies Survey', *Publications of the Astronomical Society of the Pacific*, 115, 928–952.

Koch, T. (1998) 'Story telling: is it really research?', *Journal of Advanced Nursing*, 28 (6) 1182–1190.

Labov, W. (1969) The logic of non-standard English, in Giglioli, P.-P. (ed) *Language and Social Context*, London, Penguin, pp. 179–216.

Lakoff, G. and Johnson, M. (1980) *Metaphors We Live By*, Chicago, IL, and London, University of Chicago Press.

Lederach, J.P. (1997) *Building Peace: Sustainable Reconciliation in Divided Societies*, Washington, DC, United States Institute of Peace Press.

Luling, V. (1982) *Aborigines*, London, MacDonald.

Maclean, A. (1993) *The Elimination of Morality: Reflections on Utilitarianism and Bioethics*, Routledge, London.

MacSwain, R. (2006) 'Above, beside, within: the Anglican theology of Austin Farrer', *Journal of Anglican Studies*, 4 (1) 33–58.

Mair, J.M.M. (1970) 'Psychologists are human too', in Bannister, D. (ed) *Perspectives in Personal Construct Theory*, London, Academic Press, pp. 157–184.

March, K.S. (1983) 'Weaving, writing and gender', *Man* (NS), 18 (4) 729–744.

Markevitch, M. et al (2000) 'Chandra observations of ABELL 2142: survival of dense subcluster cores in a merger', *The Astrophysical Journal*, 541 (2) 542–549.

McGuire, B. (2008) *Seven Years to Save the Planet: The Questions ... and Answers*, London, Weidenfeld and Nicolson.

Mithen, S. (1996) *The Prehistory of the Mind: A Search for the Origins of Art, Religion and Science*, London, Thames and Hudson.

Nightingale, F. (1859) *Notes on Nursing*, London, Harrison.

Nocci and Ohtou (2003) [AUTHORS TO COMPLETE]

Parody, A. (2004) *Eats, Shites & Leaves: Crap English and How to Use It*, London, Michael O'Mara Books.

Postman, N. and Weingartner, C. (1977) *Teaching as a Subversive Activity*, London, Penguin.

Pratley, R. (1998) *Spelling it Out*, London, BBC Publications.

Raban, B. (1982) *Guides to Assessment in Education: Reading*, London and Basingstoke, Macmillan Education.

Radcliffe, A. (2000) Personal communication.

Rawls, J. (1971) *A Theory of Justice*, Oxford, Oxford University Press.

Rezaee, Z. (2009) *Corporate Governance and Ethics*, Hoboken, NJ, John Wiley and Sons Inc.

'Rules for writing good' (1979) Originally printed in *The Leaflet: The Journal of the New England Association of Teachers of English*. Available at http://www.9types.com/type4board/messages/6280.html (Accessed 25 February 2010).

Salmon, W. (1984) *Logic*, 3rd edn, Englewood Cliffs, NJ, Prentice-Hall.

Schachenmayer, J., Pupillo, G. and Daley, A.J. (2010) 'Time-dependent currents of one-dimensional bosons in an optical lattice', *New Journal of Physics*, 12, 1–17.

Shoosmith, H. (1928) *Spelling and Punctuation*, London, University Tutorial Press.

Shorter Oxford English Dictionary (2007) Sixth Edition, Oxford, Oxford University Press.

Smith, A. (1981) *The Wealth of Nations*, Indianapolis, IN, Liberty Fund Press.

Solomon, R. and Winch, C. (1994) *Computing and Calculating for Arts and Social Science Students*, Buckingham, Open University Press.

Spencer, J. (1989) 'Anthropology as a kind of writing', *Man*, 24 (1) 145–164.

Thomson, A. (1996) *Critical Reasoning: A Practical Introduction*, London, Routledge.

Toulmin, S. (2003) *The Uses of Argument*, Cambridge, Cambridge University Press.

Truss, L. (2003) *Eats, Shoots & Leaves*, London, Profile.

Umotoni, H. (2010) *What is the place of forgiveness in Gacaca?* Dissertation submitted as part of the dissertation module for BA (Hons) Peace Studies and International Relations, Leeds, Leeds Metropolitan University.

Warburton, N. (1996) *Thinking – A to Z*, London, Routledge.

Ward, K. (2008) *Why there Almost Certainly is a God: Doubting Dawkins*, Oxford, Lion Hudson plc.

Williams, K. (1989) *Study Skills*, Basingstoke, Macmillan.

Williams, M. (1990) 'It's only words', *Labour and Trade Union Review*, p. 4.

Winch, C. (1985) 'Women, reason and education', *Journal of Philosophy of Education*, 19 (1), 91–98.

Wynne, P. (1985) Personal communication.

York, D.J. et al (2000) 'The Sloan Digital Sky Survey', *The Astronomical Journal*, 120, 1579–1587.

Zucker, D.B., Kniazev, A.Y., Bell, E.F., Delgado, D.M., Grebel, E.K., Rix, H.W., Rockosi, C.M., Holtzman, J.A., Walterbos, R.A.N., Ivezic, Z., Brinkmann, J., Brewington, H., Harvanek, M., Kleinman, S.J., Krzesinski, J., Lamb, D.Q., Long, D., Newman, P.R., Nitta, A. and Snedden, S.A. (2004) 'A new giant stellar structure in the outer halo of M31', *The Astrophysical Journal*, 612, L117–L120.

Index